(Great Britain) Folklore Society

Folk-Lore Society

Relics of Popular Antiquities

(Great Britain) Folklore Society

Folk-Lore Society
Relics of Popular Antiquities

ISBN/EAN: 9783744776790

Printed in Europe, USA, Canada, Australia, Japan

Cover: Foto ©Thomas Meinert / pixelio.de

More available books at **www.hansebooks.com**

The Folk-Lore Society,

FOR COLLECTING AND PRINTING

RELICS OF POPULAR ANTIQUITIES, &c.

ESTABLISHED IN

THE YEAR MDCCCLXXVIII.

Alter et Idem.

PUBLICATIONS

OF

THE FOLK-LORE SOCIETY.

III.

THE

FOLK-LORE RECORD,

VOL. II.

CONTAINING—

LONDON:
PRINTED FOR THE FOLK-LORE SOCIETY,
BY MESSRS. NICHOLS & SONS,
25, PARLIAMENT STREET, WESTMINSTER, S.W.

1879.

PREFACE.

I HAVE been asked to contribute a preface to the *Folk-Lore Record*, and regret that want of time for due preparation prevents me from writing anything at all complete or adequate about the objects of the Society. Compelled to be brief, I must select one or two points on which I have already written with, perhaps, damnable iteration. The readers of the *Record* must pardon me if, like the narrators of the fairy stories we collect and study, I tell a twice-told tale.

The science of Folk-Lore examines the things that are the oldest, and most permanent, and most widely distributed, in human institutions. It is not meant, of course, that every caprice of rural or social superstition is old, and permanent, and widely distributed. I have never heard that cannibals scruple to dine when there are thirteen in company ; or that Assyrians, Egyptians, and Andaman islanders, think it a perilous thing to walk under a ladder. It is not even in every English county that the robin redbreast's appearance in a house is a sign of approaching death, and very probably Spanish peasants do not hold, like the Scotch, that the yellowhammer "drinks a drop of the deil's blood every May morning." But, setting aside the accidents of folk-lore, we find the great mass of the more essential popular customs and beliefs existing in almost identical shape, among peoples modern and ancient, peoples barbarous and civilized, peoples of the eastern and the western hemispheres, and of the Australian continent. Let me give two or three examples, chosen at random, of the singularly wide distribution of certain practices. In the Dionysiac mysteries the ancient Greeks were accustomed to daub their naked bodies over with clay and dirt; this was part of the ritual, and, to explain a custom which seemed senseless, the initiators told a puerile story about Bacchus and the pirates. This same custom of daubing young neophytes all over with dirt is part of that rite which, among Australian black fellows and among certain African tribes, answers roughly to confirmation in the Christian Church. Will any one say that the dirty practice of the Greeks was an invention of their own civilisation, and that black fellows and negroes retain this, and not much else, from a culture which they once shared with Aryans? Or is it not more probable that a rite, originally savage, was not discarded by the Greeks as they passed from savagery to civilisation? This example has not, to my knowledge, any counterpart in modern folk-lore. Let us take another instance. French and Scotch peasants are or were in the habit of burning the bed on which a patient died, of spreading the ashes smooth on the floor, and of examining these next day to see whether the *revenant* of the dead had marked them with his feet. An inspector of natives in Australia (who does not seem ever to have heard of the Scotch and French superstition) found Australians carefully smoothing sand round the grave of a tribesman, and watching every morning for the print of his ghostly tread. Now here, we may say with some confidence, is an instance of a savage belief perpetuated in Europe among Catholic and Presbyterian peasants just as a savage rite was perpetuated by civilised and religious Greeks.

These two examples must stand as too scanty proof of the asser-
tion that the folk-lore of civilized is often identical with the superstitions of savage races, and that superstitious practices are among
the most widely and evenly distributed of human institutions. Now
when we find widely and evenly distributed on the earth's surface
the rude flint tools of men, we regard these as the oldest examples
of human skill. Are we not equally justified in regarding the
widely and evenly distributed beliefs in ghosts, kelpies, fairies,
wild women of the forests (which are precisely the same in Brittany as in New Caledonia), as among the oldest examples of the
working of human fancy? And, to go a step further, is not the
nursery-tale which you find among Celts, Germans, Basques,
Bechuanas, Aztecs, and Egyptians, obviously a relic of human
imagination, constructed in an age when people now civilised were
in the same intellectual condition as people still savage? The flint
arrow-head picked up from a British camp is like that which is
buried with an Algonquin chief, or which is discovered in Egyptian soil, or on the plain of Marathon, or which tips the reed of a
modern Samoyed. Again, the popular tales of modern Samoyeds
are often obviously related in plot and incident to, and identical
in tone and style with, those which are deciphered from Egyptian
papyri, or are imbedded in the Vedas, or are collected from the
lips of Basques in the Pyrenees, Germans in the Black Forest,
Celts in Barra, Zulus by the Buffalo River. It is a common
error to suppose that, because a tale is found in the Veda, the
Veda is its original source. But, in point of fact, the Veda is
only the oldest *literary* document in which we meet the tale.
It probably existed long before the Vedaic age, just as the story
of *Cupid and Psyche* is older than Apuleius, or the *Black Bull
o' Norroway* older than Sidney's *Arcadia*. The Vedaic priests
and minstrels found and used a pre-existent tale, just as the
country people at Bristol explain the tower, called "Cook's
Folly," by a story at least as old as the time of Rhamses II.

To return to the analogy of the arrow-heads, how is the essential identity in form of the British, the Red Indian, the Greek, the Egyptian flint arrow-head, explained? Obviously by the simple fact that on English, American, Greek, and Egyptian soil there once existed races as simple, and as necessarily driven to the use of stone implements, as are the modern savages, who still use tools of flint. No one will say that people, after acquiring the art of using metals, will prefer to resort as a general rule to the employment of stone. No; the arrow-heads in the ground attest the ancient presence of barbarism on Greek, English, and Egyptian soil. Let us turn again to the fairy tales. I am anxious to make out a parallel between them and the arrow-heads. I conceive that they are savage and early in character, that in style and type of incident they bear the marks of savage fancy as clearly as the arrow-head bears the marks of the rude stone hammer. And I conclude that many popular tales among Greeks, ancient and modern, Egyptians, Vedic Aryans, Basques, Celts, Germans, are just as plainly relics and survivals of the savage stage of fancy as the flint arrow-heads in European soil, and the rude clay pipkins of Celtic graves and of the modern cotters in the Hebrides, are relics and survivals of savage art and manufacture.

When we want to study flint weapons, palæolithic or neolithic, we visit the museums and easily find great store of these articles. But it is not quite so easy to study savage fairy-lore. One may recommend the Red Indian legends collected by Schoolcraft, the Zulu tales of Callaway, the New Zealand legends in Sir George Grey's works, the publications of Bleek, and of the South African Folk-Lore Society. A shorter way is to read Mr. F. A. Farrer's chapter on "Savage Fairy-Lore" (*Primitive Manners and Customs*, Chatto and Windus, 1879), where very many barbarous fairy stories are pleasantly discussed. These fictions of peoples still rude are, almost certainly, not importations from European neighbours. They are often intertwined with the legends of the pedigree and origin of the tribe. In other cases they are kept secret and mysterious by the least progressive and cultivated members of the race, the old women. Again, we may be pretty sure that European collectors have not much misrepresented the savage legends, because each collection lends testimony to the authenticity of the others. Collectors who know nothing of each other bring the same class of tale from every quarter of the globe. This is a point on which the reader can only convince himself by examining the collections. He will find that all the savage tales have the same features, of which the most marked is the attribution of speech and intelligence like that of men to plants, stones, trees, animals, stars, the sun and the moon. Man's fancy has not yet taken a distinction between himself and the things in the world. All nature exists in his consciousness, and his consciousness in nature, in a confused nebulous way. In savage tales the sun sits by the roadside and takes a wife; the frog goes a-wooing; the galaxy is a handful of ashes thrown up into the sky by a girl; the Pleiades among the Tasmanians were mortal girls; the Eskimo say that "some of the stars have been men, and others different sorts of fishes and animals." Now this same confusion of fancy actually exists among contemporary savages. They address bears, beavers, and lizards, as if they could be heard and answered. Their whole family laws turn on the theory that they are descended from animals and plants.

Turn now to modern European *märchen*, those collected in Russia, the West Highlands, Germany, Brittany, everywhere. Do not the animals and inanimate things play the same familiar part, as protectors, enemies, friends, walking and talking with men? Again, does not classical mythology, as in the Metamorphoses of Ovid, make Callisto a bear, and the bear a star, and another bear the ancestor of the Arcadians, while an aspara-

gus plant was the ancestress of an Athenian γένος? Do not
wood-worms and ravens talk to Melampus as familiarly as does
the mantis to characters in Bushman folk-lore? Is not the
Greek mythology, from the maiming of Uranus (as savage as
anything in New Zealand legend) to the tale of Cupid and Psyche
(which is found among the Zulus), a confused tissue of barbarous
invention underlying the delicate embroidery of true Greek
fancy? It is to account for this ferocity of incident, for cruelties,
incest, and patent absurdities, that the solar theory chiefly
exists. Is it not simpler to say these absurdities and horrors
are survivals of savage fancy, of a stage of fancy which still
exists, and, where it exists, produces stories as like Greek myths
as neolithic are like palæolithic instruments?

I would willingly go on from the discussing this mark of
savage fancy to discuss the *incidents* of the tales of contemporary
barbarous races. We should find, first, that they are generally
fanciful explanations of something in nature that excited curiosity;
second, that they introduce the manners of savage life, especially
the taboo, which forbids all manner of innocent acts under
mysterious supernatural penalties. Then one would show this
taboo in modern fairy tales and ancient mythology. It was
for breaking a taboo that Psyche lost Cupid, Urvasi her lovers,
the Scotch lassie lost the Brown Bull o' Norroway, and Eve,—
Paradise. A dozen other examples might be given, and the
explanatory craze might be traced; but for that part of the
subject it is enough to refer to Mr. Farrer's book, already
cited. I must cite an essay of my own for facts about another
branch of this inquiry. I have tried to prove (*Fortnightly
Review*, May 1873) that savage germs of classical myths exist,
in a wild and barbarous form, among non-Aryan races, and to
demonstrate that the savage is the older not the later form of
the myth.

Briefly stated, the view of folk-lore here suggested is this.

Man started from a savage origin, in a savage state he gave his fancy free play, and devised many curious and cumbrous rites. As he rose to civilisation he never wholly laid aside anything he had once acquired. His barbarous legends were polished into epics and national traditions, his rude ritual became the basis of a more polished cult. But all men did not advance with equal rapidity, and the peasant class retained something very much nearer the old savage legends than the cultivated and elaborate myths. These peasant legends survived as *märchen* in the mouths of old nurses, and even now, while they often resemble in plot and incident the greater myths of Greece, retain a still closer likeness to the legends of Zulus and Bechuanas.

If this view be correct (and it is supported by the comparative study of savage and civilised proverbs), the germ of Greek and other great mythologies is to be sought in the known qualities of the savage fancy, and in the habits of the savage mind, not in a fancied stage of society in which everybody spoke allegorically about the sun and the clouds, and then forgot the meaning of what he had said. If opponents of this theory do not deny that men passed through the savage stage we must ask them if they think it probable that the savage imaginative *data* were ever wholly laid aside, and, if so, at what time?

The purpose of this hurried sketch will have been fulfilled if it induces students of folk-lore to make anthropology part of their method. Folk-lore is the study of survivals, and possibly there is no stage of human experience, however early and incomplete, from which something in our institutions does not still survive. The theory above stated comes to this : men of every race started from an original condition of reckless fancy, to which all combinations and incidents seemed fit for imaginative art. They also started, in the region of morals, from barbarism. As men advanced, and became differentiated into

what we call races, the primitive data of savage fancy were
also differentiated.   But the religious instinct preserved so
much of the old material that even Greek mythology retained
many points identical with savage legend.

A. LANG.

THE NEO-LATIN FAY.

THERE was in archaic Italy a race of immortal damsels, whom the old natives—the *Prisci Latini* at least—agreed to call *Fatuae*.[*]

This quaint old-world name, unhackneyed by classical dictionaries, has a suggestive ring about it that should promise a solution of the long-debated but imperfectly-treated question, Who were the Fays—the *fate* of later Italy, the *fées* of mediæval France. For it is perfectly clear that *fatua*, *fata*, and *fée* are all one and the same word.[†]

But are these Fays the true daughters of the *Fatuae*, having a full right to their parents' name, or are they impostors only, who have stolen it? That is the question.

The question can only be satisfactorily handled by determining, in the first place, the nature and qualities of the *Fatua*, and comparing the result with what can be equally well ascertained of the true mediæval Fay. If in their nature and attributes both agree with each other, there will ensue but one conclusion, viz., that the Fay is a pro-

---

[*] Donatus, the grammarian and commentator (or it may be Calphurnius), in a note to the Eunuchus (Act 5, sc. 9, in Westerhovius's edition of Terence, reprinted in 1830, Leipzig, p. 233), says, "A fando fatuus dicitur. Inde Fauni Fatui, et nymphae Fatuae dictae sunt . . . . Nam Fauni quoque Dii sunt" In the Frankfort edition by Lindenbrogius, 1623, p. 20, only the following passage is given: "Nam Fatui quoque Dii sunt, qui et Fauni dicuntur." Macrobius says the Fatuae were called Faunae also (Sat. lib. i. c. 12). One of the oldest Latin folk-stories made the first Fatua to be the sister and wife of King Faunus, himself the first of the Fauns (Lactantius, de falsa religione, lib. i.) See also *post* the quotation from Marcianus Capella.

[†] The medial "t," in accordance with a law of Celtic phonetics, being elided, the word "fée" has been formed.

17

duct of the mythology once prevalent in the Italian mother country
and her colonies.

The *Fatuae* were beautiful and ever young. They were immortal,
or at least so long of life that poor transient mortals in their restricted
mental grasp could scantly realise the difference between such longe-
vity and complete eternity.

They lived on earth, but in places inaccessible to man, near lakes,
woods, and fountains, in natural caves, whose beauty can only be
appreciated by those whose lot is cast in the warm lands, where cool
retirement is a boon.

But, though this seclusion protected them from the voluntary in-
trusion of man, the *Fatuae* did not always deny themselves his society.
There were occasions when they exhibited to him their matchless
beauty ; at times rejecting their own *Fatui*, they admitted man to a
blissful *consortium*.

They had unlimited powers of injuring mankind ; but for this we
must suppose a reasonable and sufficient provocation.*

Egeria may be taken as a type of the *Fatuae*, her sisters. She is
a nymph with some of the Roman Folk-lorists, a goddess with others,
virtually the same state of existence.

She lives alone in a cavern, out of which flows a rivulet, the cavern
being in a wood on a height in Latium. She falls in love with king

---

* Marcianus Capella, lib. ii. p. 45, Eyssenhardt's edition: "Ipsam quoque
terram, qua hominibus invia est, referciunt longaevorum chori, qui habitant
silvas nemora lucos lacus fontes ac fluvios, appellanturque Panes Fauni Fontes
Satyri Silvani Nymphae Fatui Fatuaeque vel Fautuae vel etiam Fanae a quibus
fana dicta sunt quod solent divinare. Hi omnes post prolixum aevum mori-
untur ut homines, sed tamen et praesciendi et incursandi et nocendi habent
praesentissimam potestatem." When Tiberius placed his imitation nymphs in
the island of Capri they emerged to the gaze of the spectators from " caves and
hollow rocks "(Suet. vit. Tiber. lib. 3). The perfect immortality of the Fatuae
is shown in the application of the name "dea" to Egeria ; see *post*. The Latin
name for those who had become mad with love on seeing a *Fatua*, generally
reflected in a fountain, was *lymphaticus*. Sextus Pompeius Festus (sub voce
lymphae) says, "Lymphae dictae sunt a nymphis, vulgo autem memoriae proditum
est, quicunque speciem quandam e fonte, id est effigiem nymphae, viderint,
furendi non fecisse finem. Quos Graeci νυμφολήπτους appellant."

Numa, and admits him nightly to wise and charming converse, unseen by mortals.

Her wisdom apart, she is Calypso without her island. But her lover, unlike the fickle Greek, is constant and grateful.*

When Greece imported her culture, her poetry, and her folk-tales into old Italy, the Italians recognised in the Greek nymphs their own *Fatuae*, such as I have described them. The only novelty which the Greek nymph exhibited to them was her island. In that one particular the Hellenic love of navigation made an interesting, though non-essential, deviation. The island was thus to become an incident even of Italian folk-lore. The nymph was now to have her abode in a cave in an island as before it had been on a height.

Of the Greek nymphs generally, we have full knowledge. They were a brevet race of immortal women, the daughters of gods and goddesses, for whom no special employment could be found in the official government of the world and the heavens.

They were perennially young and beautiful, but left to lead a lotus-eating life of vacuous enjoyment, save only when the calm was broken by love-making, or the revenge which sometimes followed it.

They were neglected, or perhaps avoided, by the free-and-easy society of the Hellenic Pantheon.† As they brooded in solitude over beauties to which display was denied, can it be wondered at that their hearts in search of sympathy turned sometimes towards mere mortal man? Nymphs, therefore, would sometimes descend to fall in love with heroes, and to entertain them in their sacred abodes, endowing them during their sojourn with their own perennity.‡

* Liv. lib. 1, c. 19: " Simulat (*i.e.*, Numa) sibi cum dea Egeria congressus nocturnos esse." Acron (*Commentarii in Q. Horatium Flaccum*, Havthal's edition, vol. ii. p. 511) says, "Egeria nympha dicebatur loqui cum Numa Pompilio in Albano monte." So Sextus Pompeius Festus (de verborum significatione), a professed antiquary, says, " Egeria nympha." Lactantius (de falsa religione, lib. i.), who, like other Latin fathers, knew the folk-lore of his country well, calls her " dea," and says Numa met her nightly in a dark cavern in a wood, and that out of the cavern flowed a never-failing stream. There is some meaning in this last mentioned feature.

† See Calypso's speech to Hermes (Odyss. lib. v. v. 118 *et seqq*).

‡ Odyss. lib. v. v. 120, *et seqq*. Eos loved Orion in Ortygia. Demeter loved

But these fickle, hollow-hearted mortals too often showed themselves unworthy of an immortal's love and of a share in her immor·
tality. In the presence of divine beauty and preternatural culture
they sighed for terrestial and transitory charms, perhaps long since
lost. They therefore returned to the inhabited earth, and upon the
renewal of its degrading contact felt the sad reimposition of suspended
years.

The Greek nymphs had an unlimited power of changing themselves
and others into any animal or object in nature. So Nemesis, when
persecuted by Zeus with his unacceptable love, transformed herself
into any fish that the ocean engendered, or any beast that the vast
continent could produce.* So Thetis, scorning her human suitor,
Peleus, who was forced upon her by the selfish policy of Zeus, tried
precisely the same self-mutations, but equally in vain.†

Of this beautiful caste Calypso is the loveliest representative. Herself and her island were each a *chef-d'œuvre*.

When Paganism received its blow all of it did not perish. Much
of the minor machinery still held out against the new religion, or, per-

---

Jason. Odysseus would have been immortal and ever young if he had only
remained with Calypso (v. 135 *et seq.*).

> " Τὸν μὲν ἐγώ φιλεόν τε καὶ ἔτρεφον, ἠδὲ ἔφασκον
> Θήσειν ἀθάνατον καὶ ἀγήραον ἤματα πάντα."

Again, at v. 208,—

> "'Ενθάδε κ'αὖθι μένων σὺν ἐμοὶ τόδι δῶμα φυλάσσοις
> 'Αθανατός τ' εἴης."

In the *Talegonia* (Welsher's *Der Epische Cyclus*, vol. ii. p. 544) Circe made
Telemachus and Penelope immortal, and then married Telemachus, letting her
son Telegonus wed Penelope ("ἡ δὲ αὐτοὺς ἀθανάτους ποιεῖ, καὶ συνοικεῖ τῇ μὲν
Πηνελόπῃ Τηλέγονος, Κίρκη δὲ Τηλέμαχος ")

* Welcher's *Der Epische Cyclus* (vol. ii., p. 513). He quotes a passage in
the Kypria out of Athenaeus (7). It is a very good specimen of the power of
writing of the Cyclic poets.

† See the authorities quoted by Paley in his *Homeri quae nunc extant an
reliquis Cycli carminibus antiquiora jure habita sint* (at note 1, p. 15). He
says, " Mortali nubere cum nollet Thetis in varios se formas mutavit." Circe's
power of transfigurating her lovers requires no reference.

haps, much of what was graceful only was compassionately permitted to survive. Among the idealisms thus favoured with continued life the *Fatuae* were the most prominent. Under their old name, to be afterwards softened to *Fate*, they still retained their ancient influence over the Latin mind.

That this is the state of the case as regards the Fays is easily demonstrable from their own evidence.

They are beautiful, ever young, and immortal.

Each one lives alone, or in the midst of maidens, her ministers, inferior to her only in beauty, but equally young and immortal.

Each lives in a palace situate in some inaccessible country, or concealed from human eyes by glamour,* or in some island of the ocean unknown to scientific geography, and always unapproachable save through the guidance of herself or some special commissioner of her own.

No male relative is at hand to influence and control her.

Being young and beautiful her heart is as emotional as such a combination should make it, and she is susceptible of love towards even a human, whenever the world produces such an one as may warrant that condescension.

The husband thus selected is carried off by the gracious immortal to her own happy abode. There he passes years shorter than moments. There he participates in the youth and immortality which are the capital of his young and immortal wife. But in that island only, and in the presence only of the Fay, can he retain these precious gifts. He may live there, if he be only constant, until the crack of doom, as perennial as his mistress.

But, alas! as all rules are best proved by their exceptions, some discontented sybarites, whom a folded rose-leaf will disturb, have sought permission to quit even this fulness of delight, and by returning to earth they have forfeited the charter by which they enjoyed it.

The Fays have supernatural powers. They can turn an offender

---

* Such as the abode of the Lady of the Lake (see Keightley's *Fairy Mythology*, vol. i. p. 51).

into any shape that will most degrade or punish him. Equally they can change themselves at will.

This is the general *status* and condition of Fays.

But though the mediæval Fay has a palace for her fixed abode she still, for some purposes, adheres to the cave which had been the appanage of the Latin *Fatua*, or the Greek nymph. It is, however, an occasional resort only, not a fixed habitation, as it had been to Egeria and Calypso.*

There is one other characteristic of the Fay which deserves consideration—her faculty of prescience. The mediæval Fay has been so constantly represented in the embroidered stories of Perrault and his countrywomen as controlling the destiny of individuals by endowing them with properties beyond what nature has given them, and by ensuring them inordinate wealth and worldly success, that the theorists who have held them to be the Latin *Fata* have had some excuse for their opinion. But, for all this, the approximation of the Fays to the Fates is without a real foundation.† The *Fatuae*, as being part of a well-organised Pantheon, could never have thus interfered with the functions of the *Parcae*, who alone of all goddesses could shape destinies. The *Fatuae* had foreknowledge of events, and could foretell them.‡ That probably led to the orignal confusion, which was increased afterwards by the correspondence of the names. So also Calypso foreknew each trial that was in store for Odysseus,§ though she warned him only in general terms of the consequences which would attend his foolish election to leave one so fair in order to stretch himself again upon the rack of this rough world.

---

* In *La Gatta Cenerentola* (Pent. first day, sixth tale) the fay of the island of Sardinia, young and most beautiful, lives in a cavern or resorts to one. In *O che Viola* (Comparetti, No. 48), the *fate*, though they have a palace, resort to a cave.

† Even M. Loys Bruyère (*Contes Populaires de la Grande Bretagne*, Introduction, p. xl.) has given to this theory the support of his eminent authority.

‡ Marcianus Capella (*ante*) attributes a general foreknowledge to all Fatuae. Lactantius (de falsa religione, lib. i.) says that Fatua, the wife of Faunus, foretold to women their fates (mulieribus ata canere consuevisset).

§ Odyss. lib. v. v. 206, *et seq.*

There was an old Latin tradition that besides the *Fatuae* there were *Fatui* also. This belief, though never very popular, was not forgotten in Italy when Basile wrote, and it still lingers in Sicily. The male Fay was and is called *Fato.** He seems never to have been much of a favourite either with humanity or his own female counterparts. We know that in Horace's time the nymphs fled from the Fauns—in other words, the *Fatui*—for they were the same beings.†

Beings such as these *Fatuae*, nymphs, *fate*, susceptible, constant, beautiful—the dream of graceful intellects—have no point of contact with the Teutonic and Scandinavian elves, multitudinous, gregarious, homely, and vulgar, squalid in habits, and mischievous rather than powerful.

The nature and traditions of the Fays repugn all ascription to this coarse source, and my preceding remarks have, I think, sufficiently shown that Ariosto was right when, following the traditions of his country, he identified them with the nymphs of antiquity.‡

Before laying before the reader the two folk-tales with which it is my special object to make him acquainted as illustrating remarkably the identity of the Fay with the *Fatua*, I will first briefly recapitulate the better known stories of Ogier, Partenopex, Lanval, Graelent, and Sir Gawayne, which all bear on the same point.

Ogier is attracted to the isle of Avalon through the irresistible powers of Morgan the Fay, who loves him for his chivalry.§ She espouses and rejuvenates him, first placing him under a spell which will make him forget family, friends, and country. He lives on in her palace, in the midst of Fay-ladies (*dames faees*) who attend upon her and him. A year of the life he thus leads is less than a month to another man. One day Morgan removes the spell, and memory rushes in upon him. Ogier desires to return to earth once more to

---

* See the *Pentamerone* and also *Pitré*.
† Lib. iii. Od. xviii.: "Faune nympharum fugientum amator."
‡ Canto 1.—Dei cinque aggiunti al Furioso:—
"Queste ch'or fate dagli antichi foro,
Già dette ninfe e dee con piu bel nome."
§ Keightley's *Fairy Mythology*, vol. i., p. 74, *et seqq.*

chastise the infidels, who are ravaging France. Morgan grants the permission, and lends him an enchanted horse upon which to make the journey. As Ogier stays too long away, and is taking advantage of his rejuvenescence to marry a young earthly bride, Morgan proceeds to the spot, and takes him back to Avalon, whence he has never since returned. We have here Calypso's island, and we shall soon meet again the magic horse, which facilitates the return of the fickle lover to earth.

In the romance of Partenopex of Blois the Fay Malior carries off the hero to an island, where he henceforth lives in entire felicity, and is never more seen on earth.*

So it is with Lanval and Graelent, who are both relegated to the same enviable and insular life, each with a Fay.†

So Gawayne married a Fay, and was carried away by her into "faerie," or the land of Fays.‡ This is the older and better legend, which Sir Thomas Mallory has ignored altogether. The tale of the Fata Collina, so charmingly told by Professor Comparetti in his incomparable collection of the folk-tales of Italy, recites the same Calypso-like story, in this instance, however, ending happily.§

The two folk-tales which, as I have intimated, it is my intention to invoke, are the one French, the other Italian.

The French story is, I venture to think, though it was published a century and a half ago, unknown in this country. The Italian has

---

* Keightley, *ante*, p. 49.

† *Poesies de Marie de France* (Roquefort), *Lai de Lanval*, p. 202, *et seq. Lai de Graelent*, p. 486, *et seq.*

‡ It is a curious circumstance that we have not this story in a perfect form. We have the two parts only which together help to make up the whole. There is a ballad which recounts the marriage of Sir Gawayne to the Fay, and no more. (See Dr. Percy's folio, edited by Messrs. Hales and Furnival, vol. i. p. 103, *et seq.*) But Sir Gawayne's retirement with his wife into Fairyland is referred to by Chaucer only (*The Squieres Tale*) :—

"That Gawcyn with his olde courtesye,
"They he were come again out of fayrie," &c.

§ See a paper in the *Folk-Lore Record*, vol. i. intituled "Some Italian Folk-Lore."

only recently been committed to writing. Both are substantially identical, notably so in the touching manner in which they recount the fate of the inconstant wretch who could tire of perennial beauty, even though his own assurance of immortality was conditioned on his fidelity.

The French tale is contained in a novel of Madame d'Aulnoy, entitled *Histoire d'Hypolite Comte de Douglas*, and occurs in the second part.*

A gentleman, who has disguised himself as an artist's assistant, is called upon by a gay French abbess to amuse her while his master is engaged upon her portrait, and he complies with the request by telling her the following "*conte approchant de ceux des fées.*"

A young king of Russia, named Adolphus, having successfully terminated a war with some neighbouring people, who are strangely called Muscovites, devotes himself to bear-hunting. At the close of one day, whilst separated from his companions, he is overtaken by a terrific tempest. After long wandering through the deepening gloom, he discovers a light at a distance, and finds, on approaching, that it issues from a cavern at the foot of a high mountain. He hesitates at first, but, as the souls of princes have something nobler and prouder than those of other men, he enters, his hand on the hilt of his sword. At the noise he makes on entering, a very old woman appears from the depth of the rock. She shows an extreme astonishment, saying, " Do you know, Sir, who lives here ? " " No," said the king; " I do not." " This is the abode of Æolus, king of the winds, and his children," is the reply. " I am their mother. They are all out now, each occupied in his own way, doing good or doing harm in the world."

Hereupon the West Wind comes in, and blows up the fire. After him drop in Æolus and most of the other winds. They are all wet through ; their cheeks are puffed out, and their hair disordered. Their manners were rough and uncivil, and when they spoke to the King of Russia they nearly froze him. They were recounting each one his day's work of destruction, when their mother interrupted them, asking

* I quote a Brussels edition of 1713 (p. 206, *et seqq*).

them if they had met their brother Zephyrus on the road. Thereupon
the latter, who is a very beautiful youth, arrives, and excuses his delay
by explaining to his mother that he had been all day in the gardens
of the Princess Felicity, a most lovely and enchanting person by his
description.

"In what country does she live ? " asks the king. " In the island
of Felicity," answers Zephyr. The whole party then retire to rest,
the king with Zephyr, who has the cleanest and least cold part of the
cavern. The king, however, is so overcome with the description of
the lady, that Zephyr yields to his importunities, and consents to
carry him next day through the air, and drop him upon the island.
Zephyr, besides the promise, gives him a cloak green on one side,
which will render him invisible if he turns the green on the outside.

Zephyr and the king start early the next morning, and before the
end of the day the king descends upon the island, with his cloak
turned on the green side. The princess is living in a magnificent
palace, attended only by beautiful and accomplished ladies, the eldest
of whom is only eighteen years of age.

The king effects his entrance into the palace, and finally discovers
himself to the princess, who takes him for the phœnix. She accepts
him for her husband, and they thenceforth pass a time of unsurpass-
able happiness, when suddenly the king takes to considering how long
he has been in the island. " A week," he says, if he consults his
heart, but his memory says three months. The princess tells him, with
a laugh, that he has been there three hundred years. The ungrateful
man then wishes to revisit the world, and the princess reluctantly gives
her consent, for she has a sorrowful foreboding that the parting is for
ever. She gives him magnificent arms and a horse, and warns him
not to set foot to the earth until he shall have reached his own
country.

He promises everything and starts. His fairy horse takes him through
the ocean, and over every intervening land with winged speed, without
stopping or resting. One evening the king and his horse arrived at
a narrow stony lane fenced with thorns. There they found their way
blocked by a cart upset across it. The cart was laden with old worn-

out wings, and the driver, an old man, was lying under it. The king was about to turn away and leap the hedge, when the old man implored his assistance. The king alighted from the horse to go to his assistance, when suddenly the old man rose up of himself and seized the king. " At last, Prince of Russia," said he, in a terrible voice, "I have found you. My name is Time. I have worn out all the wings that this cart is loaded with in going round the world in search of you, but now I have you." With these words he put his hand on the king's mouth and stifled him. Just at this moment Zephryrus flew by, and seeing his friend in this sad condition he endeavoured to restore him to life, but in vain. He flew away with him to the island of Happiness, where the princess was equally powerless to undo the work of time. Henceforth the island was no longer worthy of its name.

There can be no doubt that this is a genuine folk-tale of France. In the countess's days French folk-lore was *in viridi observantia.* There was a floating unwritten *corpus* of romance more or less accessible to every family connected with the rural districts of France, and in this she found the materials of her " Ile de Felicité." A part of the tale as it still existed in Brittany in popular tradition was taken down in writing at the end of the last century. For in a book quoted by the learned Rev. Edward Davies as " Voyage dans le Finisterre en 1794 et 1795," there occurs a tale, stated to be oral, which may be briefed as follows :—

" The young son of a prince of St. Pol de Leon, while wandering alone upon the seashore, is overtaken by a tempest. He repairs for shelter to a cavern, which proves to be inhabited by the goddess of nature. Her sons, the winds, enter. Under their influence the child's limbs become mortally cold. But, as repose is not made for them, they rush out again, and Zephyr, her spoiled child, enters. Zephyr afterwards takes up the prince's son and carries him round the world," &c. &c. *

Between this passage and the preliminary portion of the countess's tale the resemblance is striking. The rest of the *voyageur's* story

---

* Davies's *Celtic Researches,* pp. 558—560.

is made up of stealings from Marcianus Capella, the whole being a garbling of a portion of genuine Armorican folk-tale to make druidical philosophy out of it.

What, however, is most interesting of all is, that the identical story told by the countess is still a folk-tale of Italy, and Professor Comparetti has for the first time recorded it in a way which will charm all readers. It comes from Monferrato, and is No. 50 in his collection of " Racconti." It is as follows :—

" There was once a poor widow, who, with her boy, lived in an out-of-the-way hut. When he was eighteen or twenty years old the son said to his mother, ' Mammy, I wish to go and seek my fortune, and I will stay away until I have found it; and, if I find it, you also shall be well off.'

The young fellow went away and travelled round the world for a whole year. But fortune had not found him. One night he entered a wood, and finding a cottage there, he knocked at the door. An old man came out, and consented to give him a lodging for the night.

Next morning the old man asked him what he went seeking for in those places, and the young man told him. ' My dear boy,' said the old man, ' Fortune comes once every hundred years, and if she is not caught then she is not caught again. But mind, to-morrow evening exactly the hundred years terminate, and she must come. Thou must be sharp to the very minute at midnight. Thou must crouch down behind the wood that is upon the bank of the brook. Three most beautiful girls will come there, and they will undress themselves for bathing. Look out for their being quite naked, and then take up the clothes of the one that stands in the middle, and carry them off. If she wants them, take out the book of command that is in the pocket, and thou art safe.' .

" The young man said yes to all this. But when the night came, not being accustomed to watch, he fell asleep, and the first night he caught nothing. In the morning he went to the old man and told him that he had seen nothing. ' But wast thou awake?' ' No.' ' Then if thou art a fool, it is thy own loss.'

The second night was a repetition of the first.

On the third night the old man gave him a hemp comb, and said

to him, ' If sleep comes to thee rub thy back on the comb, and thou
wilt wake up.'   And so it was ; for that scratching was stronger than
sleep ; and when the three girls came the young man was all attention, and scarcely had they undressed themselves, when he forthwith
carries off the clothes of the one who stood in the middle. The other
two dressed themselves and went away. The third had no choice but
to run after the young man and get her clothes back. He gave them
to her but kept the book of command, and with that he did what he
wished, and, as he had a wish to marry Fortune, she could not help
but marry him.

It happened one day that he was obliged to make a journey. He
locked up the book in a chest, and said to his mother, ' If my wife
wishes for anything, don't give it to her until I have returned.'   No
sooner was he gone than the wife told the mother-in-law that she
wished to go to mass, and wanted the book that was in the chest.
But the mother-in-law would not give it her on 'any account Then
the wife begged and prayed so hard, that finally the poor mother-in-
law sent for a blacksmith and made him force open the chest. When
the book she wished for was given her, Fortune said to the mother-in-
law, ' Farewell, farewell ; I am going. If your son wishes to come
and find me, or wishes to hear of me, let him come to the Island of
Happiness. There nobody ever dies, everybody is happy, and years
seem minutes.' After a time the son came home, and the mother said
to him, ' Thy wife has gone to the Island of Happiness. If thou
wishest to find her, go to that country.' The son began to despair,
and to cry out, ' Oh, poor me ! I shall never see her more.' But
afterwards, when he came to think it over, he said, ' Happen what
may, I will go and seek her.'

Accordingly he journeys along until he comes to a place where
there were robbers, who had a table-cloth that on being spread produced food of every kind ; a pair of shoes that being put on went a
hundred miles in a minute ; and a cloak that rendered its wearer invisible.

The three robbers said to the young man, ' See, we are disputing
who is to have the one or the other of these things. Act thou as
judge.' He replies, ' I must first see for myself what these are, and

afterwards I will give judgment.' Accordingly he spread the table-cloth, and forthwith the dishes came out, and, as he was hungry, he ate. Afterwards he put on the mantle and the shoes, and asked the robbers ' Do you still see me ?' ' No,' said they. ' Then, good-bye,' he says, 'till the day of ' never ' ' " (*a rivederci il giorno del mai*).

And away and away with those shoes, till he came to the rock of Thunder, and there it seemed that hell was coming down and stones and crags were falling with a great noise. He says to Thunder, ' Halloa, my fine fellow (*brav' uomo*), I have a table-cloth here that lays the dinner; stop a bit, and come and eat ;' and Thunder stopped and ate. And the young man said to him, ' Do you happen to know where the Island of Happiness is ?' ' No; but I have a sister, Flash of Lightning (*Saetta*), that lives five hundred thousand thousands of miles away, and if thou art good to go there she will tell thee.'

In two or three days he arrived there, and Flash of Lightning sent out a gleam of light that made it seem day. The young man asked her where was the Island of Happiness. But not even she knew. So she sent him to her brother Thunderbolt. And the young man roams and roams, and at last finds Thunderbolt, who was throwing down steeples and towers and trees, and even the tops of mountains, and he made him stop and tell him what he wanted to know. Thunderbolt told him he should have asked his seven cousins, the winds. But none of them knew, except South-East, who roams everywhere.

South-East not only told the young man where the Island of Happiness was, but gave him a push with his breath that sent him on.

Arriving at the House of Fortune, which was on the island, the young man put his cloak on, and so without being seen he passed through the window and entered the room where the three sisters were. The one that had been his wife was just then saying, ' If I had not been afraid of staying there where people die, and I had been able to have carried away my husband, I should be well pleased.'

The young man then showed himself, and said, ' Here I am.' She was quite pleased, and said, ' Now I wish to be always with you.'

He stayed a short time with his wife, and then said, ' I wish to go away for a short time and find my mother.' ' What is it thou wantest to go and do ? There is no more of her now, not even ashes.' ' How so ; it is only two months since I came here.' ' It will be more than two hundred years. But if thou wishest to go take care, for thy cloak and thy shoes are no longer of any use. I will give thee a horse that will do a year's travelling in one step, and I will come with thee, and won't leave thee.'

Travelling along with Fortune, the young man fell in with a cart, in which was a lean woman who had worn out a cartload of shoes with long travelling. When she saw him the woman pretended to fall down out of the cart, to see if he would help her up. If he had touched her he would have died for certain.

But Fortune was with him, and called out, ' Take care, that is Death ;' and he left the woman and went his way.

Afterwards he met the Devil on horseback, looking like a great lord, and the horse from much exercise had worn out his legs. He also fell down from his horse, and the young man almost ran to assist, but Fortune turned round and called out, ' Take care ;' and the young man went on without more ado to his own country. But no one there knew him, and there was not one even of the oldest persons who remembered him. Seeing this, he perceived that in the world people get old and people die. So he got on his horse again, and set off with Fortune, and returned with her to the Island of Happiness, and there he never died, but is living still."

Though with these two stories my object is satisfied, I cannot forbear before ending my paper informing the reader that the French and the Italian tales have their double in Ireland.

In that country an oral tradition exists in connection with a large cave which is situated at Coolagarrouroe, Kilbenny, near Mitchelstown, in the county of Cork. The cave is called Uaimh na caorac glaise— the cavern of the grey sheep. Mr. William Williams, a native of the district, on being appealed to by the late Mr. John O'Daly, the well-known bookseller, of Anglesea Street, Dublin, sent him the following brief account of the tradition :—

" Oisin went into the cave, and met a beautiful damsel, after crossing the stream lived with her for (as he fancied) a few days, wished to revisit the Fenians, obtained consent at last on condition of not alighting from a white steed with which she furnished him, stating that it was three hundred years since he came to the cave. He proceeded till he met a carrier whose cart, containing a bag of sand, was upset. He asked Oisin to help him. Unable to raise the bag with one hand, he alighted, on which the steed fled, leaving him a withered, decrepit, blind old man.*

In the same volume which contains Mr. Williams's statement is also a poem entitled Tir na nog (Land of Youth), edited by Mr. Bryan O'Looney, of Monreel. The original Irish poem is the composition of Michael Comyn, and was written about A.D. 1749.† But, though of so late a date, it is none the less valuable as an exponent of an ancient Gathelian folk-tale, the tradition which I have just stated, and it takes a shape which also is of considerable antiquity, that of a dialogue between Oisin and S. Patrick. Oisin recounts to the saint that his father Fionn and his sons and warriors were out hunting one day, when there suddenly appeared to them a beautiful golden-haired young maiden, riding a slender white steed. She tells Fionn that she has fallen in love with Oisin, and intends taking him away with her to the land of Youth. She has heard reports of his prowess and his beauty, and wishes to marry him.

Oisin assents with rapture, though he parts with tears from his father and his friends. He mounts the steed with the maiden in front. The two riders turn their faces due west, and the horse plunges into the sea.

They finally arrive at the Land of Youth, and Oisin is duly married to the princess, whose name is Niamh (Niav). He lives in the island for three hundred years, and then suddenly bethinks himself he should like to see Fionn and the Fianna. It is useless to expostulate with him, and the princess, who knows what will happen, lends him the white horse, and warns him thus :—

---

* *Transactions of the Ossianic Society*, vol. iv. pp. 232, 233.
† *Ib.* p. 230.

> Remember, O Oisin, what I am saying,
> If thou layest foot on level ground,
> Thou shalt not come again for ever
> To this fine land in which I am myself.

She impresses this warning upon him three times, besides telling him that the Fenians are all gone, and that Ireland is quite changed He departs, however, upon the white steed, and arrives safe in Ireland, where he wanders about to every resort of his family, but all to no purpose. At last he meets with a multitude of men in Glenasmole, some of whom are lying under a large slab of marble, which they are unable to dislodge. Oisin's assistance is asked, and he generously gives it. But in leaning over his horse, to take up the stone with one hand, the girth breaks, and he falls. Straightway the white horse fled away on his way home, and Oisin became aged, decrepit, and blind.*

Kennedy in his *Legendary Fictions* of the Irish Celts has a tale called the " Old age of Oisin,"† which is on all fours with Michael Comyn's poem. The curious incident of the overturned cart, contained in the tradition as recorded by Mr. Williams, as well as in the French and Italian stories, is, however, omitted by Mr. Kennedy, equally as it is in the Irish poem.

That the Irish version is very ancient cannot be doubted. It is inseparably attached, as we have seen, to an untrodden and wild locality—an unerring evidence of antiquity. It is moreover ascribed to a chief personage of the Fenian cyclus—the oldest form of the poetry and tradition of Ireland.

These two circumstances are wholly inconsistent with its being an importation from France in the shape of a translation out of *Hypolite Comte de Duglas*. Ireland has her own native version of *Peau d'âne*—the princess Catskin‡—without owing anything to France for it. Why then should she be under an obligation to that country for her form of the " Island of Happiness ? "

* *Transactions of the Ossianic Society*, vol. iv. pp. 234—270.
† P. 240 *et seq.*
‡ This long lost folk-tale of Ireland, made famous by Oliver Goldsmith's allusion to it in the *Vicar of Wakefield*, has been recovered by Mr. Patrick

All things considered, there is no reason why the folk-tale of "Tir na nog" should not be as old as the original story of the island of loving, rejuvenating Calypso, or older still—a part of that light, intellectual baggage which the Aryans carried with them out of India into Europe.

HENRY CHARLES COOTE.

Kennedy, and is to be found in his *Fireside Stories of Ireland*. The public of the three kingdoms is under an obligation to Mr. Kennedy for this and his cognate book, the *Legendary Fictions of the Irish Celts*. Both were wanted, and both are excellently well done. Goldsmith's other allusion, viz., to "Kaul Dereg," though somewhat mysterious to Englishmen, is well understood in Ireland.

MALAGASY FOLK-LORE AND POPULAR SUPERSTITIONS.

THE Folk-Lore of the various tribes inhabiting Madagascar has been as yet but slightly studied, and no one has up to the present time made any systematic examination of the curious superstitious beliefs which are found in the island. But as there exists a considerable amount of information on these points scattered through different books—notes of journeys, miscellaneous pamphlets, and magazines published only in Madagascar—which are quite inaccessible to the general reader, it will perhaps be worth while to collect these together in the present paper, in the hope that attention may be directed to the subject, and that those who reside in the island may be led to inquire more minutely into the noteworthy facts which still invite research.

That there is reason to suspect the existence of much more that is curious in Folk-*Lore* may be inferred from the fact that within the last three or four years a large number of most interesting Folk-*Tales* have been discovered, of the existence of which, for the most part, we who had resided in the country for several years had no suspicion. But, as these Folk-Tales are sufficiently important to require a separate paper to themselves, we shall not refer to them now, but endeavour, by grouping our information under various heads, to show how much there is of interest in the Folk-Lore, properly so called. And, as this is closely connected with the primitive religious beliefs of the Malagasy tribes, a second paper might be hereafter supplied giving various particulars as to the idolatry and religious beliefs and practices of the people of Madagascar, and the notions they entertain about a Supreme Being.

1.—*Animals.*

It may, perhaps, be convenient to commence by describing some of the superstitions which exist among the Malagasy as connected with animals.

As is the case almost throughout the world, *serpents* are held in great dread, although, unlike most tropical countries, Madagascar is singularly free from noxious reptiles of this order. In the greater part of the interior there are no venomous snakes, and there are probably only two or three species at most which are harmful in the warmer coast plains. But curiously enough, with this dislike of the reptile there exists also, as in other countries again, a belief in its connection with the healing art; for one of the chief idols of the central province, which was the god of healing and of medicine, was held also to be the patron of serpents, and to be able to employ them as the agents of his anger should any one become obnoxious to him. And so, when this idol, Ramàhavàly, was carried abroad, his attendants used each of them to carry a serpent in his hand, which, as it writhed and twined about him, inspired terror in the beholders.

There is a curious belief about a species of serpent called *màrolòngo,* which inhabits the mounds made by a white ant called *vìtsikàmbo.* Mr. Grainge, in his notes of a visit to the North-west Coast, says : "We noticed a large number of earthen mounds, varying from one to two-and-a-half feet in height ; these were the nest of a large ant, credited by the people with uncommon sagacity. We were told that they make regular snake-traps in the lower part of these nests, easy enough for the snake to enter, but impossible for it to get out of. When one is caught the ants are said to treat it with great care, bringing it an abundant and regular supply of food until it becomes fat enough for their purpose ; and then, according to native belief, it is killed and eaten by them." "There is no doubt," says another resident (Rev. R. Toy), "that the belief is most universal among the natives. I have been assured most confidently over and over again that it is a fact that snakes are kept and fattened by the ants as above described."

A much more formidable reptile in Madagascar than the serpent is the *crocodile*, which swarms in every river and lake, and is not a little destructive to human life. About this creature, accordingly, a good deal of fable has been evolved from the imagination of the people; and from their dread of its power they will never kill one except in retaliation for one of their friends or neighbours who has been destroyed by a crocodile. They believe that the wanton destruction of one of these reptiles will be followed by the loss of human life, in accordance with the principle of *lex talionis*. The inhabitants living in the neighbourhood of the lake Itàsy, to the west of the central province, are accustomed to make a yearly proclamation to the crocodiles, warning them that they will revenge the death of some of their friends by killing as many *voày* in return, and warning the well-disposed crocodiles to keep out of the way, as they have no quarrel with them, but only with their evil-minded reptiles who have taken human life. On the principle of "taking a hair of the dog that bit them," a crocodile's tooth is worn as an amulet or charm, and silver ornaments made in that shape formed a chief part of the adornment of the people in former times (see frontispiece to *History of Madagascar*, vol. i.), while a golden crocodile's tooth formed the central ornament in the royal crown. From this dread of the supposed supernatural power of the crocodile, it is invoked by prayers rather than attacked; even the shaking of a spear over a stream is dreaded as likely to give offence to the reptiles and provoke their vengeance the next time the offender ventures on the water; while to throw dung into the water was a heinous offence.

Mr. Grainge mentions that along the river Bétsibòka the people believe that "crocodiles live chiefly on stones, stealing cattle, pigs, and people merely as a relish to the harder fare. Also, that, smitten by the charms of the pretty little divers and other water-birds, they choose their mates from among them, and so crocodiles' eggs are produced."* Among the Antankàrana, in the extreme north of Madagascar, the people believe that the spirits of their chiefs pass into crocodiles, those of inferior people being transformed into other animals; and doubtless this belief leads to their being unmolested except in the cases already mentioned.

The belief in a kind of transmigration of souls is also connected

* *Antanànarìvo Annual*, No. i. p. 16.

with other animals besides the crocodile. The pretty species of lemur
called Babacoote is believed by the Betàniména tribe to be an
embodiment of the spirits of their ancestors, and therefore they look
with horror upon killing them. They have as much repugnance to
killing the harmless and timid little Aye-Aye, so interesting to naturalists, although it is not quite clear that it is from the same notion
respecting them. Accordingly, it is very difficult to obtain one, as tho
natives believe that any one killing an Aye-Aye will die within the
year, and that evil will follow from their even seeing one of them.*
Dr. Sandwith, who procured the first specimen sent to England, from
which the creature was described by Professor Owen, was only able to
overcome this dread by offering the large sum of fifty dollars for a
single animal.

The spirits of those who die unburied are believed to be doomed
to associate with, if not to become, wild cats, owls, and bats. And
there is much the same opinion with regard to the spirits of certain
criminals, especially those who are killed for supposed sorcery. The
above-mentioned animals are therefore all of evil omen, and in most
parts of the country the people look with horror upon the keeping of a
wild or native cat, those who have one in their houses being regarded
as familiar with the black art. This cat is called kàry, and is a beautifully marked animal, with stripings of black on a grey ground. The
European cat, on the other hand, which is called sàka, is rather
prized, and fetches a good price in the markets.

There is also in many parts of the country a dislike to goats, and
also to pigs. Repeated proclamations have been made about the
latter animals, ordering their removal to a distance of several miles
from the capital city, and some tribes and families will not eat their
flesh, considering it unclean.

The most valuable and plentiful of all the animals found in Madagascar, the large humped buffalo, has some curious legendary history
connected with it. A king called Ralàmbo, the eleventh on the list of
Hova sovereigns, is held in memory as the first who ventured to use it
as food. It is said that before his time it was called jamòka, a word

---

* Monograph on the Aye-Aye (Chiromys Madagascariensis); by Richard
Owen, D.C.L. F.R.S. &c. 1863.

which is still in use as an adjective, meaning "gentle, easy, not harsh." But since then it has been called *omby*. This name is said in the story to be derived from the circumstance that Ralàmbo said " *Omby, omby* " (Enough, enough!), when the folds were filled with cattle. But it looks very much as if the story were invented to account for the word, which is most likely the same as the Swahìli *ngombé*. It has been conjectured that before Ralàmbo's time the ox had retained (in that part of Madagascar, at least) the semi-sacred character which it still bears among many nations, as with certain Himalayan tribes, the Veddahs of Ceylon, the Kaffirs, and some peoples in the valley of the White Nile. The correctness of this supposition is confirmed by the fact that amongst several Malagasy tribes the office of killing an ox is one which belongs only to the chief, who was, it must be remembered, a sort of high priest among his people. Thus, Drury says, " Few in this part of the island [south-west provinces] will eat any beef unless it is killed by one descended from a race of kings. My master and his brother, to execute these high offices, were sometimes obliged to go five or six miles to kill an ox."[*] Among the Taimòro people, on the south-east coast, the writer found the same custom to prevail. At a large village called Ambòtaka we were told that no bird or animal must be killed for food except by some one belonging to the family of the king. A relic of this custom still remains among the Hovas, for at the Fandròana, or New Year's festival, the fattened oxen to be killed are driven into the royal courtyard to be blessed by the sovereign. An ox without blemish is killed, and the hump being cut off is brought to the sovereign to be tasted, as a sort of first-fruits. After this the people take their cattle home and kill them. Connected with this doubtless is the fact that in many Malagasy tribes they do not kill oxen, although they have them in great abundance, unless at funerals or other very important occasions.

In former times the Bétsiléo killed oxen only at reaping times, while the Tanàla kill chiefly at planting time; but on these occasions there is evidently some religious significance in this bullock killing. The Tanàla are said to offer a great deal of the flesh upon altars in their fields.

---

[*] *The Adventures of Robert Drury*, p. 153, ed. 1807.

Another noteworthy circumstance connected with the ox is that the rump is the royal share of every ox killed. As Dr. Davidson has pointed out, " the very name anatomists give to this part is suggestive. It is called the *sacrum*, or sacred part—the part devoted to the gods in Greece and Rome. But, tracing this up to a higher source, we find that in the Levitical law this part was specially directed to be offered to the Lord."* See Lev. iii. 6-11.

It is also worth notice that the same part of a fowl (*vòdi-akòho*) is the proper portion to be given by children or inferiors to their parents or superiors; while the same portion of a sheep is what is given by a man to the father and mother of the girl whom he marries. This is now always a money present, but it retains the original name, *vòdi-òndry*, and makes a marriage legal and binding.

These three animals, it may also be observed, are those esteemed by the Malagasy as proper to be sacrificed. These sacrifices were sometimes holocausts, but more frequently what are called meat-offerings in the Mosaic law, being feasted upon by the offerers ; while the blood and fat, as representing the life and the best part of the animal, were alone offered. These portions of the victim were smeared upon the upright stones of the tombs as offerings to the ancestors, and also upon other sacred stones and places.

Mr. Richardson says that the following curious notion in connection with oxen exists in some parts of the country: " The top of a large ant-hill is frequently taken off and thrown at the rump of an ox that persists in returning to the town where it has been bought, and it is a belief firmly held by the cattle dealers that the animal will never return to its former owner after the operation."†

The buffalo being by far the largest and most powerful land animal known to the Malagasy is continually used in their poetical and figurative language as the emblem and embodiment of strength and majesty, much as the bull was employed by the ancient Assyrians, and the lion by Western Asiatic and European nations. Thus, the kings were saluted as *òmbelàhy*, " bulls;" and the same expression frequently occurs in forms of benediction at the circumcision and other

---

* *Sunday Magazine*, 1873, p. 674.
† *Antanànarìvo Annual*, No. iii. p. 85.

festivities. In some tribes the chief is saluted as *Bíby*, a word usually meaning "animal" or "living creature," but probably intended as a figurative way of saying that he possesses all the power of the noblest animal forms. Bull-fighting was formerly a favourite amusement with the Malagasy, and there are words for numerous charms which were supposed to make a favourite animal victorious and to disable his antagonist.

In the rejoicings connected with the ceremonies at the circumcision the ox has a prominent place. In the songs which are sung the animal is called by a special name, *Vòrihàngy*, instead of the common name, *òmby*. And every portion of the animal is apportioned to a particular person; every one taking part in the slaughter of the ox having his proper share, as well as the old, the newly-delivered, the visitors, &c. This song is a kind of chant, with a chorus which is repeated at the end of every line, while the name of the ox (*vòrihàngy*) is also repeated in every stanza. Thus, leaving out the repetitions, the horns, the hoofs, the tongue, the ears and eyes of the animal, are each celebrated as having their special office; while the brain is the share of the newly-delivered, the head to the beater of the drum, the neck to the owner of the axe, the hump to the children undergoing the ceremony, the shoulder to the fetchers of the sacred water employed, the sirloin to the circumcisers, the breast to the visitors, the ribs to make bodkins for parting the hair, the dewlap to the blowers of the conch shells, and so on, until every part of the creature has been appropriated, and all concerned in the ceremonies or the killing have had their proper share of the meat.

Another ancient saying as to the uses of the ox thus apportions the different parts of the animal: "Its horns to the maker of spoons, its teeth to the plaiters of straw, its ears to make medicine for a rash, its hump to make fat, its rump to the sovereign, its feet to the oil-maker, its spleen to the old men, its liver to the old women, its lights to fathers and mothers-in-law, its tripe to the owner of the rope, its neck to the owner of the axe, its haunch to the herald, its tail to the weaver, its suet to the soap-maker, its hide to the drum-maker, its head to the chief orator, its eyes to make beads, its hoofs to the gun-maker," &c.

2.—Birds.

Turning from the quadrupeds to the *birds*, it has already been remarked that owls were considered of ill-omen ; and no one who has heard the unearthly screech of some of the Madagascar owls can wonder that they should be held in disfavour by a superstitious people. But there is another bird which is also looked upon with dread should it fly across the path a person is taking. ' This is the *Tàkatra*, a bird which builds a very large nest resembling an immense heap of hay or grass when viewed from below. No business of importance would be undertaken by a Hova in former times were his path crossed by one of these birds; and if it crossed the path before the chief idols these were obliged to return to their houses. It was also believed that any one destroying the nest of the *tàkatra* would be seized with leprosy.

Among the Tanàla people the diviners foretell events "by means of good and bad birds, according to their notes, or the way they take in flying, and they profess to know whether they bring good or evil. They look upon the kite as being a bird of much evil omen. Should its droppings fall upon the head of any one, he is watched as sure to die ; the people mourn for him and kill oxen to ward off the impending death."*

Then again, the laying by a fowl of an unusually large egg is regarded as ominous either of some extraordinary good or evil, while an unusually small egg is feared as foreboding evil. Something of the same feeling comes up in the name given to a small insect which attacks the young rice-plants. It is called *Ondrikélin' Andriamànitra*, " God's lamb ;" it appears to be regarded as an instrument of divine anger for men's wickedness.

The fables respecting animals and birds are numerous, and sometimes very amusing, as giving ingenious reasons for their respective habits, likes and dislikes, &c. Thus there are conversations between " The Crocodile and the Wild Hog," " The Wild Hog and the Rat," " The Wild Hog and the Chameleon," " The Hedgehog and the Rat," " The Kingfisher and the Great Moth," " The Sìtry and the

* *Antanànarìvo Annual*, No. ii. p. 98.

Antsiàntsy " (two species of lizards), " The Wild Cat and the Rat," " The Hawk and the Fowl," " The Fly and the Ant," &c. &c.

3.—*Fabulous Animals.*

But besides these well-known animals the native imagination has pictured several wonderful creatures which have no existence except in the fancy of some story-teller of a past age. Among these is the *Songòmby*, a beast said to be the size of an ox, but of wonderful swiftness and addicted to human flesh. Then there is the *Tòkan-dia* or *Tòkan-tòngotra* (" the single-footed "), a creature whose fore and hind legs are said to be each joined, so that it has only two feet altogether; also a beast of incredible swiftness, eating men, and only going abroad by night. Then there is the *Làlomèna*, a beast with red horns and as big as an ox, but living in water. But besides these fabulous stories there are others of strange serpents, described as of marvellous power, which very possibly have a basis of truth, since it has been ascertained that there is a species of boa in the western part of the island which drops from trees upon oxen and passing travellers.

But there is another creature also spoken of by the Malagasy, especially by the Bétsiléo, in which there seems to be a curious mixture of fact and fable. This is the *Fanàny* or the *Fanànim-pito-lòha* (" the Fanàny with seven heads "). This creature is variously described as a lizard, a worm, and a serpent, and is believed to come from the corpse of those of noble blood, and to be, in fact, an embodiment of their spirits. After the completion of the revolting practice of treating the bodies of such people (by so compressing the corpse that a putrid liquid exudes from the foot), the pots containing the liquid portion are taken great care of, for the corpse cannot be buried until a small worm appears in one or other of them. Two or three months are said to frequently elapse before this takes place. After the worm has increased in size the body may be buried; while the earthen pot with the worm is placed in the grave; but in it is also fixed a long bamboo reaching up to the outer air through an opening at the top. After six or eight months they say that this worm climbs up the path prepared for it and comes into the village. It is then like a lizard in appearance, and called *fanàny*. The relatives of the deceased proceed to question the creature, asking if it is Such an one, and believe that they get an infallibly correct answer by its lifting its head. Thus assured, they make assurance doubly sure by fetching a plate off which the deceased ate his or her last meal, and in this plate the blood from an ox's ear, together with rum, are poured. The *fanàny's* drinking these liquids leaves no doubt as to its identity. A clean cloth is then spread, upon which the creature steps, and it is borne into the village with feasting and rejoicing. It is finally carried back to the tomb from which it emerged; there it remains (so they say) and becomes the guardian deity of the people living near, and grows to an enormous size.

The Rev. J. Richardson, from whose account the foregoing description is taken, says, that, although he has never seen the *fanàny* itself, he knows for certain that the bamboo and earthen pot in the tomb, &c. are arranged as described. He adds: "And I have heard from the lips of the chief prince of one of the tribes, when his mother was dead, ' She has not yet appeared in the earthen pot, and so I cannot bury her body.' Of this prince's mother I know that for nearly three months from the time of her decease, as also the decease of her sister, and until the *fanàny* appeared, the people in the whole district were not allowed to dig or plant. There was danger of a famine, and the Hova authorities were obliged to interfere and hasten the appearance of this *fanàny*."*

In a native account of this marvellous creature it is said to have seven heads, whence its name, and each head has horns. At its death it swells to the size of a mountain, so that the villages near are uninhabitable from the effluvium; while there are other equally apocryphal stories of its ascending up to heaven, and of its taking refuge in the sea, where only it could have space to move about. The narrator says that the *fanàny* seen by him was the size and had the appearance of a small water-snake called *tòmpondràno*. He confesses that he saw only one of its seven heads, but the people accounted for this deficiency by saying that the specimen he saw was

* *Antanànarìvo Annual*, No. i. p. 74.

still young. Evidently the doctrine of development was urgently needed in this case.

4.—*Trees and Plants.*

There are several *trees* which have a somewhat sacred character among the Malagasy. Among these are the *Fàno*, a species of mimosa, which is frequently found growing over and around the tombs of the Vazimba. The tombs of these ancient people were held in extreme veneration, and also the tree growing over them; and the seeds, which are contained in large pods a foot long, and resemble small beans, were commonly used in the working of the divination or *sikìdy*. Another tree connected with idol-worship is the *Hàsina*, a species of pandanus, often attaining a considerable size, and branching in its growth. The name of the tree implies its sacred character, *màsina* being the adjective used to describe consecrated or sacred things.

Another tree called *Zàhana* (*bignonia articulata*), an evergreen with dark glossy leaves and pink flowers, is one frequently seen growing in Imérina (the central province of the island) as ornamental timber. But there is an old superstition regarding it, and still believed in by many, to the effect that any one planting it in his grounds will meet with an early, if not sudden, death.

In the southern parts of Madagascar, among the Bàra and Tanòsy, the Tamarind tree (one of the finest of the trees growing in the island), and also the Baobab, have each a sacred character. In this latter tree there is a certain part considered as specially belonging to God. Portions of the tree are coloured black, white, and yellow, bound with mats, and decorated with charms.

Among the Sakalava, a tree called *hàzomànitra* ("fragrant wood") is planted at the birth of the first child, as a witness that the father acknowledges it as his own.

The Malagasy do not, like the Polynesians, make much use of flowers in their festivities; but it was formerly the custom that those who accompanied the Queen, on her return from the ancient to the present capital, should all be decorated with flowers. The effect produced by several thousands of people, with their heads or head-dresses all adorned with flowers, was often extremely pleasing. Some flowers used to be considered as acceptable offerings to the idols; thus a pink-petalled flowering plant, called *vonénina*, was proper to be brought to the tutelar deity of the reigning family, while the other idols had also their appropriate flower offerings.

Flowers were also carried in the joyful procession which was formed of the friends and relatives of those people who had been cleared of guilt by the *tangéna* ordeal, and were then termed *madio*, "clean," or cleared of blame. These were fastened to small wands, and carried in the hand.

An edible arum, called *sàonjo*, is always eaten at a Hova house-warming. But occasionally, possibly on the principle that " one man's meat is another man's poison," some of the most nourishing vegetables are *fàdy*, or tabooed, by certain individuals or families. Thus, I was once warned that I could not enter a certain house if I had amongst my property any arrowroot prepared from the manioc root, as that was *fàdy* to the owner of the house.

5.—*Lucky and Unlucky Days and Times.*

Leaving now the natural objects, animal and vegetable, with which superstitious notions are associated in Madagascar, something may be said about *days and times*. The wide-spread belief in lucky and unlucky days is common to all the tribes in the island. The Malagasy month is, of course, a lunar one ; indeed, the word for moon and month are the same. In some parts of the country there seems little use of a sevenfold division of time, but the days from one new moon to another are called by twelve names. These are the very same as the month-names, some having two other three days respectively, which are distinguished as *vàva, vònto*, and *fàra*, or *vòdy* (" mouth or opening," " swelling or increase," and " end or close " of that name. The Hova names for the months are all of Arabic origin, while those used on the coast are compounds of native words ; but, curiously enough, although these words, with slight variations in their form, are the same on both the eastern and western sides of the island, they are not synchronous. So that while the order of the twelve names is the same, the month Vòlambìta, for instance, is four months later in the east of Madagascar than on the western side of it. From the double meaning of month-names a very complicated system of lucky and unlucky times was formerly in use among the Hovas. Thus, out of the twenty-eight days of the month, twelve only are lucky. The *vàva*, or first days of some months, were especially disastrous to the children born on them, in some cases to the offspring of the people generally, and in others, to those born of the family or in the household of the sovereign. These were usually put to death by placing the new-born infant's head, face downwards, in a shallow wooden dish filled with lukewarm water. In certain cases, however, this fate might be averted by making prescribed offerings, or by undergoing an ordeal, as will be presently described. On the other hand, some days were considered as favourable for planting, commencing house-building, going on a journey, or a war expedition, &c.

Each tribe, however, has customs peculiar to itself. Thus, among the southern Tanàla we found that eight days in each month were considered unlucky, viz. those called Tsàratà, three days; Alakaòsy, two days; and Alijàdy, three days; and that children born on those days were put to death in the manner above described, so that a fourth of all who are born are destroyed.

Then we also learned that with them every day throughout each month has its *fàdy* or food which must not be eaten when travelling on that day. Thus, on the first day silkworms must not be eaten; on the second Indian corn is prohibited; and so on successively, with sugar-cane, bananas, sweet potatoes, rice, yams, honey, earth-nuts, beans, *kàtsaka*, and *vòamàho*.

Among the Sihànaka tribe the people of a village called Anòrohorò are said to be almost like wild men, and are extremely superstitious, being addicted to astrology and the observance of days. Among them the twelve months have each their qualities of good or bad, and the month is also divided into the same number of parts; each day, even, they divide into a number of parts from morning to evening. And if a stranger comes to them on a day which they consider unlucky, or on one of the divisions of the day or of the month which is of bad omen, they will not allow him to enter the village, but make him remain outside, and there they bring him food. Should he, however, persist in coming in they say he will certainly come to harm, either dying in the town, or being so ill as to lose his senses, or will be lost and not find how to advance or retreat, becoming hopelessly adrift among the rushes on the water. For, as this village is situated in the midst of a dense thicket of papyrus, there is no road to it except by canoe.*

Among the Bàra, if a child is born on a day which is unlucky to either its father only or its mother only, it is not put to death, but if born on a day of evil omen to both parents it is buried alive in an ant-hill. The unfortunate infant thus destroyed is called *nébo*, a term also employed as indicating the strongest reproach.†

Among the Tanàla one of the months called Faosa is extremely unlucky. " No one works on that month, no one changes his place of abode or goes about. If any one happens to be in the fields when the month comes in there he remains. Almost all children born in that month are buried alive in the distant forest ; but, should the parents determine to let one live, they fetch the ômbiàsy or diviner." This functionary makes an expiatory bath, consisting of certain grass, herbs, and other articles placed in water, in which the child is bathed. This ceremony puts an end to the child's evil days, and the water and its contents are buried.‡

Among one clan of the Sàkalàva all children born on Tuesdays are put to death, while almost every family has a day similarly ill-omened to their newly-born offspring.

The month called by the Hova Alakàosy was esteemed very unlucky; and among them and other Malagasy tribes the waning of the moon is an unfavourable time for any important undertaking. Among the Antankàrana the dead are only buried immediately after the new moon appears.

Before the destruction of idolatry in Imérina in 1869 every idol had a day sacred to it, on which day those who were especially its votaries abstained from work. Until quite lately the Sunday or Thursday

* *Antanànarivo Annual*, No. iii. p. 61.
† *Lights and Shadows*, App. i. p. 5.
‡ *Antanànarivo Annual*, No. ii. p. 100.

were the lucky days for the Hova sovereign to go on a journey or commence any undertaking.

6.—Ordeals.

Reference was just now made to a certain ceremony by which a child might be preserved from death although born on an unlucky day. There are, however, many different ordeals in use among the Malagasy tribes, of which a short description may now be given.

Foremost among these is the well-known one of the *Tangéna* or poison ordeal.

The Tangéna is a small and handsome tree growing in the warmer parts of the island, and the poison is procured from the nut of its fruit. This in a small quantity acts as an emetic, but in a larger dose as a virulent poison. The chief use of the tangéna ordeal was for the detection of witchcraft, by which the African races "understand the use of poisonous drugs for evil purposes." Dr. Davidson remarks * that the word " is in fact equivalent to the Φαρμακεία of the Greeks ; and as the terms Φαρμακός and *veneficus* were applied by the ancients to signify alike a physician, a sorcerer, and a poisoner, so in many of the African languages the same peculiarity obtains. This arises from the fact that among these and other primitive races the physiological effect of drugs, whether poisonous or medicinal, are ascribed to some magical power, either inherent in the substance itself or imparted to it by sorcery. Medicines are thus employed as charms both for causing and curing disease."

The use of *some* poison as an ordeal in Madagascar is probably of very ancient date, but it seems possible that the tangéna itself has not been used for a very long period. It was employed chiefly for the detection of infamous crimes when ordinary evidence could not be obtained, such as witchcraft and treason ; and it was believed that there was inherent in the fruit some supernatural power, a kind of " searcher of hearts," which entered into the suspected person, and either cleared him of guilt or convicted him. The mode in which it was administered was by giving a portion of the nut rubbed down in water or the juice of a

* *Journal of Anatomy and Physiology*, vol. viii. p. 97.

banana, the culprit having previously eaten a little rice and swallowed
three small square-shaped pieces of a fowl's skin.   Tepid water was
after a few minutes administered to cause vomiting, and the proof of
innocence was the rejection of these three pieces uninjured.   But even
if the ordeal was fairly administered there was an amount of risk of
poisoning; and, as it was frequently used to get rid of obnoxious persons, by a little management it could easily be made to yield an
unfavourable result.

One of the most remarkable things in connection with this ordeal
was the implicit faith of the people generally in its supernatural power,
so that they would often demand of the authorities that it should be
administered to them to clear them of any possible suspicion, and
this notwithstanding the certainty that some would fall victims to
their credulity.   As whole villages sometimes took the tangéna, the
mortality caused by it was very great, and it was a fearful means of
destruction with an appearance of fair dealing.

I have been told by native friends, who had been obliged to take the
ordeal during the persecution of Christianity, that they were not freed
from suspicion even after the pieces of skin had been rejected, but
that for a day or two afterwards they were closely watched, and dared
not even spit to get rid of the bitter taste caused by the poison.   In
that case they would have been put to death all the same.

Among the Tanàla, or forest tribes, some other ordeals are in use,
and it is curious that two of these are called *tangéna*, with another word
added, as if the word had become equivalent to "ordeal" in meaning.*

One of these is termed *Tangén-Janahàry, i.e.* " the Creator's ordeal,"
and is administered as follows: Water is heated in a pot, and as
the water begins to boil some pieces of quartz, called *vàto vélona*
(*i.e.* " living stones "), are slung in the water, so as not to touch the
bottom of the pot.   When this is done the accused person is ordered
to take the stone out of the pot, putting his hand under the stone, and
bringing it out lying on the palm of the hand; he must then put the
stone into cold water.   He is then carefully watched until the next
day, and should his hand not blister he is declared innocent.   Yet if
the accused himself should be the first to declare his hand unblistered

he is accounted guilty, and if accused of stealing he must pay the stipulated fine. The hand not blistering, and the accused having waited for others to declare him innocent, his accuser must give him one slave, and he is set free.

Another ordeal is that of *Tangém-boày*, the " ordeal by crocodile." In this test the person suspected of wrong-doing is taken to a river in which there are many crocodiles. The people are assembled there. A man stands behind the accused and strikes the water thrice, and addresses the crocodiles, begging them to show whether the culprit is guilty or otherwise. He is then made to swim across the river and back again, and if he successfully accomplishes this, and is not hurt by the crocodiles, then the accusers are fined four oxen ; the swimmer gets two, the king one, and the councillors one.* It may be presumed that few escape this ordeal with life.

Still another ordeal is called *Kodéo*, a word of obscure meaning. In this ceremony the accused is set upon a rice-mortar, and he is made to mutter. A man then approaches holding a large stick, with which he thrice strikes the earth, and thrice cuts the hair of the accused, throwing it to God, who is invoked to show his guilt or innocence by certain signs. Should the person be guilty it is said that he at once begins to tremble, to be purged, and to vomit; and some of them, although they do not die as they sit there, do not escape, for the lightning, it is said, soon strikes their houses. If, although guilty, he finds favour with his judges, they invoke God's mercy for him and purify him by lustration. Should the person be innocent he is sprinkled with water in which silver rings have been allowed to stand to make him well.

The drinking of the *Vòkoka*, or water mixed with earth taken from the tomb of a former sovereign, as a test of allegiance, may also be regarded as a species of ordeal.

Another ordeal must be mentioned which was formerly in use in Imérina. In the case of children born in the month of Alakàosy it was possible to avert the necessity of actually destroying them by

---

* For a romantic story founded on this custom see *Chambers's Journal*, p. 309, Dec. 1, 1849, " The Trial by Caiman," by Percy B. St. John.

placing them at the entrance of the cattle-fold of the village, the oxen being driven over the spot where the hapless infant was laid. Should it happen that through any freak of the animals the child was avoided by them and so escaped death from their hoofs, it was considered to have overcome the evil fate, and its life was spared. It was usually sent away into some sequestered village, and not acknowledged as its father's offspring until some time had elapsed. It was believed that those children who escaped through this ordeal would live to be extremely rich. It is said that the present Prime Minister of Madagascar was thus exposed as an infant, having been born in the ill-fatèd month, but he escaped injury, and so has lived to be the most powerful chief minister the country has ever had as its ruler.

There is still one more custom in use in Madagascar having the character of an ordeal. This is called *Ràno-àn'òrona,* " water in the nose," and is a test which is made by putting water in the nostrils, this being supposed to cause the guilty party to sneeze. So that if a person accuses another of theft the accused will say, " Come, let us both put water in our nostrils, if you dare test it, and see whether I stole or not ?"

7.—*Folk-Lore of Home and Family Life.*

A few words may now be said about some popular Malagasy beliefs and superstitions having reference chiefly to home and family life.

The mention of sneezing just now reminds us that the world-wide superstition of some evil influence being at work when any one sneezes is equally prevalent in Madagascar. Thus, when a child sneezes its mother or nurse always repeats the common benediction, " *Hotahìn Andriamànitra hianao,*" " God bless you," exactly as is done in Europe and other parts of the world.

When a child loses one of its first or milk teeth the tooth is thrown over the house, a practice closely corresponding to what is common in some parts of England. Toothache is believed to be caused by a small worm in the offending tooth, and so the sufferer is described as being *maràry òlitra,* " poorly through the worm."

There is a common belief that the first spittle produced after waking iu the morning has medicinal virtue in healing a sore ear or eye. It is then called *ròra mafàitra*, " bitter or disagreeable saliva." And when a Malagasy passes anything with an offensive smell, as, for instance, a dead dog on the roadside, he always spits, as a kind of antidote.

On entering a house, especially a royal house, it is improper to use the *left* foot on first stepping into it; one must "put one's best (or right) foot foremost." Then again, it is improper to lean against a chief's house, and it is considered highly indecorous to sit upon any royal property, such as cases of goods, &c.

In many parts of Madagascar it is common when giving a present of food for the donor to taste part of it himself as an assurance that it is given in good faith, and may confidently be eaten without any suspicion of its being poisoned. Much the same feeling is expressed in old forms of salutation, as *Sàrasàra tsy ambàka*, the two latter words meaning "not deceived, overreached, or beguiled." This is no super-fluous assurance in some portions of the island, for the Bàra are said to live in such constant suspicion and dread of an enemy that they never wash in their houses, but only in the open air. And even then they only wash one side of the face at the time, leaving one eye open, and one hand grasping gun and spear.*

In the arrangements of a Hova house in the central province the sacred portion of it is always at the north-east corner, where, in time of war, the women sing the *ràry*, a kind of chant or invocation imploring victory for their husbands and friends. The following is one of these chants :—

> " Although they have many guns,
> Although they have many spears,
> Protect Thou them, O God."

The *ràry* is also made use of at other times, as when there has been injury caused by hail, lightning, or waterspouts.

In this north-east corner the fixed bedstead always has its head towards the north, for the Hovas invariably sleep with their heads towards the north or east. Even in their tombs the dead are also laid in this direction, never with the head towards west or south. The

* *Antanànarìvo Annual*, No. ii. p. 47.

entrance to the tomb is always on the western side. Other tribes, however, are not so particular as the Hovas about the position of their tombs.

In building a house the first corner-post set up is always at this sacred part of it. Several kinds of plants are attached to its base, and on the top is fixed a piece of silver chain, a sort of assurance that the owner will always have money in his dwelling. In the case of a royal house the post is sprinkled by the sovereign with sacred water brought from a special spring, and an invocation is pronounced imploring a blessing on the building.

8.—*Lucky and Unlucky Numbers, Actions, &c.*

In the building of a house for the late sovereign all the measurements were regulated by the Queen's own *réfy*, or fathom, that is, the space between the tips of her fingers when the arms were extended; and smaller dimensions were according to her span, a most awkward and troublesome fettering of the European architect in making his drawings. Besides this, no dimension was, if possible, of the unlucky numbers, six and eight. These are considered as of bad omen, because *énina*, six, is the same in sound as the root of the word *manénina*, to regret, or feel remorse ; while *válo*, eight, is similar in sound to *miválo*, to abjectly beg pardon, and also to *fàhaválo*, an enemy. The word *fàhatélo*, third, is also used for enemy, possibly on the principle that "three are no company," so that it also has some disfavour attaching to it, as has also the word *fàhasìvy*, ninth, in some tribes at least, amongst whom it is used to denote a malignant kind of spirit or ghost.

Mr. Richardson says that the Bàra have a strong dislike to the singular number. "They will take nothing singly. You must offer two, and sometimes they will spend an hour or two in matching two beads. They call two ' one person' (*iraika amin' olo*). If you offer one they always ask, '*Aïa ny váliny ?*' (Where is its partner?)" *

* *Lights and Shadows*, App. i. p. ix.

Perhaps, however, this love of the plural arises from nothing more than their covetous habit of mind, in short, by an apparent paradox, from their love of " Number One."

But of course some numbers are lucky, especially twelve, a number which appears in many connections. Thus, the sovereign has *twelve* wives; there are *twelve* capital crimes, and *twelve* men who are appointed executioners for such offences; while in proclamations *twelve* royal ancestors are often spoken of, and also the *twelve* ancient towns in Imérina, or, as they are usually on hills, they are called the " twelve sacred mountains."

The left hand and side appear to be regarded as more appropriate in circumstances of mourning than the right. Thus, after leaving off mourning for a deceased relation the youngest son or daughter puts a little grease on the left side of the neck by the little finger of the left hand, a custom known as *mitendrilo*.

There are numerous acts and customs which are *fâdy* or tabooed in different parts of the country. Thus in some villages it is forbidden to enter with burdens carried by one man only; all must be borne by two men. Then "there is a belief prevalent among the carriers of burdens that if a woman should stride over their poles the skin of the shoulders of the bearers will certainly peel off the next time of taking up the burden. A cooking-pot may not be used for ladling water out of a stream, or be put into a pool; an infringement of this is looked upon as a sure precursor of a wet day." Similar weather is expected should a man die on a journey and be buried on the downs where he dies.*

Mention might be made in a paper on Malagasy *names* of much that is curious in connection with them, but there are two or three facts that may be perhaps more appropriately considered as illustrations of folk-lore. For instance, it is often difficult to get persons to tell you their name; if asked, their attendants or slaves will reply for them. Indeed in some places it is *fâdy* for a person to pronounce his own name. Mr. Grainge says, " Chatting with an old Sàkalàva while the men were packing up, we happened to ask him his name,

* Rev. J. Richardson, in *Antanànarìvo Annual*, No. iii. p. 84.

whereupon he politely requested us to ask one of his servants standing
by. On expressing our astonishment that he should have forgotten
this, he told us that it was *fàdy* for one of his tribe to pronounce his
own name. We found this was perfectly true in that district."*

There is a custom called *Tatào*, which consists in placing on the
head a portion of the rice, honey, and meat eaten at the New Year's
feast. But it is also employed on other occasions ; thus, when crossing a stream which is dangerous either from the strength of the current or the number of crocodiles in it, those who have passed in safety
take a handful of the water and put it on their heads, apparently as a
sign of thanksgiving. This practice seems to be a relic of some
ancient form of worship.

9.—*Sickness and Death.*

It will be readily supposed that amongst the Malagasy there are
many strange observances and beliefs connected with death. Some
of these would be more appropriately described in papers on their
Burial Customs and on their Language, but there are others more
strictly belonging to the present subject.

At the death of a sovereign there are a number of things which
become *fàdy*, and must not be done for a specified time, usually
extending over several months, and in some cases lasting a year.
Thus at the death of Radâma I. not only was almost every one ordered
to shave the head, but to use no showy dress or ornaments or
unguents, not to ride on horseback, or be carried in a palanquin ; not
to weave silk, or make pottery, or work in the precious metals, or manufacture sugar ; no carpentry work was to be done, or writing, or
plaiting of straw; no salutations were to be used, or musical instruments played, and dancing and singing were prohibited ; no beds,
tables, or chairs were to be used, and no spirits were to be drunk.†
At the decease of the late Queen Ràsohérina in 1868 it was ordered
that no musical instrument should be played, that there be no building

---

* *Antanànarivo Annual*, No. i. p. 24.
† *History of Madagascar*, vol. ii. p. 398.

in clay, or manufacture of pottery, that no one lie on a bed, or spin, or prepare silk, and in case of death the corpse was to be buried without any killing of bullocks or the usual ceremonies.

The trouble the Malagasy take about their tombs is partly accounted for by their belief that the spirit of the departed is unrestful if the body remains unburied. But there also exists a general belief throughout the country in pollution as connected with death. Thus no one who has been at a funeral can enter the palace or approach the sovereign unless a month has elapsed, and no corpse is allowed to be buried in the capital city, or to remain in it beyond a very short time. The rough bier on which the body is carried is thrown away in the neighbourhood of the grave as polluted; no one would dare to use it even for firewood, but it is left to decay with the weather. Besides this, after a funeral the mourners all wash their dress, or at the least dip a portion of it in running water, a ceremony which is called *àfana*, "freed from," and is supposed to carry away the uncleanness contracted from contact with or proximity to a corpse.

Among the Sàkalàva such is the dread of death that when it occurs in one of their villages they break up their settlement, and remove to a distance before rebuilding their slight houses. They seem to believe that the spirit of the deceased will haunt the spot, and do some harm to those who stayed where it had lived in the flesh. This perpetual fleeing before death of course prevents the population from becoming settled in its habits, and produces a most unsubstantial style of house-building. The same notion is also found among the Bàra.*

Something of the same superstition prevails in other tribes. Thus the Sihànaka do not pull down the house or go away from the village, as do the Sàkalàva, but they leave it, and allow it to fall to pieces of itself. Such deserted dwellings they call *tràno fòlaka*, "broken houses."†

These same people, when taking a corpse to the grave, have an earthen dish filled with burning cowdung carried on a man's head, and this is placed at the headstone. They say that the reason of this is

---

* *Antanànarìvo Annual*, No. ii. p. 46.
† Ibid. No. iii. p. 66.

that the dead person may be able to get fire should he chance to
be cold.

"When the corpse has been placed in the grave a man knocks at
the door of the tomb, or on the stone covering it, should there be no
door, and calls out, ' O thou, Such an one, whoever it is that has
bewitched you, let him not hide, let him not be concealed, but break
him upon the rock, that the children may see it, that the women may
see it ; ' and all there also join in the adjuration."*

Among this same tribe, should any one happen to be seriously ill,
he is taken secretly out of the village and conveyed to some out-of-
the-way place, where no one is allowed to see him except those who
nurse him.†

It is said that among the southern Tanàla the people are accustomed, when any of their relatives are ill and become insensible, to
take and place them in a part of the forest where they throw their
dead ; and should the unfortunate creatures so cast away revive and
return to the village they stone them and kill them outright.

Among these same Tanàla they call sudden death *fòla-mànta*
("broken-unripe "), and " such deaths are ascribed to witchcraft. The
diviner is fetched, and he consults the oracle ; and wrapping up some
grains of black sand, places them on the head of the corpse, saying,
'He who is caught carrying his cloth (*i. e.* his dress) within a month is
mine.' They think that the black sand will make the person who
bewitched the deceased to go about naked ; and, therefore, should such
a one be caught at such practices during the month he is killed."‡

10.— *Witchcraft and Charms.*

It will be inferred from the above, what indeed is the fact, that
those who practise witchcraft are accustomed to go about naked, but
this is, of course, done by night, and the *làmba* or outer dress is carried on the head. To dance on tombs is said to be another action
commonly done by *mpàmosàvy* or sorcerers.

* *Antanànarìvo Annual*, No. iii. p. 65.
† Ibid. p. 63.
‡ Ibid. No. ii. p. 98.

Although to practise sorcery was a capital crime, it appears to have been very prevalent; indeed the sorcery which consists in a use of charms of various kinds is still practised almost all over the island. When it was wished to do injury to any one, a basket containing various small articles, each having a symbolic meaning, was laid at his door. Shortly before the revolution in 1863, Mr. Ellis had such charms betokening evil to him laid at his door or window for more than a week. "This charm consisted of a small basket, three or four inches in diameter and depth, in which were two pieces of granite stone, called 'death stones.' A hole was burned in the basket, which indicated calamity by fire. Amongst the contents were hedge-hog's bristles, parts of scorpions or centipedes, hair, earth said to be from a grave, and other strange ingredients."*

Charms or òdy (òly, in some parts of the country) are used for all sorts of purposes: thus there are òdifàty, a cordial for exhilarating in circumstances of extreme sorrow or danger; òdifítìa, a philtre or love charm; òdimahéry or òdiràtsy, a malignant charm, &c. There were also certain charms thrown towards an enemy before a battle as a means of insuring victory. And as soon as one goes away from the Christianised portions of Madagascar one meets with numbers of charms worn by the people, and designed to protect from various evils or to procure certain benefits. Thus, among the Bàra, Tanàla, and East-coast tribes, every one carries charms round his neck. These are small pieces of wood, some being smeared with animal oil, and others with castor-oil, those belonging to rich people being ornamented with beads and anointed with fat. Occasionally these charms are tied round their knees, or fastened round the chest; some are small pieces of wood shaped like a little canoe; others are lemur's bones, both from the hands and feet; others are small wooden figures of men; others are figures of women, or of oxen, with a variety of other small objects. "This lemur's foot," said the people, "we call tsimòkotra, and it is a charm against fatigue; and the meaning of this little canoe is, that we shall not be upset, and if we swim we shall get across safely." And the little human figures they call a charm for obtaining spoil and get-ting plenty of slaves; and the figure of a woman is to aid in obtaining

* *Madagascar Revisited*, p. 271.

women ; and as to the figure of an ox, they say of it that those who possess it will get abundance of cattle.* There are other charms also called *sàmpilàhy* or *òdibàsy*, that is, charms against a gun. These are pieces of a bullock's horn, from three to five or six inches of the tip ; they are ornamented with tin, or with small beads worked in patterns ; the cavity is nearly filled with the ashes of certain trees or plants of supposed magical power, and mixed with fat and bees'-wax; in this composition are stuck a number of large needles. These *òdibàsy* are supposed to render the wearer invulnerable, being an unfailing protection against a musket-ball.

Mr. Richardson says of these Bàra people : " The charms are very numerous ; " and, in addition to the gun charm just described, " the men wear from two to twenty-nine (the greatest number I counted), others on the head, or slung from the shoulder and across the breast." " They have unbounded confidence in these charms, and will not part with them except on exorbitant terms." " Should you show a man that his charms are useless, he will only agree to the belief that you have a more powerful charm than his own, and which he is prepared to buy at any price." † According to the same authority, the Bàra have many prohibited acts (*fàdy* or tabooed), for which fines are imposed. Thus " for sitting or reclining on another person's bed, a fine of one ox, or to be shot. For striding over a person, or for striding over the foot even, the same. For brushing a person's face or any part of his body even with any part of your clothing, the same. For using spoons, plates, or drinking vessels belonging to another person, the same. Children while young are exempt from the penalties; but, when a child arrives at an age when he may be trusted with a spear, he is given in charge of his mother, who takes him from home for a month, and instructs him in his duty to his fellow-men, especially urging him to beware of incurring a fine, or running the risk of being shot. On his return, should he commit any of the above offences, the father will pay the fine, but disinherit his child; and on the second offence will drive him from the place." ‡

---

* *Antanànarìvo Annual*, No. ii. p. 63.
† *Lights and Shadows*, App. i. p. vii.
‡ Ibid. p. vi.

Among such customs may be counted one found among the Sihanàka. In a certain place is a small hole, into which, if you can pitch a stone, you will be rich and prosperous.* Among these people also, as amongst other tribes, a white earth is plastered over the face as a cure for certain complaints. The Hovas are also accustomed to put patches of this substance on their faces on some festive occasions. Thus at the coronation of Queen Rànavàlona I. her majesty's forehead was marked with this white clay, which is called, probably from this use of it, *tàny ràvo*, or "joyful earth."

The charms which were used to procure victory in the bull-fights have already been mentioned ; and many charms are also employed to secure a favourable result in the *tangéna* ordeal.

There is a curious custom formerly in use among the Bétsileo, and still practised by other southern tribes, which is called *Sàlamànga*, a kind of incantation to induce the "spirit of evil," which they believe possesses every one who is ill, to leave the body in which it is and pass into other bodies. Mr. G. A. Shaw, in his *Notes of a Journey to Ikongo* (South-east Madagascar), and also from information he has kindly supplied me with, gives the following particulars of the ceremonies employed:—" To compass this object many forms are gone through under the direction of a diviner. On the roof of the house were placed pieces of white wood, pointed and painted in cross bars of black and red, and stuck in the thatch near the ridge, so as to resemble the horns of the old-fashioned Malagasy houses. About three feet from the door was planted a forked branch of a tree, also resembling horns, having the bark peeled off from the joint upwards. Those in the roof were to induce the spirit to ascend them and so leave the house. That near the door is to prevent any stranger, or any one coming from a house of mourning, from entering the house, as that would break the spell. Then twice every day a dance is performed. The *òdy* or household charms are brought into the court-yard and placed on the wooden rice-mortar together with a dollar. A cloth or mat is spread over this, and upon the whole the sick person is seated dressed in a most curious fashion. One had on, among other

* *Antanànarìvo Annual*, No. ii. p. 14.

ornaments, a conical fool's cap, decked with leaves and flowers, and a great tassel at the tip. Then drums and bamboos were beaten, and the native guitar, banjo, and flute played, the whole village forming a circle round the sick person and clapping hands, while the women and girls sang a monotonous refrain. Then a woman of rank appointed for the occasion began to dance, while another, seated behind the sick persons, began to beat a worn-out spade, suspended by a string, with a hatchet, quite close to their ears, making a horrid din. I thought as I stood by that if it wanted anything to make an indisposed person downright ill this would be a good recipe. The idea of this is to drive the *àngatra* (evil spirit) possessing the sick person into one of those dancing. But the two sick persons sat perfectly motionless, while the drums were beaten louder and louder, and more and more voices and hands joined in the chant and the clapping until it reached a perfect shriek; when I was rather astonished by seeing the two sick girls jump up and commence dancing round the inside of the circle formed by the performers. All this goes on twice, and sometimes three times, a day, and if the sick persons are not speedily cured appeal is made to the diviners, who tell them that not enough rum has been brought, or enough beef, or that the persons dancing are not of high enough rank, or anything else for an excuse."

Numerous other curious practices, which are all closely connected with folk-lore and superstitious beliefs, might be described, as shown in the worship of idols, in sacrifices and offerings for atonement and expiation, in sacred stones and places, the belief in guardian demons and water-sprites, in divination, the native ideas about ghosts and shades, and the customs connected with the New Year's festival, and the practices of circumcision and blood covenants, &c. These may possibly form the subject of another paper if the foregoing proves of interest to the members of the Folk-Lore Society.

JAMES SIBREE, Jun.

POPULAR HISTORY OF THE CUCKOO.

" Sumer is icumen in,
  Lhude sing cuccu;
  Groweth sed, and bloweth med,*
  And springth the wde† nu,
             Sing, cuccu !

" Awe‡ bleteth after lomb,
  Lhouth§ after calve cu,
  Bulluc sterteth,‖ buck verteth,¶
          Mŭrie, sing cuccu !

" Cuccu, cuccu, well sings thu, cuccu,
  Ne swike** thu naver nu,
  Sing, cuccu, nu, sing, cuccu,
  Sing, cuccu, sing, cuccu, nu."
      —*Oldest English Song, about* 1250 (RITSON'S *version.*)

" Tempus adest veris, cuculus, modo rumpe soporem."
                      Ascribed to BEDE.

POPULAR compend of the natural history of the cuckoo might be drawn up from the various opinions afloat regarding this darling bird, and the strains of the rural muse in which these conclusions are embodied.

William Howitt, in his genial *Book of the Seasons*, adduces a rustic rhyme of the shire of Norfolk, which commemorates, in faithful

---

* Meadow.   † Weed.   ‡ Ewe.   § Loweth.
‖ Leaps about, gambles; " startles."—*Scottice.*
¶ Goeth to harbour in the vert or fern.—*Sir J. Hawkins.*
** Cease.

characters, the several epochs by which its summer pilgrimage in our clime is distinguished,—

> "In April, the cuckoo shows his bill ;
> In May, he sings both night and day ;
> In June, he altereth his tune ;
> In July, he prepares to fly ;
> Come August, go he must."

The uneducated Suffolk man, in abhorrence of the sibilant *s*, gives it thus,—

> " In April, the cuckoo show his bill ;
> In May, he sing both night and day ;
> In June, he change his tune ;
> In July, away he fly :
> But in August, away he must."

The Hants song is a monologue,—

> " In April, come I will ;
> In May, I prepare to stay ;
> In June, I change my tune ;
> In July, I prepare to fly ;
> In August, go I must."

Thus runs the Devonian version,—

> " In March, the guku beginth to sarch ;
> In Aperal, he beginth to tell ;
> In May, he beginth to lay ;
> In June, he alterth 'is tune ;
> In July, away a dith vly."*

And other districts still further vary the lay.   In Gloucester the saying is to this purport,—

> " The cuckoo comes in April,
> Sings a song in May,
> Then in June another tune,
> And then he flies away."

---

* In Bray's *Borders of the Tamar and Tavy* there is a different version:—
> " In the month of April, he opens his bill ;
> In the month of May, he singeth all day ;
> In the month of June, he alters his tune ;
> In the month of July, away he doth fly."

This, in Wiltshire, is converted into,—

> " The cuckoo comes in April,
>   Stays the month of May,
>   Sings a song at Midsummer,
>   And then a goes away."*

Then there are other variations,—

One asks—   " Cuckoo, cuckoo !
            What do you do ? "

Answer—   " In April, I open my bill;
            In May, I sing night and day ;
            In June, I change my tune ;
            In July, away I fly ;
            In August, go I must."

> " In April, come he will ;
>   In flowery May, he doth sing all day ;
>   In leafy June, he doth change his tune ;
>   In bright July, he doth begin to fly ;
>   In August, go he must."

In Sussex it is added, as if an afterthought,—

> " If he stay until September,
>   'Tis as much as the oldest man can remember."†

With not less admirable reference to the calendar of nature, in disclosing gems and odoriferous blossoms, the author of the *Address to the Cuckoo,* saluting the " blithe new-comer," tells us,—

> " What time the daisy decks the green,
>   Thy certain voice we hear ;
>   Hast thou a star to guide thy path,
>   And mark the rolling year ?

> " What time the pea puts on the bloom,
>   Thou fliest the vocal vale ;
>   An annual guest in other lands,
>   Another spring to hail."

---

* These rhymes are from the *Gardeners' Chronicle*, 1850, and the *Athenæum*, 1846.

† *Athenæum, ibid.*

The first two lines, however, are a re-adaptation of Shakspeare's,—

> " When daisies pied, and violets blue,
>   And lady-smocks all silver white,
>   And cuckoo-buds of yellow hue,
>   Do paint the meadows with delight,
>   The cuckoo then on every tree
>   Sings cuckoo !"

In Northumberland also the working-man cherishes his traditionary song of the seasons ; he, too, adduces some incident in the mysterious tale not generally observed or known :—

> " The cuckoo comes of mid March,
>   And cucks of mid Aperill ;
>   And gauns away of midsummer month,
>   When the corn begins to fill."

Accordant with this is the version of the South of Scotland, part of ancient Northumbria : —

> " The cuckoo comes in the middle of March,
>   And sings in the middle of April ;
>   And passes away at the Lammas-tide,
>   When the corn begins to fill."
>   *Peebles-shire.**

The cuckoo sometimes makes its appearance considerably prior to the date when the leafing woods and the sunny vales re-echo its " two-fold shout."

A common English couplet says :—

> " The first cock of hay
>   Frights the cuckoo away."

The Lanarkshire ploughman believes that " the cookoo comes wi' a haw leaf, and gangs away wi' a bear (four-rowed barley) head." It is also said in the West of Scotland that the cuckooo flies away on the first sight she obtains of barley in the ear.

The Rev. Gilbert White, of Selborne, in his calendar gives the earliest and latest days of the cuckoo's arrival as the 7th and 26th of April. In Cornwall, Mr. Couch, from 1810 to 1836, found it to be

---

* *Round the Grange Farm*, p. 108.

from April 19th to May 18th.* Mr. Henry Doubleday, of Epping, says, " The male cuckoo arrives about the middle of April (seldom earlier than the 13th or later than the 20th) in the southern counties."† Mr. Marsham, at Stratton, in Norfolk (in his tables laid before the Royal Society) from 1753 to 1788, observed its earliest song from April 16th to May 7th. In the north of Yorkshire it sings about the 26th or 27th of April. Mr. Selby found that it arrived at Twizell House from April 26th to May 4th. Mr. Hepburn gives April 24th as the period for East Lothian; while I, not so far north as his locality, but at a greater altitude, find it to be from April 29th to May 15th; in exceptional years as early as April 7th; but for the most part after the beginning of May; thus corroborating the testimony of an old Scottish poet:—

> " In May begins the golk to gail."
> ALEX. SCOTT'S *Gratulation to the Moneth of May.*

The latest periods I ever saw old cuckoos were the 2nd and 4th of August, 1860-61. Young cuckoos are fledged at this period, but those seen, the one in Berwickshire and the other in Northumberland, wore the old plumage. In East Lothian the date of departure for young birds is August 23rd. Those I saw were most likely stragglers, for Jenner states that " Old cuckoos take their final leave of the country the first week in July," and Mr. Selby says the period of departure of the old birds " seldom or never extends beyond the first week in July ;" and Mr. Couch corroborates this. " At the beginning of July the old birds disappear altogether at nearly the same day." The epoch of the cuckoo's temporary visit to Germany is from St. Tiburt's day (April 14th) to the feast of St. John the Baptist (June 24th); rarely to the feast of St. James, July 25th ; but in Italy not seldom protracted to the end of July.‡

It is the popular belief in some parts of the country that the cuckoo

---

* *Cornish Fauna,* p. 18.

† *Gardeners' Chronicle,* 1851, p. 485.

‡ Wolfgang Franzii *Hist. Animalium,* pars ii. a Johanne Cypriano ; Francofurti et Lipsiæ, 1712, 4to. pp. 1299, 1304.

always makes its appearance on the 21st of April.* In Sussex the 14th of April is called " First Cuckoo Day."† In Scotland it is phrased, " the gowk has come hame." The 20th of April is the fair-day of Tenbury, in Worcestershire, and there is a belief in that county that you never hear the cuckoo till Tenbury fair-day, or after Pershore fair-day, which is the 26th of June.‡ In Wales it is considered unlucky to hear the cuckoo before the 6th of April, but " you will have pros-perity," is the common saying, " for the whole year if you hear it on the 28th."§

In Scotland the coming of the lapwing to its breeding haunts from its winter residence on the coast, about the beginning of March, is heralded by several days of tempestuous weather, called from local names of the bird " a peesweep or teuchit storm." So,

> " When well-apparell'd April on the heel
> Of limping winter treads,"

the advent of the cuckoo calls forth the old season's spite, and the consequence is, a "gowk storm." Hence, in Craven, in Yorkshire, it is said—

> " In the month of Averil,
> The gowk comes over the hill
> In a shower of rain."

The expression, a " gowk storm," is connected with a remarkable historical incident. " The Marquis of Argyle, being executed for his complicity in the Cromwellian usurpation, his son succeeded to the title of Earl of Argyle only. He had repaired to London, in order to make some interest at court, and had been persuaded that some of the minions of Lord Clarendon—then at the head of affairs—would, for a thousand pounds, undertake to procure for him that minister's patron-age and favour. Argyle, upon this, wrote a confidential letter to Lord Duffus, in which he told him that providing he could raise a thousand pounds he would be able to obtain the protection of the

---

* Chambers' *Book of Days*, i. p. 530.
† Hone's *Every Day Book*, i. p. 466.
‡ *Notes and Queries*, 2nd series, i. p. 249.
§ Dyer's *English Folk-Lore*, p. 57.

English minister; that in such a case he trusted the present would prove but a *gowk storm;* and, after some depreciating expressions concerning the prevailing party in the Scottish Parliament, he added, that 'then the king would see their tricks.' This letter fell into the hands of Middleton (who then guided the Scottish realm), who determined that for expressions, so innocent and simple, being, in fact, the natural language of a rival courtier, Argyle would be brought to trial for *leasing-making.* Argyle was condemned to lose his head and forfeit his estate. He was respited, but was detained a prisoner till the end of Middleton's government."[*]

As a prognosticator of weather, "when it appears, the first claps of thunder are heard in the sky announcing the season of heat."[†] "The Germans connect the cuckoo with good weather, and countrymen do not like to hear it before June, because, they say, the sooner he comes, the sooner will he go." (Chambers' *Popular Rhymes,* p. 193.) In Switzerland, when the cuckoo ventures near a town, especially if it enters it, it forebodes rain or a great storm; and some fear a dearth when it approaches houses. There it continues in full note till St. John's Day in summer, but, if cultivators hear it later, they dread that the wine of Zurich will that season be sour.[‡] In Germany, if it sings after St. John's Day, grapes ripen with difficulty, and a scarcity of the produce of the earth will result.[§]

The bad weather it brings with it is little to its own advantage. A Welsh distich tells how—

> " The first week of May
> Frights the cuckoo away."[‖]

In the rigorous weather of early May his voice becomes hoarse; hence the German rustics allege that then his voice is frozen.[¶]

---

[*] *Tales of a Grandfather,* vol. ii. p. 191-3 (2nd series).
[†] Gubernatis' *Zoological Mythology,* ii. p. 231.
[‡] *C. Plinii Secundi, Des wijdt-vermaerden Natuur-kondigers vijf Boecken.* Amsterdam, 1662, 12mo, p. 383.
[§] Wolfgang Franz. pars ii. p. 1304.
[‖] Mary Howitt's *Pictorial Calendar of Nature.*
[¶] Wolfgang Franz. *ubi sup.*

In some parts of England the spring quarter is known as "Cuckoo time." In Shakspeare (*Love's Labour Lost*) the cuckoo represents *Ver*, or the spring. An eclogue attributed to the Venerable Bede, inscribed "Cuculus," describes the conflict of spring and winter. Winter is at length told to cease his importunity, and allow the harbinger of spring to arrive with all her grateful accompaniments, which every one is anxious to welcome. In a second eclogue two shepherds bewail the cuckoo's death which shall no more arouse the spring with its gladsome lays.* According to Grimm, the commencement of spring is expressed in the old German law by the formula, "When the cuckoo cries (wan der gauch gucket);" and the Anglo-Saxon, Codex Exoniensis, of the song of St. Guthlac, ascribes to this bird the announcement of the year, "geacas geár budon"—cuculi annum nuntiavere. Thus also Spenser—

> "The merry cuckoo, messenger of spring,
> His trumpet shrill hath thrice already sounded."

And Lyly—

> "Hark ! how the jolly cuckoos sing
> Cuckoo ! to welcome in the spring."

And with equal felicity, Grahame—

> "How sweet the first sound of the cuckoo's note ;
> Whence is the magic pleasure of the sound ?
> How do we long recall the very tree,
> Or bush, near which we stood, when on the ear
> The unexpected note cuckoo ! again,
> And yet again, came down the budding vale !
> It is the voice of spring among the trees;
> It tells of lengthening days, of coming bloom ;
> It is the symphony of many a song."†

It is a popular saw that—

> "On the third of April
> Comes in the cuckoo and nightingale."

---

* *Ibid*, p. 1305. The entire pieces are said to be inserted in Dornavii *Amphitheatro*, fol. 456-7. The second may be the mediæval poem quoted in a note in Gubernatis' *Zool. Mythol.* p. 233, as preserved in Uhland's *Schriften*, vol. iii. where the subject of lament is that the bird would be swallowed up in crossing the sea.

† *Birds of Scotland*, p. 57.

Ray also records that " the nightingale and cuckoo sing both in one month;" but the hidden meaning may intend to contrast the quality of each bird's song, for, according to the line of King James I.,

" Unlike the cukkow to the Phylomene ;"

or, as Portia declares, after speaking of the nightingale,

" He knows me as the blind man knows the cuckoo,
By the bad voice."

The cuckoo and the nightingale may be thus placed in contrariety, in recollection of the fable that relates the contest of the two very dissimilar birds for pre-eminence in song. According to the story, the ass being judge, assigned the prize to the cuckoo, for the reason that he understood what it said; but the nightingale, whose music was beyond its comprehension, appealed from the unjust sentence to man, who alone could properly appreciate it, and the judgment was reversed.[*] A German song of the sixteenth century given in Uhland's *Schriften*, iii. p. 25, places the nightingale in opposition to the cuckoo. The Hon. Horace Walpole and Miss Mitford agree in the expression of their annoyance that the frequency of the cuckoo's note should overpower those of the unrivalled songster. Of date Strawberry Hill, June 25, 1778, " I have found but one inconvenience," says Walpole, " which is the host of cuckoos." " It is very disagreeable that the nightingale should sing but half-a-dozen songs, and the other beasts squall for two months together."[†] The lady is still more indignant about " the unison of the most delightful, the most various, and the most powerful of all our songsters, with that tiresome, monotonous, detestable bird."[‡] Not such was the judgment of Fingal, King of Men.

" Sweet is the song of the three sons of Meardha,
The cuckoo's note in early summer,
And the echo of loud laughter in the wood." [§]

---

[*] Gubernatis' *Zoological Mythology*, 235-6. Broderip's *Zoological Recreations*, pp. 70, 71.

[†] *Correspondence of Horace Walpole*, iv. p. 110. London, 1820.

[‡] *Life of Mary Russell Mitford*, by Rev. A. G. L'Estrange, i. p. 192.

[§] Kennedy's *Fictions of the Irish Celts*, p. 240.

This, like the expression of the ancient German song of May, is the unvitiated utterance of unsophisticated nature—

> " The cuckoo with its song makes every one gay."

" In some places," remarks the Rev. T. F. Thiselton Dyer, " there is a popular prognostication from the fact of the cuckoo or nightingale being first heard.   Thus the poet Milton, in his ' Sonnet to the Nightingale,' says :—

> ' Thy liquid notes that close the eve of day,
>   First heard before the shallow cuckoo's bill
>   Portends success in love.'

" This piece of Folk-Lore is also alluded to by Chaucer in his poem entitled ' The Cuckoo and the Nightingale.'   In the modernised version by Wordsworth, it is said :—

> ' But tossing lately on a sleepless bed,
>   I of a token thought which lovers need :
>   How among them it was a common tale,
>   That it was good to hear the nightingale,
>   Ere the vile cuckoo's note be uttered.' " *

It has been a fond conceit with many, that husbandmen ought to be guided at seed-time by the indications that natural phenomena supply of the suitability of the season for engaging in their operations. It prevailed among the ancients, who drew the omens they could most depend on from birds ; and Stillingfleet, of blue-stocking memory, familiarized us again with the notion.   Thus Hesiod, the earliest Georgical writer, informs us " That if it should happen to rain three days together when the cuckoo sings among the oak-trees, then late sowing will be as good as early sowing." †   According to Aristophanes, " The cuckoo formerly governed all Egypt and Phœnicia, because when that bird appeared it was time for wheat and barley harvest."‡ Looking forward to the return of fine weather in spring, the Norfolk

---

* *English Folk-Lore*, p. 73.
† Stillingfleet's *Tracts*, p. 225.
‡ Stillingfleet's *Select Works*, ii. 390.

people say " When the cuckoo has picked up the dirt."* Lord Bacon
also makes the remark, " Swallows, batts, cuckoos, &c. that come towards summer, if they come early, show a hot summer to follow."†
From some such observation it may have been that a Norwich farmer
wrote in the *Bath Papers*, vol. v. page 266, " Sept. 9, 1789. The
present appearance for the greatest appearance of barley is from the
seed sown on the earliest sound of the cuckoo, and while the buds of
blackthorn were yet turgid, than what was delayed to the frequent
note of the former, and the expansion of bloom in the latter." It
may have been a popular idea to sow barley then, for we find it in
Grahame's *British Georgics*—

> " Soon as the earliest swallow skims the mead,
>   The barley sowing is by some begun ;
>   While others wait until her clay-built nest,
>   Completed, in the window corner hang ;
>   Or till the school-boy mock the cuckoo's note."

Thus also, " it was a custom among the farmers in the southern
counties of Scotland never to sow their peas till the swallows made
their appearance."‡ This is primitive practice, but, if the farmer was
to place dependence upon such pet times, he would soon become liable
to the same reproach as the vine-dressers mentioned by Pliny
(lib. xviii. c. 26), " Who were anciently called cuckoos, *i.e.* slothful,
because they deferred cutting their vines till that bird began to sing,
which was later than the right time."§ In Berwickshire " gowk
oats " are those sown after the 1st of April. It is said of an early
March, " There will be no gowk oats this year." " In some districts
the following proverb is much used :

> ' Cuckoo oats and woodcock hay
>   Make a farmer run away.'

---

* R. Taylor, in *Ann. Nat. Hist.* xiii. p. 403.

† *Sylva Sylvarum*, p. 174.

‡ Thomas Wilkie's MSS.

§ *Horat. Sat.* i. 7, v. 23. There is more on this reproach in Cyprian's *Annotations on Wolfgang Franz.* pp. 1305-6, a book I have several times referred to,
and in Gubernatis' *Zool. Mythol.* ii. p. 233.

This phrase, says a correspondent of *Notes and Queries* (3rd series, vol. v. p. 450), means that if the spring is so backward that the oats cannot be sown till the cuckoo is heard, or the autumn so wet that the latter-math crop of hay cannot be gathered in till the woodcocks come over, the farmer is sure to suffer great loss. In Norfolk, too, one may frequently hear the poorer classes quoting the subjoined rhyme with reference to their agricultural pursuits :

> ' When the weirling shrieks at night,
> Sow the seed with the morning light ;
> But 'ware when the cuckoo swells its throat,
> Harvest flies from the mooncall's note.'

' When the cuckoo purls its feathers, the housewife should become chary of her eggs,' is a popular saying in many parts of the country."* Another agricultural omen, taken from this bird, is given by Ray—

> " When the cuckoo comes to the bare thorn,
> Sell your cow and buy you corn ;
> But when she comes to the full bit,
> Sell your corn and buy you sheep."

" It portends misfortune to the Servian haiduken when the kukavitza (cuckoo) appears early and comes out of the black wood, but good luck when his cry comes from the green wood."—(Grimm).

Everything about this bird is matter of wonder. The time is not long past when the cuckoo was feigned to derive its summer sustenance from the eggs of helpless warblers, whose trim nests it rifled :—

> " The cuckoo's a bonny bird, he whistles as he flies ;
> He brings us good tidings, he tells us no lies.
> He sucks little birds' eggs, to make his voice clear ;
> And never sings cuckoo ! till summer draws near.
> Sings cuckoo in April, cuckoo in May,
> Cuckoo in June, and then flies away."†

---

* Dyer's *Folk-Lore*, pp. 60, 61. See also *Notes and Queries*, 4th ser. i. pp. 533-4, and ii. p. 22.

　† Var. 1. " And never sings cuckoo till the springtime of year."
　　　2. " And when he sings cuckoo the summer is near."
　　　3. " He drinks the cold water to make his voice clear,
　　　　　And he'll come again in the spring of next year."
　　　4. " He sucks the sweet flowers to make his voice clear."
　　　5. " That she may sing cuckoo three months of the year."

The Germans think that the cuckoo cannot cry till he has eaten a bird's egg. Hence, perhaps, the Spanish proverb, " I am like the cuckou, which sing not until I have my stomach full." * I should not wonder if the common opinion is correct after all. Some of its kindred are omnivorous. On Audubon's authority, the yellow-billed cuckoo of America robs smaller birds of their eggs, which it sucks on all occasions. In two cuckoos that I examined—an old one in May, and a young bird in August, the food consisted of caterpillars, rough and smooth, the shards of beetles, immense quantity of the aphides (plant lice) of fir-trees in the young one, two or three seeds, a few stones, and some blades and roots of grass. Swainson was of opinion that from the form of its nostrils, analogous to those of the toucans, it is facilitated in the discovery of the nests of those species in which it deposits its eggs by its superior powers of smell.† It carries its own egg in its mouth, that it intends to place with a foster-mother. In Ireland one was shot, when the egg dropped from its mouth entire, and was ascertained to be a cuckoo egg.‡ " I have," says Mr. Edwin Lees, " seen the cuckoo flying along very early in the morning with an egg in its mouth, most likely its own, which it was conveying to the nest of some little warbler, according to its well-known and singular economy."§ Le Vaillant killed several specimens of an African cuckoo (*Cuculus auratus*) transporting eggs in this manner. Other observers have seen a cuckoo with an egg in its bill, but considered that it was practising robbery.

From this delicious speech-invigorating element, then, to go on with the popular view, it is, that it acquires that lucid intonation and unfettered utterance that enables it to keep the spring-tide groves so long resonant to its "wandering voice." When the date of the feathered tribes' solicitude is completed, and instead of fragile eggs, and callow young ones, in slim, unprotected abodes, full-fledged broods flutter amid the boughs, and scuttle down into the brake beyond

* Dialogues appended to Minshen's *Spanish Dictionary*, 1623.
† *Magazine of Zoology and Botany*, i. p. 431.
‡ *Dublin Nat. Hist. Review*, January, 1855, p. 25.
§ *Pictures of Nature around the Malvern Hills*, p. 16.

the reach of the prying intruder, its once mellow notes grow hoarser and huskier, imperfect and reduplicate, until at length the bird's melodious functions are entirely suspended.

> "In April the cuckoo can sing his song by rote ;
> In June of tune she cannot sing a note ;
> At first, *koo-koo, koo-koo,* sing shrill can she do ;
> At last *kooke, kooke, kooke,* six *kookes* for one *koo.*"

This is what Southey calls a "stuttering cuckoo." "A.D. 1815. By Mr. Leathes's I heard a stuttering cuckoo, whose note was cuc-cuckoo, cuccuckoo ; after three or four of which he brought out the word rightly."* This is a circumstance well known to country observers. The period of silence in Berwickshire is from June 26 to July 2 ; the latest date of hearing the cuckoo in East Lothian was July 3. Near London "A Southern Faunist" had heard it even to the 9th of July. (*Gent. Mag.* 1792, p. 506). In the course of six-teen years Mr. Marwick never heard it after the 26th of June. (*Linn. Trans.* vol. i.) "Cuckoo first heard April 27, last heard June 27. Mean of eleven years." (*Jenyns' Observ.*) :—

> "Nor does she cease
> Her changeless note, until the broom, full blown,
> Give warning that her time for flight has come."
> GRAHAME.

To its far extending, *harrying* excursions, then, it would be said, we owe the never steady, ever-shifting intensity of its voice ; now near, now remote, now clear, and now stifled, now silent, and now hurried in breathless succession, now—

> "Babbling only to the vale
> Of sunshine and of flowers,"

and now indistinctly stirring the ancient silence of the upland waste. And in Berwickshire it is the persuasion that to this cause is to be ascribed its harsher second note, uttered among the leafy thickets at uncertain intervals. This is only heard when the vagabond bird has pounced upon some nest, and, being interpreted, implies "muck it

---

* Southey's *Common-Place Book,* iv. p. 535.

out," *i. e.*, make a complete clearance. Unfortunately for the poet's credit, this note, as observation can testify, is repeated by one of the birds when in pursuit of its mate ; it is also heard when it leaves a branch, and occasionally both sexes are said to utter it when disturbed. I have seen two cuckoos crossing a moor, one silent, and the foremost uttering both " cuckoo " and " muck it out." How could Kit North affirm, " She is always mute as she flies ? " * It is now pretty certain that both sexes can utter the cuckoo cry. There is still a third note, of a peculiar character, as if it had borrowed the " blutter " of the curlew; seldom heard, except by those traversing the sides of the mountain glens, which the birds frequent in pairing time. It has not obtained popular notice.

A correspondent to *Long Ago* (p. 205), from North Notts, gives a belief of some of the country people, that the male calls " cuckoo " thrice in succession, and the female twice; properly adding that " this rule will not hold." It is also imagined that when the cuckoo is converted into a hawk he can whistle and sing.—*Ibid.* When the common note changes towards the end of the season, rain is approaching. (North Yorkshire, *Notes and Queries*, 4th ser. ii. 355.)

In the South of England the cuckoo appears to be regarded as *he*, while in the North and in Scotland it is spoken of as *she*, and as the only one of the species. I once asked a man if he did not think it was the cock that sung. " I dinna ken," was the reply ; " I never see nane but ane." The Slavonians always represent the bird as a female—Zezhulice, who sits on an oak and bewails the transitoriness of spring. " The Servian kukavitza was a maiden who long bewailed her brother's death, until she was changed into the bird, the grey kukavitza (' the plain-song cuckoo gray '); so also in Russian songs it is a bird of mourning and melancholy, and Russian traditions speak of her as a young maiden changed by an enchantress." †

" In Italy," says Gubernatis, " we say, ' the years of the cuckoo,' and in Piedmont, ' as old as a cuckoo,' to indicate great age. A mediæval eclogue ascribes to the cuckoo the years of the sun, ' Phœbo comes

---

* *Noctes Ambrosianæ*, iv. p. 19.

† Grimm's *Deutsche Mythologie*, in *Ann. Nat. Hist.* xiii. p. 405.

annus in ævum.' As no one sees how the cuckoo disappears it is supposed that it never dies, that it is always the same cuckoo that sings year after year in the same wood." *

In her presumed egg-hunting excursions the cuckoo is pursued by troops of small birds, all up on the defensive and twittering in dismay, for they have misapprehended her homely gray vesture and equivocal shape for those of a hawk. One only of that numerous train has she selected as her bosom friend; it is her inseparable associate, and becomes her tool. In some places this shadow of authority, usually a meadow pipit or "moss cheeper" (*Anthus pratensis*), is entitled "the cuckoo's titling," and why the connection exists no one can divine, unless it be that the cuckoo has secret intentions of engaging a foster-nurse to attend to the duties of incubation, for which in her own person she has no hearty relish or deeply urgent desire. It is the opinion of the Durham labourer that this small bird is the "cuckoo's Sandie." The cuckoo is of the *hawk kind*, and inclines to regale herself with the dainties of wild game and so forth, but "has neither the beak, the toes, the claws, the courage, nor the strength of a bird of prey." She assumes this bird as her eaterer, who dismembers the birds they contrive to catch and feeds her therewith; hence the protection vouchsafed and the inexplicable union. A correspondent of *The Gentleman's Magazine* for 1796, p. 117, says, "The peasantry of Devon and Cornwall believe the cuckoo feeds on the eggs of other birds, and that *the little bird*, as they call it, accompanying him (the *Yunx Torquilla*, wryneck or summer bird) searches for them for that purpose and feeds him." The wryneck prefers the South of England, and has generally been considered not to be distributed further north than Morpeth, although there are several instances recorded of its occurrence in Scotland. It precedes the cuckoo's arrival by about a week, and is variously known as the "cuckoo's maiden, mate, or marrow," and the "cuckoo's attendant, messenger, or harbinger." Its Swedish name is Göktita. Mr. Broderip relates that in this country a pair of red-backed shrikes have been seen feeding a young

* *Zoological Mythology*, ii. p. 235.

cuckoo, and hence probably the provincial name for the shrike, as in
Herefordshire for instance, where it is called " the cuckoo's maid." *
In the moorland districts, for often there,

> " From the neighbouring vales,
> The cuckoo straggling up to the hill tops
> Shouteth faint tidings of some gladder place,"

its common follower is the meadow pipit. In some parts of Scotland
this is termed the teeting, in Orkney the titing, and in Yorkshire the
moor-tite. This nearly resembles tätting, the Swedish name for the
common sparrow. But we have another titling (Tyttlingur, Icelandic,
a sparrow) in the hedge-sparrow (*Accentor modularis*), called also the
hemp-sparrow, the latter a name in Sweden for the domestic sparrow.
Muffett calls his Curruca, whatever he may have meant by the term,
" the titling, eucknel, or unfortunate nurse, for the cuckoo ever lays his
egg in the titling's nest."† The *Complaynt of Scotland* says, " The
titlene followit the goilk, and gart her sing guk, guk." Its diminu-
tive size contrasted with that of its patron has originated the proverb, " Like the cuckoo and the tit-lark," " the cuckoo and the little
bird," " the gowk and the titling," applied to two disproportionately
sized animals or to one who obsequiously follows another. " Many
an old apple-woman at the fairs," says Galt in *Sir Andrew Wylie*,
" on seeing the gouk and the titling approach (as two boys were
called) watched their tempting piles of toys and delectables with gleg
een' and staff grasped to repel some pawkie aggression."

In Ireland, the charitable wish is sometimes heard, if two people
are quarrelling, " May you never hear the cuckoo nor the little bird
that follows it." It is believed that the latter bird is ever trying to
get into the cuckoo's mouth. If this should once happen, " the end
of the world 'ould come." (*Long Ago*, p. 248.)

From the notion that in her predatory vocation, with " Sandie " as
provider, she talks more than she works, has arisen a popular reproach,
which I once picked up near Newcastle—

---

* *Zoological Recreations*, p. 75.
† Muffett's *Health's Improvement*, p. 105.

> " Cuckoo, scabb'd gowk,
>   Mickle said, little wrought."

Ray, in his *Proverbs*, has " as scabbed as a cuckoo," and in
Lovell's *History of Animals, &c.* p. 193, Oxford, 1661, it is related
" their feathers came off in winter, and they are scabbed." " As
scabbed as a cuckoo," says a correspondent of *Science Gossip*, 1866,
p. 184, " is a common saying in Yorkshire, and I certainly never
had hold of any living thing from which such an amount of scurf
comes off as from a young cuckoo." The Annotator on *Franzius*,
part ii. p. 1306, says, " the cuckoo is an unclean, nasty bird, particularly in winter, when, having lost its feathers, its body is scabbed all
over, whence there is a proverb among us—'a man scabbed as a
cuckoo.' "

That the cuckoo is a hawk is no recent fabrication.   Aristotle, and
after him Pliny, mentions that it was the belief of some, that during a
portion of the year it was converted by the alteration of its voice, shape,
and plumage, into a real bird of prey ; but the first of these naturalists
was not convinced—for their physical structure did not correspond, and
he knew that hawks killed cuckoos and ate them, which they would
not have done had they been consanguineous.   In the South of Yorkshire, as Mr. Heppenstall once wrote to me, " the young bird is taken
for a hawk, and is said to turn to one in winter."   " In Plutarch (*Life
of Aratos*) the cuckoo asks the other birds why they flee from his
sight, inasmuch as he is not ferocious ; the birds answer that they
fear in him the future sparrow-hawk." (*Zool. Mythol.* ii. p. 235.)·

The old cuckoo being accounted predaceous, no wonder that its offspring fleshed itself by making a meal of its foster-parents.   " In se
nutricem convertit " (Pliny) was true natural history in the days of
Shakspeare.

> " The hedge-sparrow fed the cuckoo so long,
>   That it had its head bit off by its young."
>   *King Lear.*

> " And being fed by us, you us'd us so
>   As that ungentle gull, the cuckoo's bird,
>   Useth the sparrow : did oppress our nest ;

Grew by our feeding to so great a bulk
That even our love durst not come near your sight,
For fear of swallowing."

King Henry IV.

It was at one time also blamed for devouring all its companions in the nest; because, as soon as the young cuckoo emerged from the shell, all appearance of birds or eggs was removed from the nest.* But it was shown by Jenner that it chucks these overboard by rising with a sudden spring after it has crept beneath them and got the luckless *gorblets* into a hollow on its back. To the supposed ungracious treatment of its nurse, responds the German proverb, " Thou rewardest me as the cuckoo did the hedge-sparrow." Among the Declamations of Philip Melancthon there is one—tom. i. p. 643— " On the Ingratitude of the Cuckoo," an oration delivered in the year 1537. There are some extracts from it in Cyprian's *Notes on Franzius*, ii. p. 1302. The French have a proverb, " Ingrat comme un coucou."

The cuckoo moults about the end of March.† When it reaches Europe it looks so feeble that it was fabled that it had been transported on the back of the kite (Isodori *Orig.* lib. xii. cvii.) Its low short flights at this period are not from weakness, but that it may select its food, which is then principally on or near the ground. The birds are then so lean as to justify the French proverb, " Maigre comme un coucou "—as lean as a cuckoo. The young birds in autumn are very fat, and their flesh was considered a delicacy in ancient, as it still is in modern, Italy.

Everyone has heard of the " seven sleepers," once " devoutly believed in as an almanac, who formed a favourite nursery chant "—

" Seven sleepers there be—
The bat, the bee, the butterflee,
The cuckoo and the swallow,
The kittiwake and the corn-craik,
Sleep a' in a little hollie."

* Constable's *Edinburgh Magazine*, April, 1818.
† *Edinburgh Phil. Journal*, n.s. v. (1828), p. 200.

How confirmatory of these first lines in physical lore is Willoughby's tale, which, however, he did not believe, of the cuckoo torpid in a bundle of feathers in the hollow of an old tree, which shouted cuckoo in the midst of winter when aroused by the heat of a stove ; or that other Bewick tells of, which giving its captors the slip in spring, as it fled across the Tyne, wickedly cried " Cuckoo !" all along as it went. But the notion is a very old one.

> " But the warm sun thaws the benumbed earth,
> And makes it tender ; gives a sacred birth
> To the dead swallow, wakes in a hollow tree
> The drowsy cuckoo and the humble bee."
>
> CAREW.

> " Thick-lined with moss, which, though to little boot,
> Seemed as a shelter it had lending been
> Against cold winter's storms and wreakful teen ;
> For in his hollow trunk and perished grain
> The cuckoo now had many a winter lain."
>
> BROWNE.

A story of similar import is told in Agricola *De Animantibus Subterraneis,* of which the date as a separate work is 1549; but in another form, 1521. Gesner alludes to it as a fable of Swiss origin. In *Gassendus Physicæ,* &c. the cuckoo is said to have issued from a Christmas log in Champagne. A very circumstantial relation of a like occurrence is given by Jean Faber in his book on the *Animals of Mexico,* Rome, 1628, which may be found quoted in Cyprian's *Notes on Franzius,* p. 1304. Aristotle asserts "that many birds, and not a few as some imagine, hide themselves in holes ;" and that " sage philosopher," Alexander Ross, puts on the cope-stone : " Swallows, cuckoows, dormise, &c. live all the winter without any chilification or action of the stomach."[*] It is from the reported deplumed condition of the cuckoo in winter that the proverb originates, " As naked as a cuckoo," which I have heard in Northumberland applied to a prodigal. " As naked as the cuckoo in Christmas " occurs in Dekker's *Gull's Hornbook,* 1609 (Hindley's Reprint, p. 20).

---

[*] *Arcana Microcosmi,* p. 20.

What, then, becomes of the cuckoos when they disappear? They are, it seems, committed to the custody of an irascible old woman in Sussex, to whose fits of temper is owing the irregular distribution of the birds throughout the rest of the country. In spring the cuckoo-keeper "fills her apron with them, and—if she is in a good humour—allows several to take flight, but only permits one or two to escape if anything has happened to sour her temper."*

A notion prevailed at Lorbottle, a small inland town in Northumberland, that the cuckoo was the cause of summer. These silly folks, popularly known as "the coves of Lorbottle," agreed that, if she could be secured "within a pinfold there," they would never have winter more. One particular plantation was noted, whither she was accustomed most frequently to repair, and utter her notes earliest and most mellow. It was evidently a favourite haunt, where she loved to linger. This it was determined to environ with a wall, to render her stay perpetual, and give her unquiet footsteps rest. They were encouraged to this also by the short flights the bird takes in spring. The wall was reared in haste and with solicitude, but, alas, just as it was completed and a home prepared, the capricious and ungrateful bird glided quietly over the top, "and flapped her well-fledged wings and sped away." Thus perished all hopes of Lorbottle's being blessed with a never-ending summer. It is still, however, a fondly cherished opinion among the seniors of the place that if the wall had only been elevated *a little higher* the darling project would have been achieved.

"Certain Cornishmen," according to Mr. Hunt, "built a wall around the cuckoo to prevent that bird from leaving the county, and thus insure an early spring. When built the bird flew out, crying, 'Cuckoo! cuckoo!' 'If we had put one course more on the wall we should a' kept 'n in,' said they."†

A similar design was once entertained by that sage race, the wise men of Gotham. They, too, attempted to hedge in the cuckoo.‡ The story is as follows:—On an eminence about a mile south of Gotham, a

---

* *Folk-Lore Record*, i. p. 17.
† *Popular Romances of the West of England*, p. 426
‡ *Gentleman's Magazine*, June, 1796, p. 636.

village of Nottinghamshire, stands a bush known as the "Cuckoo Bush," which represents an older one connected with one of the legends that has given notoriety to that place. King John was once marching towards Nottingham, and intended to pass through Gotham meadow; but the villagers, believing that the ground over which a king went became for ever afterwards a public road, to save their right of common, contrived means for preventing the king from going in that direction. The king, incensed, sent messengers to inquire the reason of their incivility, intending, doubtless, to punish them, by fine or otherwise, for their rude behaviour. When the king's servants arrived "they found some of the inhabitants endeavouring to drown an eel in a pond; some dragging their carts and waggons to the top of a barn to shade a wood from the sun's rays; some tumbling cheeses down a hill in the expectation that they would find their way to Nottingham market; and some employed in hedging in a cuckoo which had perched upon an old bush. In short, they were all employed in such a manner as convinced the king's officers that they were a village of *fools*, and consequently unworthy of his majesty's notice. They, of course, having outwitted the king, imagined that they were *wise*. Hence arose the saying, 'The wise fools of Gotham.'"*

An original "Merry Tale," as reprinted by J. O. Halliwell, of the Gothamites and the cuckoo, is this: "On a time the men of Gotham would fain have *pinn'd* (*sic*) in the cuckoo, whereby she should sing all the year; and in the midst of the town they had a hedge made round in compass, and they had got a cuckow, and put her into it, and said, ' Sing here, and you shall lack neither meat nor drink all the year.' The cuckow, when she perceived herself encompassed within the hedge, she flew away. ' A vengeance on her,' said the wise men, ' we made not our hedge high enough.'" (*Notes and Queries*, 4th ser. vol. iv. pp. 305-6.)

The wise men of Somersetshire once attempted to solve the mysteries of cuckoo-life by building a high wall round an unfledged cuckoo, in which they fed and kept it like a prisoner of state. "The

---

* Chambers' *Book of Days*, i. pp. 462-3.

bird quietly grubbed until it was fledged, when it spread its wings and easily flew over the high wall and escaped. The wise men had forgotten to roof their enclosure—they had penned the cuckoo but had forgotten that it would fly." Hence they were derisively called "Cuckoo-penners." (*Ibid.*)

Fulke Greville, Lord Brook (1554-1628), declares—

> "Fools only hedge the cuckoo in."

The cuckoo is singular among British birds, so admirable in their domestic relations, for consigning its eggs and young to the care and nurture of another, which is silly enough not to detect the guile. Whence does this, one would suppose, unnatural alienation of the parent from its offspring spring ; and that—

> "She, alone of all the innumerous feathered tribes,
> Passes a stranger's life without a home ?"

" According to the Bohemian creed, the festivals of the Virgin Mary used to be held sacred, even by animals ; and birds, for instance, took particular care not to work at their nests on those days. The cuckoo, having infringed that custom, was cursed, and obliged to wander perpetually, without ever a nest of its own."* In Denmark a different solution has been arrived at. "If you wish to know why the cuckoo builds no nest of its own," that Mr. Horace Marryat can easily explain according to the belief in Denmark. "When in early spring-time the voice of the cuckoo is first heard in the woods, every village girl kisses her hand and asks the question, ' Cuckoo ! cuckoo ! when shall I be married ?' and the old folks, borne down with age and rheumatism, inquire, ' Cuckoo, when shall I be released from this world's care ?' The bird, in answer, continues singing, ' Cuckoo !' as many times as years will elapse before the object of their desires will come to pass. But as some old people live to an advanced age, and many girls die old maids, the poor bird has so much to do in answering the questions put to her, that the building season goes by ; she has no

* Baron Ernouf on Bohemian Superstitions, in *Revue Contemporaine*, 1861.

time to make her nest but lays her egg in that of the hedge-sparrow."*
The opinion of the muirland shepherds on the Borders is, that the
blame, at least, attaches not to the female party, but is attributable to
the brutish behaviour of the male.   He, a very Saturn among birds—
if allowed his will—would speedily exterminate the cuckoo race.
Such is his inveteracy against eggs or offspring, that, if the female
attempted incubation, he would forthwith expel her from the nest,
break the eggs, and gobble up in his wrath their entire valuable contents.   Therefore, to preserve the breed, she must have recourse to all
those expedients by which she contrives to have the egg conveyed
out of his reach, and palmed upon some foolish dupe, that in the
enthusiasm of hatching cannot distinguish an egg from a pebble-stone.
On account of the stratagems which she employs to effect this, the
Greeks, contrary to other nations, considered her as being endued with
peculiar sagacity, and had a proverb, which has been rendered,
" Coccyce astutior," *i.e.*, 'cuter than the cuckoo (Erasmi *Adagia*).
She—

> " Doom'd
> Never the sympathetic joy to know,
> That warms the mother cowering o'er her young,
> Some stranger robs ; and to that stranger's love
> Her egg commits, unnatural ; the nurse,
> Deluded, the voracious nestling feeds
> With toil unceasing ; and amaz'd beholds
> Its form gigantic and discordant hue."
>   GISBORNE.

From this imposition of its offspring upon an alien, unaware of the
deceit, has sprung the connection between the bird and cuckoldism
which pervades nearly every language in Europe, and also occurs in
the East among the Arabians.   Hence the Welsh proverb, " When
thou hearest the cuckoo cry, take timely heed to thy ways, for it may
be that he warns thee to a straighter line of duty ;" and thus it is
" the cuckold's quirister " of Green ; and Shakspeare's

> " Word of fear
> Unpleasant to a married ear."

---

* *Jutland and the Danish Isles*, i. p. 270.

But the idea in this country is literary rather than indigenous, and may have been derived from the Normans. In the passage from classic to mediæval periods, the application of the term has been transferred from the paramour to the husband.*

The cuckoo's connnection with marriage ceremonies may date from the period when Jupiter or Zeus wooed Juno or Hera, who presided over marriages, in the shape of a cuckoo on Mount Thornax, which afterwards obtained from that circumstance the name of Coccyx or Coccygia. (Pausanias, *Corinth.* cap. xxxvi.) Pausanias, *Corinth.* cap. xvii. saw in a temple of Juno fifteen stadia from Mycenæ, a town of Argolis, a statue of the goddess in ivory, of very great size, the work of Polycletes. She wore a crown on which were represented the graces and the seasons, and held a pomegranate, emblem of fertility, in one hand, and a sceptre, on which was placed a cuckoo, in the other. In a bas-relief representing the marriage of Zeus and Hera, a cuckoo sits upon the god's sceptre. "According to Mannhardt the cuckoo is the messenger of Thor, the god in whose gift were health and strength, length of days and marriage blessings, and therefore it is that people call upon the bird to tell how long they have to live, how soon they will be married, and how many children they shall have; and that in Schaumburg the person who acts at a wedding as master of ceremonies carries a cuckoo on his staff." (Mannhardt, *Die Götterwelt der Deutschen und Nordischen Völker*, p. 198.)† In Germany of old the cuckoo was carried on the fist, like a hawk, to the church.

> "Another on his fist, a spar hawke, or fawcone,
> Or else a cokow."‡

Jealousy, in Chaucer's *Canterbury Tales*, had a "cukkow sittyng on hire hand."

Gubernatis says that the song of the cuckoo was considered a good omen to whoever intended to marry. "In the popular song of the

---

* See Chambers' *Book of Days*, i. p. 531 ; Gubernatis' *Zool. Mythol.* ii. p. 234 ; Cyprian's *Annotations on Franzius*, p. 1300.

† Kelly's *European Traditions and Folk-Lore*, p. 98 ; see also Cyprian's *Notes on Franzius*, pp. 1296-7.

‡ Brant's *Ship of Fools*, translated by Barclay, 1508.

Monferrato, sung for the Easter eggs, the landlord is cunningly
advised that it is time to marry his daughters. In Swedish and
Danish songs the cuckoo carries the wedding-nut to the nuptials."
(*Zool. Mythol.* ii. p. 232). In Sweden the "grey cuckoo up in the
tree" prophecies to unmarried lasses how many years they shall
remain single. If the bird cries oftener than ten times, they say it
sits upon a silly bough, and they pay no heed to its augury.—(*Grimm*).
In Goethe's *Fruhling's-Orakel* the prophetic bird announces to a fond
couple their approaching marriage, and the number of their children.
In its character as a derider, Gubernatis notes, that, when "children
play at hide and seek, they are accustomed in Germany and Italy, as
well as in England, to cry out ' Cuckoo ' to him who is to seek them,
in vain, as is hoped." (ii. p. 233.)

Young cuckoos are stupid creatures, and ill adapted to take care of
themselves as pets. I am told of one brought up on porridge that
got scalded to death, from flying into the pot newly off the fire ; thus
perishing amidst what it most sought after. Another may be read of
that daily consumed its "pound of flesh," but was at last choked by
attempting to swallow some moss that was in its cage. A relative,
when a boy, reared one on meal and water, and then turned it into the
garden to provide for itself on the gooseberry caterpillars, which it
soon learned to collect; but, having paid too great attention to the
inmates of some bee-hives, for it can feed on bees, it was stung to
death by the " genus irritabile."

From a similar defect of quick-wittedness are derived the terms
gowk and *gawkie*, applicable to stolid specimens of humanity. This
idea is common to other Teutonic languages, and in the Celtic, says
Mr. Douce, *coeg* and *kok* signify anything foolish.

What a "gowk's nest" is, the following anecdote will explain.
Andrew Gemmels, a Scotch beggar in the Border districts, the supposed original of Edie Ochiltree, on one occasion " went to visit one
of his patrons, a poor Scotch laird, who had recently erected an ex-
pensive and fantastic mansion, of which he was very vain, and which
but ill corresponded with his rank or his resources. The beggar was
standing leaning over his pike-staff, looking very attentively at the

edifice, when the laird came forth and accosted him, ' Weel, Andrew, you're admiring our handiworks here ?' ' Atweel am I, sir.' ' And what think ye o' them, Andrew ?' ' I juist think ye hae thrawn away twa bonny estates, and *built a gowk's nest.*' "*

A " cuckoo tune," is to harp on one string ; to weary by iteration. " Cantus Coccygis dicitur de iis, qui eadem ingerunt semper." Hence Young's sombre shading—

> " The cuckoo seasons sing
> The same dull note to such as nothing prize
> But what those seasons from the teeming earth
> To doting sense indulge."

In the golden age of the North the cuckoo's song measured time. In the mythic King Frodi's house were two maidens of the old giant race, whom he had bought as slaves. He made them grind his quern or hand-mill, out of which he used to grind peace and gold ; and was a hard taskmaster, for he kept them to the mill, nor gave them longer rest than the cuckoo's note lasted, or they could sing a song.†

It early became a proverb in Scotland that "the goik hes na sang but ane " (Sir D. Lindsay's *Papingo*). In Ferguson's *Scots Proverbs*, cited in Dean Ramsay's *Reminiscences*, we have it, " ye bried of (take after) the gowk, ye have not a rhyme but ane ;" but the more modern saying is, " You're like the gowk, you have not a rane but ane ;" or " Ye're like the cuckoo, ye have but one song ;" which is a parallel to the German, " Du singest immer einen Gesang, wie der Guckguck." And thus in the sixteenth century were the Romish clergy reproached by the Reformers :—

> " Sen ye will nocht change your indured will,
> Knawand your fault, yet will continue still ;
> Sing on—guk, guk, the blaiting of your quier ;
> False fathers of the haly kirk, the XVI. hunder yeere."‡

Like their countrymen of the present time, they liked " nane o'

---

* Constable's *Edinburgh Magazine*, Sept. 1817.
† Dasent's *Introduction to the Norse Tales*, p. 52.
‡ *Scottish Poems of the Sixteenth Century*, ii. p. 174. John Knox, nicknamed Gavin Dunbar, Archbishop of Glasgow, whom he calls a "glorious fool," as " Good *Guckstone* Glakestone."

your kind o' folk that do naething but chim-cham at the same thing ower again, like the gowk on a June day." (Hogg.) This last is Shakspeare's :—

> " He was but as the cuckoo is in June,
> Heard, not regarded."
>
> *King Henry IV.*

It is also the opening sentence of the *Gull's Hornbook*, "I sing, like the cuckoo in June, to be laughed at." In Germany when one indulges in ostentatious, silly, worthless talk, it is said, " Der guckguck ruffet seinen eignen nahmen aus " (the cuckoo proclaims his own name).   In Tennyson's *Lover's Tale* it is said, and truly:

> " We loved
> The sound of one another's voices more
> Than the grey cuckoo loves his name."

" Cuckoo-lambs " is a name given in Hertfordshire, and also in Northamptonshire, "to such lambs as are yeaned in April and May, because they fall in cuckow time." (Ellis *on Sheep*, p. 79.) " Cuckoo-malt," in Warwickshire, is "malt made in the summer months." (Halliwell's *Archaic Dictionary*). "To see the gowk in one's sleep, to be given to vagaries, (Fifeshire) ; also used as a proverbial phrase, denoting a change of mind, in consequence of conviction that one is in error." (Jamieson's *Scottish Dictionary*). " Coucou," some sort of undignified carriage in the environs of Paris, is mentioned in Miss Berry's *Journal*, iii. p. 391.

It is said of a lawless Highland chieftain, Macdonald of Saddell, Lord of Cantire, who was surnamed " Righ Fiongal," that he was accustomed to amuse himself by keeping watch from the battlements of his castle, and firing at any suspicious-looking person with a gun that he called " the cuckoo," the notes of which, as may be imagined, were listened to with less delight than those of the " blithe new-comer of the spring."[*]

The Caucasus mountains, say some authorities, derive their name

* *Glencreggan; or, a Highland Home in Cantire.* By " Cuthbert Bede." i. p. 50.

from the cuckoo. In 12 Edward III. (1337-8) Gouxhull manor, co. Lincoln, belonged to John de Roos (*Calend. Inq. post Mortem*, ii. p. 85). It is also written Gouxhill, Goushill, Goushull (*l.c*). Another Gouxhill or Goushill belonged to the Abbey of Thornton-on-Humber (vol. iii. pp. 9, 65, and vol. i. p. 107). These appear to be represented at present in Goxhill parish, co. Lincoln, and Goxhill parish, co. York. Goukwell, in Lincolnshire, 6 Ric. II. (1382), was part of the dowry of Anne, Queen of England. (*Ibid*. iii. p. 54). Gokewell or Gowkeswell Nunnery, co. Lincoln, was founded before 1185; it is written Goukeswell in *Cal. Inq. post Mort*. iii. p. 331. In 41 Edward III. Goukethorp, co. Norfolk, was a feu held from Robert de Insula (*Ibid*. ii. p. 292). Gouthorp and Gowethorp are old similar names in Yorkshire, now converted into Yawthorpe. In 8 Henry IV. (1406) Margaret, Dowager Countess of Thomas de Beauchamp, late Earl of Warwick, held a free chapel situated beneath the Park of Weggenok, which was called Coukowechirchle (*Ibid*. vol. iii. p. 312). Weggenok Park was parcel of Warwick Castle and manor. In 21 Ric. II. (1397) Thomas, Earl of Warwick, held Cukkechirch land and pasture beneath the Park of Wiggenok (iii. p. 225). Cuckfield, co. Sussex, and other corresponding place-names, can only dubiously be arranged here. In the reign of William the Lion in Scotland (1165-1214) there was a " Cukoueburn," in the territory of Clifton, Roxburghshire, pertaining to the monastery of Melrose (*Liber de Mailros*, No. 113). In Dumbartonshire, on Arden estate, there is a Gowk Hill. The Goukthropple, in old writs Golkthrapple, lands are on the estate of Cambusnethan, Lanarkshire. Godscroft, the estate of David Hume, the historian of the Douglasses and Homes, is invariably mispronounced Gowkscroft. This perversion occurs also in Teesdale. Robert Roxby, "the Reedswater Minstrel," has rendered Davyshiels, near Otterburn, famous for its "gowks;" and like him thus a Gaelic bard celebrates the charms of his mountain abode :—

> " Lond were the eagles round its precipices,—
> Sweet its cuckoos and swans."

Pennycuik in Midlothian implies the height of the cuckoo. Of the

Penycuik cuckoos, P. F. Tytler, the historian, gives us information, singularly to the purpose, in a letter to his sister. He was present in Paris when Louis XVIII. made his appearance at the theatre, 24th May, 1814. "The moment the king entered the house, the most loud and universal applause began and continued without interruption, till the people (like the cuckoos at Penicuik) had cried themselves hoarse, and the words *Vive le Roi, Vive la Duchesse, Vive Monsieur, Vive les Bourbons*, became quite inarticulate."* Quite a cuckoo scene !

" There is found a similitude," says Lord Bacon, " betweene the sound that is made by inanimate bodies, or by animate bodies that have no voice articulate, and divers letters of articulate voices; and commonly men have given such names to those sounds as doe allude unto the articulate letters. As trembling of water hath resemblance with the letter *L;* quenching of hot metalls with the letter *Z;* snarling of dogs with the letter *R;* the noise of scritch-owles with the letter *Sh;* sounds of strings with the letter *Ng;* voice of cats with the dipthong *Eu;* voice of cuckoes with the dipthong *Ou.*" The sound of the cuckoo's voice almost every people in Europe has tried to reproduce in the name given to it, and the " rude forefathers " of nations may have once prided themselves as much in their apt imitation of it as the man-miniature who—

> " Crows his cuckoo-notes
> Till all the greenwood alleys loud are ringing."

In the Greek it is, coccyx; old German, gaug, guggauch, guckguck; modern German, kukuk, kuckkuck, gukuk ; Bohemian, kokes; Servian, kukavitza; Dutch, koekoek; Islandic, gaukr; Norwegian, gouk; Swedish, goek, gjok ; Lapland, geecka ; Danish, gjoeg or gjöge ; Anglo-Saxon, gaec, geac; Latin, cuculus ; Italian, cucullo, cucco, cuco, cucho, cuccu; French, cocou, coucou, coqu; Spanish, cuco, cuclillo ; Welsh, cog, gwccw; Gaelic, cubhag, cuthag, cuag, cuach; Hindoo, kuka ; Persian, koku. Old English forms are gowke, cuccu, cuccow, cuckoe, cuckowe, cokowe, guckoe, kocok,

---

* Burgon's *Memoir of P. F. Tytler*, p. 97.

kokoke, kuckue. Scottish forms are goilk, golk, goik, gowk, gouckoo, gowkoo, gukkow, goukoo, cucu, cneko, cukkow, cockow.*

"This sound is like the cuckoo, the Welsh ambassador." (Middleton's *Trick to Catch the Old One*, Act iv. sc. 5.) It is conjectured to be so called because its notes resemble words in the Welsh language. See *Gentleman's Magazine*, 1840.†

The aliases of the cuckoo figure in the following Scotch "guess"—

> "The cuckoo and the gowk,
> The laverock and the lark,
> The mire-snipe and the heather bleat,
> How many birds is that?" Answer: Three.

The Germans nick-name him "beckenknecht," or baker's man, and explain to us how he obtained this byword, as well as his singular cry. "The bird is said to be a bewitched baker or miller boy, and thus has pale or meal-coloured feathers. In a dear season he robbed poor folks of their dough, and when God blessed the dough in the oven drew it out, plucked some off, and every time cried out as he did so, guknk! (look, look!) He was therefore punished and turned into a thievish bird who continually repeats this cry. This legend is of great antiquity." (Grimm).‡ The Norwegians have also a story about its call, which reminds us of one we have about the wood-pigeon or cushat. "Once on a time the cock, the cuckoo, and the black-cock bought a cow between them. But when they came to share it and could not agree which would buy the other out, they settled that he who woke first in the morning should have the cow. So the cock woke first, 'Now the cow's mine! now the cow's mine! hurrah! hurrah!' and he crew, and as he crew up woke the cuckoo. 'Half-cow! half-cow!' sang the cuckoo, and woke up the black-cock. 'A like share, a like share, dear friends, that's only fair! saw see! see

* Drawn up partly from Grimm. Mr. J. A. Harvie-Brown writes me that in Orkney and Shetland "gowk" and "horse-gowk" are invariably applied to the snipe, whose spring call-note is very like "gjöge, gjöge," quickly repeated.

† A different explanation is suggested in Rev. T. F. T. Dyer's *English Folk-Lore*, p. 61.

‡ Another legend of a stingy baker being thus punished, from the same source, may be found in Kelly's *European Traditions and Folk-Lore*, p. 88.

saw !' That's what the blackcock said. And now, can you tell me
which of them ought to have the cow ?"* The cuckoo often anticipates
the cock in proclaiming the dawn, and on moonlight evenings may be
heard at midnight.

The cuckoo's garland consists of several ingredients. The true
cuckoo flower is *Cardamine pratensis*, the pinks or wild rocket of the
Borders. "These flower for the most part in April," says Gerard
(*Herball*, p. 261), "when the cuckowe doth begin to sing her pleasant
notes without stammering." Stillingfleet notes that in 1755 the
cuckoo called on the 17th and the cuckoo flower was in blow on the
19th of April. The name *Flos Cuculi* is traced to Otto Brunfels,
1536, adapted from the Gauch-blume and Kukucks-blume of the
Germans. It appears in English, in Lyte's translation of *Dodonæus*,
1578, as "coccow flower." The Flemish name is cocockbloem or
coeckoecbloem. It is goje blomster in Danish, according to S.
Paulli ; blodeuyn y gôg in Welsh, but this is modern. *Lychnis flos-
cuculi* is another "cuckoo flower" derived from a German source, the
Cuculi flos Germanis of Tragus, 1552. J. Bauhin, *Hist. Plant.* iii.
p. 348, says the Germans call it gauch-blum, kuckuck-blumen, and
the French, fleur du coquu. The Flemish is coeckcock-bloemkens
and Lyte translates it cockow gillofers. In the county of Durham I
found "gilloflowers" was a common name for *Cardamine pratensis*.
In Welsh it is blodau'r góg. Shakspeare's cuckoo-flower in the
mock coronet of the mad Lear appears to have been a cereal weed.

> " Crown'd with rank fumiters and furrow weeds,
>   With harlocks, hemlocks, nettles, cuckoo-flowers,
>   Darnel, and all the idle weeds that grow in corn."

The "cuckoo-flower" of Clare, Miss Baker thinks (*Northamptonshire
Words and Phrases*, i. p. 164) is the red-flowered campion, *Lychnis
diurna*.

> " And oft, whilst scratching through briary woods
>   For tempting cuckoo-flowers and violet buds."

---

* Dasent's *Tales from the Norse*, p. 211.

He also names the cuckoo-pint, *Arum maculatum*, the cuckoo-pint flower,—

> " Where peep the gaping speckled cuckoo-flowers,
> Prizes to rambling schoolboys' vacant hours."
>
> *Poems*, p. 8.

> " These harebells all
> Seem bowing with the beautiful in song ;
> And gaping cuckoo-flower with spotted leaves,
> Seems blushing of the singing it has heard."
>
> *Rural Muse*, p. 33.

In Devonshire, according to Mr. Halliwell (*Archaic Dictionary*), the harebell (*Agraphis nutans*) is called cuckoo ; in Dumbartonshire it is gowk's hose (Jamieson). Cuckoo's stockings, as a provincial name for the harebell, is mentioned in Howitt's *Book of the Seasons*. The Welsh names are Esgidiau'r gôg, cuckoo's shoes ; and Hosanau'r gôg, cuckoo's stockings (Thomas Jones); Bwtias y gôg, cuckoo's boots. (Davies' *Welsh Botanology*.) Canterbury bells has the name of gowk's hose in the South of Scotland. In Lovell's *Herball*, Oxford, 1665, p. 72, Canterbury bells is synonymous with "cuckoo-flowers or throatwort ;" but unfortunately, at page 113, it is arranged as a double lady's-smock. The common bell-flower (*Campanula rotundifolia*), in the Gaelic list of Lightfoot's *Flora Scotica*, is written curachd-na-cuaig. This is also written curachd-na-cubhaig, and signifies the cuckoo's cap (female head-dress), and it is still known as such in the Isle of Skye, as I ascertained by inquiry. In Gaelic, *Pinguicula vulgaris*, or butterwort, is brogan-na-cuiag, cuckoo's shoes. The *Orchis mascula* is also a cuckoo flower. Turner's *Herball*, 1551, distinguishes it as goukis meat ; it is referred to in Lyte's *Dodoens*, 1578, p. 226, as cuckowes orchis, and it is so entitled in the index to Gerard's *Herball* by Johnson, 1633. The name in Wales is Hosanau'r gôg, the cuckoo's stockings or hose (Davies's *Botanology*). In the *Nomenclator Plantarum* of Benedict Berzelius, in the *Amœnitates Academiœ*, Upsal, 1759, the German guckuks-blume stands opposite to this orchis. The original cuckoo's hose may have been the cowslip; but correct application cannot be expected in every instance of popular names. In Lyte's *Dodoens*, p. 123, the French names of the cow-slip are coquu and brayes de coquu, *i.e.* cuckoo's hose in the modern acceptation. This appears to be from Ruellius, 1537, in whose work the country name is cuculi brachula. By others it is written bracha cuculi (J. Bauhin, *Hist. Plant.* iii. p. 495, 1651). In the Flemish dictionary, *Kilianus Auctus*, 1642, both brachæ cuculi and braies de cocu are interpretations for the cowslip. Miege's *French Dictionary*, 1675, Englishes coucou, as primrose. Giôkblomma is the name of cowslip in Gothland. Mr. Don (*Hist. of Plants*, i. p. 40), following Philip Miller, conjectured that the " cuckoo buds " of Shakespeare is the *Ranunculus bulbosus*, crowfoot or buttercup, which blows in May and June. Mr. Sidney Beisly (*Shakspere's Garden*, p. 42) advocates the pilewort (*Ranunculus ficaria*) as a claimant for the honour. The name may still exist in country places. The *Caltha palustris*, the showy marsh marigold, Linnæus says, conforms in time of flower-ing with the arrival of the cuckoo in Sweden, and it is still a marked feature in that country. . (Marryat's *One Year in Sweden*, i. p. 74.) Stillingfleet found the marsh marigold to blow April 7th, and the same day the cuckoo sang. (*Select Works*, ii. p. 373.) The Greek work coccyx signifies cuckoo, and likwise a young fig, and the reason given for it is that in Greece they appeared together. *Oxalis acetosella*, the wood-sorrel, bears the vagrant bird's impress in many languages. " It is called of some panis cuculi, cuckowe-breade, eyther because the cuckowes delight to feede thereon, or that it beginneth to blossome when the cuckowe beginneth to utter her voyce." (Parkinson's *Theatrum Botanicum*, p. 747.) Dr. Prior found this in the *Ortus Sanitatis*, c. xviii. (1486.) Ruellius, 1537, also gives it that name. In French it is pain du cocu, pain de coucou; in Italian, pan cuculi; in old German, gouches-ampfera ; in modern German, kukucksbrot ; other German names are gauchklee, guckgauchklee, kugugsklee (cuckoo-clover), gauchbrot, guckgauchbrot, guchenlauch, and gauchlin; in Danish, giogebrodt, giogemad, giogesyre ; in Swedish, giokmat, which name in that language *Lathyrus macrorrhizus* (Orobus tuberosus, L.) shares with it. It is the Anglo-Saxon Gacces-sure and the Welsh Suran-y-gôg ; the cuckowes meat of Turner's *Names of Herbs*, 1548.

It is the English cuckoo-sorrel, cuckoo-bread, cuckoo-spice; the Scottish gowk's meat; the border cuckoo's meat, cuckoo clover, cuckoo's sourocks; and the cuckoo-sorrel of the North of Ireland. *Tragopogon pratense*, goat's beard, has for one of its German names Gauchsbrot. "Children," says Tragus, "who eat the root while it is yet tender are wont to call it gauchbrot, *i.e.* the bread of the cuckoo, from the sweetness thereof; and, if an Apician only knew how good it was, he would never again prefer his acetarian dainties to all other herbs and roots."—(J. Bauhin, *Hist.* ii. p. 1059.) The cuckoo claims also the sweet-scented violet and the pansy, both being in Gaelic sail-chuach, the cuckoo's heel. In Irish, the first is sail covagh, according to Threlkeld's *Irish Herbal.* A pretty fancy; but the cuckoo has no heel like the lark, the fee being zygodactile, or with two toes behind and two before for grasping. *Anagallis arvensis*, the scarlet pimper-nel, is in German gauchheyl, gochheyl, and jochheyl; and in Flemish guychelheyl; gowk or fool's heel, from gauch and guych, a fool; a secondary derivative. The kind of moss called great golden maiden-hair, *Polytrichum commune*, is the gowk bear, *i.e.* cuckoo's barley, of Ayrshire. In Sweden, says the *Flora Suecica* of Linnæus, it is known as gukulijn, and giökrag. In the same country the rare and beautiful *Cypripedium calceolus*, our Lady's slipper, is guckuskor. Geckdox, in Gerard's *Herball*, *Galium aparine*, may rank here. Cocowort, Halliwell renders shepherd's purse; but this may be doubted. We have also gowk's siller, shillings or sixpences, *Rhinanthus Cristagalli;* and on the Borders cuckoo grass, *Luzula campestris*, "flowering with the primrose and the dog-violet, and pulled by children to give variety to the spring nosegay." In Boehmeri, *Commentationes Œconomico-Medico-Botanicæ:* Vitebergæ et Servestæ, 1792, 4to. *Anagallis arvensis* is called gauchblume, and rother gauchheil (p. 34); and *Avena fatua* (wild oats) is reckoned to be the gauchhaber (p. 68). Mr. James Britten states that "Cuckoos" is in Buckinghamshire and Essex applied to any spring-flowering plant which has no other name." (*Notes and Queries* 4th ser. iv. p. 467).

The cuckoo-spittle, gowk's-spittle, cuckoo's-spittens, frog-spit, toad-spit, snake's-spit, or wood-sear of England and Scotland; Kukuk-

speichel, and hexenspiechel (witch's-spit) of the Germans;* gugger-
speu of the Swiss ; gred-spott (frog-spit) of the Swedes ; giogespit of
the Danes : trold-kiaringspye of the Norwegians ; and crachat de
coucon of the French ; is a froth discharged by the young froghoppers
(*Pytelus spumarius*), which belong to the order *Hemiptera-Homoptera*
among insects, to defend them from enemies and the overpowering
effect of the solar heat. ." M. Poupart tells that as soon as the little
creature comes out of its egg it hastens to some plant, which it touches
with the tip of its body, and fastens there a drop of white liquor full
of air ; it drops a second near the first, then a third, and so on, till it
covers itself all over with a scum or froth." These get the name of
gowk-spittles, because they are at the greatest plenty " when the bird
gets hoarse, or seems by its voice to have a spittle in its throat" (Mactaggart). The dates of first appearance are, in Berwickshire, May
6, 11, 23, 24, June 8. English dates are June 16, June 2-21. One
writer considers it a kind of hardened dew, another a blight. Sibbald,
in his *Scotia Illustrata*, regarded it as an exhalation infecting plants,
which speedily corrupts and engenders vermiculi, and unless it is
wiped off it burns up the plants. The inclosed insect lives on the
juice of plants, and is often prejudicial to garden blooms. In Sweden
it is said to cause madness in cattle that feed where it abounds. The
Cardamine pratensis and *Lychnis flos-cuculi* are favourite depositories
of its spume, and some conjecture that hence arises the name of
cuckoo-flowers by which they are distinguished (Dr. Johnston's *Flora
of the Eastern Borders*, p. 33 ; Miss Baker's *Northamptonshire Words
and Phrases*, i. p. 165) ; but it has already been shown that the origin
of the name is not in our language, and has existed on the Continent
for three hundred years, whatever more. And there are plants that
it is noticed to affect as much as it does these. " The experience is,
that the froth which they call woodesare (being a kind of spittle) is
found but upon certain herbs, and those hot ones, as lavender, lavender-
cotton, sage, hyssope," &c. (Lord Bacon's *Sylva Sylvarum*, p. 104, and

---

* Mr. Broderick, erroneously, I think, identifies the witches' butter in the
tragic tale of the *Witches of Blockula* with the cuckoo-spit (*Zoolog. Recreations*, p. 72). Dr. Prior makes it *Tremella Nostoc*, one of the *Algæ*.

Sir Thomas Browne's *Vulgar Errors*, p. 237.) But there is a kind of plant that has been gifted with a name, "in respect of that kind of frothy-spattle or spume, which we call cuckoo-spittle, that more aboundeth in the bosomes of the leaves than in any other plant that is knowne," viz. *Silene inflata*, bladder campion, which Gerard denominated spattling poppy. This is the English of *Papaver spumeum*, which again is translated from the Greek *Mecon aphrodes* of Dioscorides, a plant that no one now can recognise, but which Gesner thought might be this plant. Gerard's name has not come into common use. Plants besmeared with the froth of this insect were formerly considered emblematical of cuckoldom. "There was loyal lavender," says Green, "but that was full of cuckow-spittles, to show that women's light thoughts make their husbands heavy heads." The Northumbrian name of the insect is a brock, and hence, some one told Brockett, the expression "to sweat like a brock;" but this, as is well known, is on the Borders applied to a badger. Boys take them for the early state of the cuckoo; and Isodore, with all a boy's credulity, tells how at the dog-days they inflict matricidal retribution, for then attaining perfection they rush upon her in a body and kill her with their bites. (Joh. Johnstoni *Thaumatographia*, p. 250.) Isodore, however, regarded the insects in these spittles as the offspring of the musical cicada of the South of Europe. (*Orig.* lib. xii. cap. viii.) Our countryman, Muffett, in his *Insectorum Theatrum*, 1634, pp. 122, 132, seems to be the first who had a correct conception of the nature of the "young gowk." The passage has been rendered by Sir T. Browne. (*Vulg. Err.* p. 237.) "Certaine it is that out of this some kind of locust doth proceed; for herein may be discovered a little insect of a festucine or pale green, resembling in all parts a locust, or what we call a grasshopper." Near Newcastle the small springing homoptera are called grass locusts. "Not worth a gowk spittle" is a Galloway phrase. (Mactaggart.) "Gesner asketh how any man dare be so foolish or venturous as to eat of a cuckoe, whose much spitting argueth a corrupt and excremental flesh." (Muffett's *Health's Improvement*, p. 99.)

Cuckoo holidays are few in number, and now seldom heard of

The *Morning Post* newspaper of May 17th, 1821, says : " A singular
custom prevails in Shropshire at this period of the year, which is
peculiar to that county. As soon as the first cuckoo has been heard
all the labouring classes leave work, if in the middle of the day, and
the time is devoted to mirth and jollity over what is called Cuckoo
Ale."*   " Towednack Cuckoo Feast " takes place on the nearest
Sunday to the 28th of April. " It happened in very early times,
when winters extended further into the spring than they now do,
that one of the old inhabitants resolved to be jovial, notwithstanding
the inclemency of the season; so he invited all his neighbours, and
to warm his house he placed on the burning faggots the stump of a
tree.   It began to blaze, and, inspired by the warmth and light, they
began to sing and drink ; when, lo ! with a whiz and a whir, out flew
a bird from the hollow in the stump, crying, Cuckoo! cuckoo !
The bird was caught and kept by the farmer, and he and his
friends resolved to renew the festal meeting every year at this
date, and to call it their " Cuckoo Feast." Previous to this event
Towednack had no " feasten Sunday," which made this parish a
singular exception to the rule in Cornwall.†

Many northern people at the name of *gowk* will, with all the fresh-
ness of events that indelibly impress the memory, recall the frolics of
the first and second of April, when in holiday attire defects were
inquired into of which the wearer had not a twinkling of suspicion ;
when the swain's cart dropped its back-board, but not through hasty
driving; when out-field labourers were hurried home to carry stacks
of corn that midsummer saw unremoved; when errands of urgency
were speeded to absent parties, who repaid the bearer with astounding
laughter; and when oil of hazel, essence of sloethorn, pigeon's milk,
stirrup ointment, and other nonsensical pleasantries were in suc-
cessive requisition to insure the fond *gowk's* being dispatched in
fruitless search another weary mile.   This—

> " Make-believe on April day,
>   That sent the simple heart a-fooling,"

---

* Brand's *Pop. Antiq.* ii. p. 124, Charles Knight's ed.
† Hunt's *Popular Romances of the West of England*, p. 404.

is called a " gowk's errand," "an April errand," "hunt the gowk."
Sometimes the April fool was the bearer of a missive containing this
distich,—

> " The first and second day of April,
> Hound (or hunt or send) the gowk another mile."

The reply by parties too old or too experienced to be thus played
on is—

> " April gowks are past and gone,
> You're a fool and I am none."

At Wooler, in Northumberland, those who thus resisted being made
" feul gowks," on " feul-gowk day," April 1, replied:—

> " The gowk and the titlene sit on a tree,
> Ye're a gowk as weel as me."

Such an epoch as the calling-time of this favourite bird could not
fail to have its " trivial fond records " and concomitant superstitions
observances.

At Wooler, you are told, if you are walking on a hard road, when
the cuckoo first calls, the ensuing season will be full of calamity ; but
if you should stand on soft ground it is a lucky omen.

In Scotland it is lucky to be walking when the cuckoo is first
heard—

> " Gang an' hear the gouk yell,
> Sit and see the swallow flee ;
> See the foal before its mother's ee,
> 'Twill be a thriving year wi' thee."

As a prophet, the cuckoo's oracles were believed by the Poles to be
given by the great god Zywie, the life-giver, who transformed himself
into the bird to utter them. (Grimm.) In the Tyrol the cuckoo is a
prophet of disaster. When the traveller hears it he crosses himself,
for it bears the reputation of being the devil's own bird, and the " evil
one himself, the worst of the phantoms, rejoices in adopting his
voice."* In like manner " the cuckoo that placed itself upon the

* *Tales and Legends of the Tyrol*, by Comtesse A. von Günther, p. 118.

spear of Luitprand, King of the Longobards, was considered by them as a sinister omen, as if the cuckoo were a funereal bird."[*]

The inhabitants of the little island of Rona, in the western isles of Scotland, say that the cuckoo is never seen or heard there but after the death of the Earl of Seaforth. In St. Kilda, the most remote of these isles, the cuckoo is very rarely seen, and that upon extraordinary occasions, such as the death of the proprietor, M'Leod, the steward's death, or the arrival of some notable stranger. "I was not able," says Mr. Martin, "to forbear laughing at this relation, as founded upon no reason but fancy, which I no sooner expressed than the inhabitants wondered at my incredulity, saying that all their ancestors for a series of several ages had remarked this observation to prove true; and, for further confirmation, appealed to the present steward whether he had not known this observation to have been true, both in his own and in his father's time, who was also steward before him ; and, after a particular inquiry upon the whole, he told me that both in his own and in his father's lifetime the truth of this observation had been constantly believed, and that several of the inhabitants now living have observed the cuckoo to have appeared after the death of the two last proprietors and the two last stewards, and also before the arrival of strangers several times. It was taken notice of this year before our arrival, which they also ascribe to my coming here, as the only stranger, the minister having been there before." The cuckoo is not uncommon in the outer islands, and the sweetness of its voice caught Wordsworth's attention in the remote Highlands—

> "Breaking the silence of the seas,
> Among the farthest Hebrides."

Werenfels (*Dissertation upon Superstitions*) says, "If the superstitious man has a desire to know how many years he has to live, he will inquire of the cuckoo." In the language of Wolfgang Franz, "With the superstitious ancients it was accounted Juno's bird, hence until this day our people (*i.e.* the Germans) by numbering its notes

---

[*] Gubernatis, *Zool. Mythol.* ii. p. 235.

attempt to ascertain when they will marry, nay even the length of
their life." (*Hist. Animalium*, i. p. 236.) It was a custom among
children in Yorkshire to sing round a cherry-tree :—

> " Cuckoo, cherry tree,
>   Come down and tell me,
>   How many years afore I dee."

Or in Northamptonshire :—

> " Cuckoo, cherry tree,
>   How many years am I to live,
>   One, two, three."

Each child then shook the tree, and the number of cherries which
fell betokened the sum of the years of its future life.* Mr. Broderip,
referring to the relish with which a cuckoo regaled itself with cherries,
notices an old rhyme employed by nurses to teach a child its first
words—

> " Cuckoo, cherry tree,
>   Lay an egg, bring it me."†

To which some add ;

> " Lay another, give it brother."

This fits on very well to what Grimm says, " When the cuckoo has
eaten his full of cherries three times he ceases to sing."

Again, in the West of Scotland, " the cuckoo, the first time you
hear it in spring, it is believed, cries once for every year you have yet
to live, hence great care is taken by some to count the exact number
of notes she sings on this interesting occasion."‡ This may be amply
illustrated from continental sources, for these superstitions, no less
than correspondences of speech, attest the brotherhood of nations.
Grimm says, " The popular belief still exists that whoever hears the
cry of the cuckoo for the first time in the spring, may ask him how
many more years he has to live.   In Switzerland the children cry,

---

* W. J. Thoms, *Athenæum*, 1846, p. 863.   C. W. Peach *in letter*, &c.
† *Zoological Recreations*, p. 81.
‡ *Glasgow Herald*, October, 1859.

‘ Gugger, wie lang lebi no ?’ (Cuckoo, how long shall I live yet) ;
and much the same in Lower Saxony.   In other places the rhyme is—

> ‘ Cuckoo, baker boy,
> Tell me true,
> How many years shall I live ?’

They then listen and count how often the bird repeats his cry after
this question, and the number betokens the years of their future life.”
“ Much depends upon the direction in which the cuckoo is first heard ;
if from the north (that is, the unlucky side) you will have mourning
during the year; from the east or west, his cry portends good fortune ;
from the south, then he is a proclaimer of butter.”   “ And we have a
story related by Abbot Theobald, of Eberbach, of a certain novice,
who, assuring himself of living twenty-two years longer, from having
heard the cuckoo repeat its cry just so many times, concluded that it
was needless for him to pass so long a period in mortification, and resolved to return and lead a jolly life for twenty years, thinking the
remaining two quite enough for penitence.”*   Of corresponding import
is the tale of the old wife who had such singular trust in the cuckoo’s
notes, that on her deathbed she would not admit that she was sinking,
but protested over and over again that the cuckoo had predicted she
would live five years longer, and repeated it by the erection of her
fingers, when in her last struggle she had become speechless.†

In Cornwall,‡ “ If, on first hearing the cuckoo, the sounds proceed from the right, it signifies that you will be prosperous ; or, to use
the language of the informant, a country lad, ‘ you will go right vore

---

* *Annals of Nat. Hist.* xiii. compared with *Athenæum,* 1846. The story
may be found in Cyprian’s *Annotations on Wolfgang Franzius, Hist. Animal.*
p. 1297. In Chambers’ *Book of Days,* i. p. 530, the authorship is attributed to
Cæsarius of Heisterbach, the date being 1221. Also Kelly, *Eur. F. L.* p. 98.

† *Geier de Superstitione,* c. 3, n. 37 ; in Cyprian’s *Annotations on Franzius,*
p. 841. A parallel instance is given in Chambers’ *Book of Days,* i. p. 530,
from Wright’s *Selection of Latin Stories.*

‡ *Choice Notes,* p. 90. On the other hand Mr. Pengelly say : “ Cornishmen
not only take it as a good omen to hear the cuckoo from the right, but also
from before them ; to hear him, in short, on the *starboard bow,* as a sailor would
say.”—*Long Ago,* p. 310.

in the world ; ' if from the left, ill-luck is before you." At the first call
of the bird a German peasant does the same thing as when he hears
thunder for the first time for that year ; he rolls himself several times
on the grass, and is thereby insured against pains of the back for that
season, and all the more effectually if the bird continues to call while
he is on the ground.*

The first time you hear the voice of the cuckoo, sit down on a bank,
and, pulling the stocking off the *right* leg, repeat these verses—

> " May this to me
> Now lucky be,"

and then put it on again.†

In the West of Scotland, on hearing the cuckoo for the first time,
pull off your shoes and stockings, and, if you find a hair on the sole
of the *left* foot, it will the exact colour of the hair of your future
spouse. If no hair is found, then another year of single life must
be endured."‡ " I got up the last May morning," says the Connoisseur,
No. 56, " and went into the fields to hear the cuckoo, and when I
pulled off my *left* shoe I found a hair in it exactly the same colour
with his."

> " When first the year, I heard the cuckoo sing,
> And call with welcome note the budding spring,
> I straightway set a-running with such haste,
> Deb'rah that won the smock scarce ran so fast,
> Till spent for lack of breath, quite weary grown,
> Upon a rising bank I sat adown,
> And doff'd my shoe, and by my troth I swear,
> Therein I spied this yellow frizzled hair,
> As like to Lubberkin's in curl and hue,
> As if upon his comely pate it grew."
>
>   GAY.

But the *right* foot has the most and oldest authorities in its favour.
" When the cuckoo uttered his first note," writes Carleton, in his
Traits, &c. of the Irish Peasantry, iv. p. 268, " from among the haw-

---

●* Kelly, *Europ. F. L.* p. 98, from *Mannhardt*, p. 200.

   † *Cuckoo Cries*, p. 8. By M. A. Denham.

   ‡ *Glasgow Herald*, October, 1859.

thorns, with what trembling anxiety did I, an urchin of some
eight or nine years, look under my *right* foot for the white hair whose
charm was such that by keeping it about me the first female name I
should hear was destined, I believed in my soul, to be that of my
future wife."

" Plinie reporteth that if when you first hear the cuckoo you mark
well where your *right* foot standeth, and take up of that earth, the
fleas will by no means breed, either in your house or chamber, where
any of the same earth is thrown or scattered." (*Thomas Hill,* and see
Brand.)

In some of the counties in the north-west of England, although
this belief is also ascribed to Norfolk, people believe that whatever
they chance to be doing when they first hear the cuckoo they will do
all the year.* In Berwickshire it is the common belief, that, if the
circumstances in which its note is first heard for the season be
attended to, they afford unerring signs whereby the secrets of a man's
destiny for the ensuing year may be disclosed. In whatever direction
he may be looking when its tones arrest him, there will he be on
the anniversary of that day next year. If he be gazing on the
ground he is warned of an untimely fate. (This I have also from
Mid-Lothian and Cornwall.) If he has money in his pocket it is
an omen that he shall not lack; if penniless, that the cruse of oil
shall not be replenished, and that losses and disappointments shall
be his lot. Thus also is it in Westmoreland.

" When the cry of the cuckoo is heard for the first time in the
season, it is customary in Northamptonshire to turn the money in the
pocket and wish. If within the bounds of reason it is sure to be fulfilled."† It is the same in Somersetshire. In Hull, " If when you
hear this bird you turn a penny over in your pocket, you will never be
without one all the year." It is called a " cuckoo penny."‡ In Germany, it is said, " if you have money in your purse when he first cries

---

* Howitt's *Rural Life of England,* p. 590.
† Sternberg's *Dialect and Folk-Lore of Northamptonshire,* p. 159.
‡ *Choice Notes,* p. 164.

all will go well during the year; and, if you were fasting, you will be hungry the whole year." *

But, amongst all this diversity of interpretation, such is the benevolent constitution of the human mind, such its hope for better things, that it rarely fails to discover, even in the most despondent circumstances, the presages of a bright futurity. No wonder, then, that the cuckoo's call, as the herald of good news, finds an echo in every bosom, and that, with eager anticipations, young and old are prepared to welcome its renewal.

JAMES HARDY.

---

* For some slight variations in the formula of these beliefs, see *Long Ago*, pp. 204-5; also Harland and Wilkinson's *Lancashire Folk-Lore*, p. 143.

OLD BALLAD FOLK-LORE.

"I love a ballad but even too well; if it be doleful matter, merrily set down, or a very pleasant thing indeed, and sung lamentably."

Winter's Tale, act iv. sc. iii.

A BALLAD may be called a narrative poem fit to be sung. In olden times the singers of these poems, the bards, most of whom were also poets, went from place to place, attending courts, festivals, and public gatherings of the people, and there sang or recited those poetic narratives descriptive of battles and adventures of heroes, of tournaments, and of love intrigues.* These bards were listened to with great attention, were held in high esteem, and in many cases were credited with prophetic gifts; and whether their narratives kept the level of common every-day life, or soared into the realms of fancy, still they were consistent with the habits and beliefs of the age in which they were delivered; and thus the old folk-songs, as they are aptly termed, remain to us now a vast storehouse of historical evidence of the manners and customs, of the thoughts and beliefs, of bygone times. In very ancient poetic narratives, such as Homer's, we find descriptions of hosts of supernatural beings, divinities or demigods, who superintended human affairs, public and private, and had among the human race those whom they favoured and those whom they thwarted, and so they plotted and intrigued for the advancement of their favourites and the overthrow of their enemies. Essentially the same in principle, though differing in detail and nomenclature, this form of belief was at one time common to all nations, and in northern Europe it held sway as the prevalent belief till within these few centuries; indeed, till this present.

After the introduction of Christianity the notion that these supernatural agents were really divinities gradually declined, but the belief in supernatural agencies remained. Instead, however, of regarding these beings as gods, they were now considered to be evil spirits or fallen angels

* It is worth while referring here to Bishop Percy's *Essay on the Ancient Minstrels in England*, and to Mr. Wheatley's Introduction to *Percy's Reliques*, pp. xxiv.-xliv.

in the service of the Devil, who were permitted by God to exercise power over men who had sinned.* They had the power and were permitted to appear to men in various shapes and disguises, and to speak through animate and inanimate things. Frequently they appeared in the guise of men and women, and in this form held licentious intercourse with the human race, wherefrom were begotten monsters—moral monsters and also physical, such as giants, dwarfs, and dragons. Very commonly we find old heathen notions commingling with the incidents of Scripture history, for in these old times Pagan and Christian elements presented no serious difficulties to their fusion; but, while the process of fusion went on, the differing elements interacted upon each other, and so new forms of mythological beliefs arose.

It is difficult, if not altogether impossible, now to indicate the precise forces which were instrumental in producing these modifications, but we see the results. In course of time the Devil's supernatural offspring were relegated to a subterranean realm, and their characters also underwent a change: the giants, dwarfs, and dragons of the older mythology had given place to a newer race, called elves, fairies, brownies, &c. These new races, like their progenitors, had human passions and dispositions, and were under the government of kings and queens, with a regular constitution of laws; they interested themselves in the affairs of men, and, like Homer's gods, they had their human favourites whom they aided, and their enemies whose designs they thwarted; they had wives and reared families, and cultivated the arts and sciences. The Pagan gods and demons had now given place to one supreme fiend—the

---

* Thus, in the "Master of Oxford's Catechism," written early in the fifteenth century, and printed in *Reliquæ Antiquæ*, i. 231, we have the following question and answer:—

" *C.* Where be the anjelles that God put out of heven and bycam devilles ?

" *M.* Som into hell, and som reyned in the skye, and som in the erth, and som in waters and in wodys."

Professor Skeat quotes the above in illustration of the lines from *Piers the Plowman.*

" Whan thise wikked went out, wonderwise þei fellen,
Somme in eyre, somme in erthe, and somme in helle depe."

This was, he says, an easy way for accounting for all classes of fairies, some of whom were supposed to be not malignant; for the fallen spirits were supposed to be not all equally wicked. The Rosicrusians, in like manner, placed the sylphs in the air, the gnomes in the earth, the salamanders in the fire, the nymphs in the water.—See Skeat's *Piers the Plowman*, notes, p. 105.

Christian devil, who entered personally into covenant engagements with members of the human family, they yielding him their services during life, and possession of their souls at death; and in return he gratified all their earthly desires, and gifted them with supernatural powers, so that when they pleased they could change their shape as they thought fit, and thus, unrecognised, vent their malice on those whom they disliked. These were known as witches, wizards, and warlocks.

These few preliminary remarks will enable us in some measure to comprehend the extraordinary matters contained in old Ballads, now popularly regarded as the product of the perverted fancy of early imaginative writers, but which in reality were only the common and real beliefs of the people, no doubt somewhat but not greatly heightened by the fancy of the bard. There is a rich mine of folk-lore of great historical value in these old Ballads, and, in order to direct attention to the wealth which here lies ready to the hand of those who have patience and health and learning sufficient for the task, I have culled a few specimens of these extraordinary beliefs. Most of my quotations, except when otherwise stated, are from *Illustrations of Northern Antiquities,* printed in Edinburgh in 1814. In a ballad, entitled "The little Garden of Roses, and of Laurin, King of the Dwarfs," a hero named DIETLIEB had a sister possessed of great beauty, named SIMILT. This beauty was sought after by knights of the highest fame, and she was also coveted by the Dwarf King.

> "One morn, with all her virgins, she issued to the plain;
> Dietlieb, with three noble earls, followed in her train:
> With many knights and squires she rode to an ancient linden tree;
> There in mirth and feasting lay the gallant company.
> But suddenly from their wondering gaze vanished Similt the bright,
> With arts of cunning grammary, the robber wrought the sleight.
> A Tarn-cap o'er the fair he cast, and his prize he quickly bore,
> Many a day and many a night, through forest dark and hoar.
> He bore her to his cavern, where he ruled in royalty."

Dietlieb, with his knights, searched for Similt without success; then, fearing the magic power of Laurin, they returned home, but Dietlieb was inconsolable for the loss of his sister. He consulted with an old hero, Hildebrand, who consoled him with the promise of help and with the hope of recovering his sister, and directed him how to proceed. He got other young heroes, fond of adventure, to join him in the search. In order to cause the Dwarf King to disclose himself, they tried an old device: they entered Laurin's rose garden, and trampled it down. As they had calculated, this brought Laurin visibly to them. He disguised his anger for a time.

> " In guise quite bold and chivalrous, in stirrups rich he stood;
> Not the truest blade could cut his pusens red as blood.
> Hardened was his hawberk in the gore of dragons fierce,
> And his golden bruny bright not the boldest knight might pierce.
> Around his waist a girdle he wore of magic power;
> The strength of twelve, the strongest men, it gave him in the stour.
> Cunning he was, and quaint of skill, and when his wrath arose,
> The kempt must be of mickle might could stand his weighty blows.
> Little was King Laurin, but from many precious gem
> His wondrous strength and power and his bold courage came.
> Tall at times, his stature grew, with spells of grammary;
> Then to the noblest princes fellow might he be;
> Silken was his mantle, with stones of mound inlaid,
> Sewed in two-and-seventy squares by many a cunning maid.
> His helmet, strong and trusty, was forged of the weighty gold,
> And when the dwarf did bear it his courage grew more bold.
> In the gold, with many gems, a bright carbuncle lay,
> That where he rode the darkest night grew brighter than the day.
> Upon the crown, and on the helm, birds sung their merry lay;
> Nightingales and larks did chaunt their measures blythe and gay,
> As if in greenwood flying, they tuned their minstrelsy:
> With hand of master were they wrought, and with spells of grammary.
> On his arm he bore a gilded buckler bright;
> There many sparhawks, tame and wild, were portrayed with cunning sleight;
> And a savage leopard ranging, prowling through the wood,
> Right in act to seize his prey, thirsting for their blood."

The Dwarf King's armour surpasses the armour and shield of Achilles, made by Vulcan, and so much praised by writers on Homer. In connection with this, the idea suggests itself to me that the fabrication of Achilles' shield was, by Homer's description, more a work of magic than an actual or possible product of the practical art of his time. The gorgeous array of the dwarf causes the heroes at first to imagine that he was an angel, probably St. Michael, but they soon found who he was by his ordering them to quit the garden, and to choose between death and the loss of their left feet and right hand. This ultimatum they met with many bravados, and at length the dwarf calmed down and told Dietlieb that he had his sister in his keeping, and agreed to take him to see her; and then in the most friendly manner he led the heroes into his subterranean dominions, with the following assurances:

> " There, my fellows, shall ye find pastimes blythe and gay;
> With song of birds and play of harps, a week will seem a day.
> All the merry pastimes never may I tell:
> There, without all guile or fear, in pleasure shall ye dwell.
> When the gates were opened, forth a splendour gleamed;
> Brighter than the day it shone, and around the forest beamed;
> From many a gem the splendour came, hung in the cavern bright;
> Wondering stood the heroes, when they viewed the magic light.
> The champions sped into the cave, where many dwarfs appeared:
> There the many songs of birds, and the sound of harps they heard.
> The trumpet clear resounded in the royal hall aloud
> To the deas had sped the host, when he viewed the champions proud."

After viewing the subterranean cave, the dwarf led his guests through the forest to his own palace, which surpassed in magic beauty anything they had yet seen. And the young knights were full of joy and gladness; but one with more experience was suspicious of the dwarf, and —

> " Wittich spake a warning word—Hark to my reed aright!
> The dwarf is quaint, and full of guile, then beware his cunning sleight;
> Arts he knows right marvellous. If to his hollow hill
> We follow, much I dread me, he will breed us dangerous ill."

They entered into his palace grounds through many gates, which were all fastened behind them. When they entered the palace, an old necromancer asked the dwarf what he wished him to do. The following is the reply:

> " Cast upon them, Master mine, for the love of me,
> A magic spell, that none of them may the other see.
> Upon the knights his magic charm cast the sorc'rer fell;
> None could behold his brothers, so mighty was the spell."

The knights were, however, able to see the other inhabitants of the palace and the servants, some of whom were dwarfs about two feet in height, and some giants of great stature, who danced and sang and tourneyed for the amusement of the guests. After this a feast was held, at which the young Lady Similt was introduced with great pomp. She afterwards gained audience of her brother and gave him a magic ring, which broke the spell laid upon the knights, and gave victory to any one who wore it. Regaining their armour, the knights fought their way out, carrying with them Similt and the Dwarf King. The former got married, and the Dwarf King became the fool or juggler to the Court of Bern. These extracts embrace a great many of the beliefs common among the people during the twelfth century.

I have said elsewhere * that it was an old and common belief that the souls of the departed inhabited the air, and could at the will of a necromancer be summoned to any place, and caused to act in accordance with his desires. The necromantic power was often claimed by the Church during the middle ages; and a good instance of their exercise of the power is contained in a ballad in *Illustrations of Northern Antiquities.* An old pagan warrior, after many a hard fight, is taken prisoner, and saves his life by becoming a Christian. He elects to join himself to the Friars, but must first undergo an act emblematic of having renounced his former life. He was sufficiently strong in the faith to be able to resist in the future the Devil and all his temptations. This was tested in the following manner : he was laid out on a bier as if he were a dead man, and in this state of assimilated death he was locked in the church during the night.

> " When the night was come, to the church the hero sped:
> Sudden all the ghosts appeared who by his sword lay dead.
> Many a fearfull blow they struck on the champion good;
> Ne'er such pain and woe he felt when on the field he stood;
> Sooner had he battle fonght with thousands on the field,
> Striking dints with falchion keen on his glittering shield.
> Half the night against the blows he waged the battle fierce:
> Bnt the empty air he struck where he weened their breasts to pierce.
> Little recked they for his blows, with his terror and his woe,
> E're the half the night was past his hair was white as snow;
> And when the monks to matins sped, they found him pale and cold:
> There the Ghosts in deadly swoon had left the champion bold."

There was a very old and wide-spread belief, common in heathen countries and also among Jews and Christians, which lingered on in our own country till within this century, namely, that the Devil and other evil spirits also appeared to women in the shape of men, and had issue by them. Even to this day when a youngster is doing some great mischief he is called "a devil's-get." Probably scripture narrative had much to do with the shaping and perpetuating in this country this belief. The text we refer to is in Genesis vi.: "The sons of God saw the daughters of men that they were fair; and they took them wives of all which they chose;" and "When the sons of God came in unto the daughters of men, and they bare children to them, the same became mighty men which were of old, men of renown." Female spirits were also in the habit of

---

* *Folk-Lore of the West of Scotland in this century*, p. 11.

tempting men to their embrace. In the prefatory notice to the Rev.
Robert Law's Memorialls, printed in 1818, there is the following: " A
young man near Aberdeen remarkable for his personal attractions com-
plained to the Bishop of the diocese that he was infested by a spirit in
the shape of a female ' so fair and beautiful a thing he never saw the
like,' which would come to his chamber at night and endeavour to
allure him to her embraces; the Bishop wisely advised him to remove
into another country and addict himself to fasting and prayer, which had
the desired effect." Lady Stairs, a noted witch in the seventeenth century,
was considered by the people to have been begotten in this way, and
that her husband and family were raised to great estate by the influence
of the Devil, whose offspring she was. One of the heroic ballads concerns
a case of supernatural birth. The mother of the Emperor O'tnits had
long been barren, to the great grief of her husband, but on a certain
occasion she met a dwarf named Elberich in an enchanted place, and
afterwards she bore a son who was called O'tnit. This dwarf afterwards
attached himself to the son, generally attending him in an invisible state.
We are favoured with the dwarf's age at this time. Sir Eligas, a
foreign knight, saw him, and, being surprised at his childlike appearance,
questioned him:

> " Quickly spake Sir Eligas: thou little babe alas,
> Why, far from friends and kindred, o'er the ocean didst thou pass?
> Not all so young am I as thy wits, sir champion ween,
> Fifty and three hundred years in the world have I seen."

When O'tnit regretted his inability to speak the language of the
foreign people he was travelling among, the dwarf supplies his wants:

> " Fear not, Sir O'tnit; here is a gem of mound:
> Thou will speak all languages the spacious world around;
> Each one canst thou answer from the north unto the south,
> When secretly the precious gem lies hid within thy mouth."

This is probably a perversion of the scriptural account of the gift of
tongues. These dwarfs and giants, as we have said, to serve their
favourite heroes would intrigue the one against the other. We may
cite the following instance. A dwarf named Bibunk helped a Christian
hero to frustrate the doings of a mighty giant:

> " Much loved the little wight the noble Grecian king,
> And soon upon his finger he thrust a golden ring.
> When the giant back returns, stick thy falchion in the sand,
> His hawberk soft as lead will turn; then pierce him with thy brand."

The giant, thus foiled by the Christian warrior, retired to a wood and drank of a miraculous spring, which gave him the strength of sixteen men. He also put on a silken shirt which no weapon could pierce. Nevertheless by the aid of other charms these magic powers were neutralised, and the Grecian king ultimately conquered the giant.

That some of the romantic ballads of the middle ages were founded upon a combination of Eastern fable and Bible history is evident from the following: A hero of great renown fell asleep when out alone in the woods, and was wakened by a female monster:

> "On four feet did she crawl along
> Like to a shaggie bear."

This monster besought the hero to become her lover, which he indignantly refused:

> "She took a spell of grammary, and threw it on the knight:
> Still he stood, and moved not (I tell the tale aright,)
> She took from him his falchion, unlac'd his hawberk bright,
> Mournfully Wolfdietrich cried, gone is all my might."

Then again she asked him to love her, which he again refused:

> "Another spell of might she threw upon the hero good;
> Fearfully she witched him, motionless he stood:
> He slept a sleep of grammary, for mighty was the spell,
> Down upon his glittering shield, on the sod he fell.
> All above his ears, his golden hair she cut;
> Like a fool she dight him, that his champions knew him not;
> Witless roved the hero for a year the forest round;
> On the earth his food he gather'd *as in the book is found.*"

This has evidently a reference to the story of Nebuchadnezzar, but the material of the ballad is evidently a mixture of the biblical narrative and the story of "Beauty and the Beast." After the hero was kept a year in this condition, the monster again visited him:

> "There naked, like an innocent, ran the hero bold,
> Strait the spell of grammary from his ear she did unfold:
> His wits he soon recover'd, when the spell was from his ear,
> But his vissage and his form was black and foul of cheer:
> Wilt thou win me for a wife, gentle hero say?
> Speedily he answer'd to the lady, nay."

She now desired the hero to go with her to witness her baptism, and to induce him to do so promised to restore to him his armour. On coming to her chamber there was a well there, into which she leaped:

> " Her bristly hide she left all in the flowing tide:
> Never gazing champion lovelier lady eyed."

The lady now urged him to follow her example, saying :

> " If beauteous thou wilt be,
> In the flowing fountain bathe thee speedily;
> Fair thy visage will become.
> Black and foul he leaped into the well of youth,
> But white and fair he issued with noble form forsooth."

The notion that some wells had the power of purifying and beautifying those who bathed in them is no doubt an Eastern fiction confirmed
probably in after times by the scripture narrative of the waters of
Bethesda, as this narrative made in Christian times the existence of
these wells a truth.* This old Eastern fancy passed through the middle
ages as a living faith, and was sanctioned by the Church, which consecrated wells, imparting to the waters healing and beautifying powers.
Such consecrated waters, or holy wells, are still frequented for their
healing virtues.

In the same ballad we meet the following:

> " In the giant's courtly hall winsome dwarfs appeared,
> Who the castle and the mount with cunning art had reared."

It was a popular belief in Scotland up to our own day, and probably
there are some who still hold it, that the Picts or *Pechs*, as they are
called in Scotland, were a race of dwarfs who occupied themselves in
building, especially monasteries and churches. A tradition still exists
that the High Church of Glasgow was built by the *Pechs*, and that they
had a subterranean passage passing under the Clyde from the church to
Rutherglen. A similar tradition exists in reference to Paisley Abbey.

In another ballad called " Hughdietrich and his son Wolfdietrich "
a pagan king had a beautiful daughter whom many youthful heroes
sought to marry. She possessed extraordinary witch powers, by which
she contrived the destruction of all who yielded to her terms of love.
One Christian hero, Wolfdietrich, refused the conditions imposed upon
him, and taking horse prepared to leave the castle or palace:

---

* In Barbazan, ed. 1808, iv. 180, there is a curious woodcut representing a well
of youth and the effects of bathing in it:

> " —— la fontaine de Jouent
> Qui fet rajovenir le gent."
>   COQUAIGNE.

> Now before the castle gate spurred the noble knight,
> But he viewed a swelling sea, wrought by magic sleight,
> Who caused the roaring waves to flow the burgh around
> Where grass and flowers blossomed before upon the ground:
> Into the roaring waters he spurred his courser good,
> But raging all around him rushed the magic flood ;
> The powers of the swelling waves his strength could not withstand,
> With mighty force they drove him aback upon the strand."

The hero, being thus baffled by the flood, yielded to enter her chamber. There she confessed her love for him and assured him of safety from her father, but he refused to accept her until she was baptized. This she would not submit to. Thinking to gain his liberty, he killed her father and then adroitly tied the maiden upon his horse before him and was riding away when she again exercised her witch power:

> " With magic art all o'er the lake a broad bridge threw the dame,
> But onward as they rode, still narrower it became:
> In wonder stood the hero; to the maiden he gan say,
> Damsel, truly tell, who has borne the bridge away.
> Little care I though you drown, cried dame Marpaly.
> Then graithe thee, said the hero, 'tis thou must plunge with me.
> No harm the waves can do me, with magic am I dight.
> Then speed we to the castle back, cried the Christian knight.
> Back the fearless hero turned his trusty horse,
> But down the bridge was broken by the lady's magic force.
> In his sorrow, cried the champion, help, God, in this my need!
> Say how we may hither pass, damsel right areed.
> From the courser Marpaly suddenly would fly.
> Stay thou here, thou woman fell! quickly must thou die.
> Piteously she wept, prayed him her life to save,
> He tied her to his body fast and plunged into the wave.
> In the name of God he leaped into the lake amain;
> But the water suddenly was gone; on the mead he stood again.
> Suddenly upon the mead, her garment down she threw,
> And showed her beauteous form to the wondering champion's view.
> Her hands she clasped together, on the hero did she look,
> And straight, by arts of grammary, a raven's form she took.
> High upon a tree perched the raven black.

Before and during last century it was commonly believed that if a murder was committed, no matter how secretly, should the person who committed the crime come near the murdered body the wounds which caused the death would bleed afresh. As an ordeal or test, if any person was suspected he or she was brought to see the corpse and made to touch it. If blood did not flow it was considered a proof of innocence. This belief existed in the middle ages. In the song of the Nibelungen of the eleventh century, a hero Siegfried was basely murdered, but it was not known who committed the crime until it so happened the murderer attended the funeral :

> " A marvel high and strange is seen full many a time,
> When to the murdered body nighs the man that did the crime,
> Afresh the wounds will bleed: the marvel now was found—
> That Hagan felled the champion with treason to the ground."

This proof of guilt was actually produced in a court of law so late as 1687. Philip Stanfield was supposed to have murdered his father, Sir James Stanfield, of Newmills. No direct proof could be brought against the son, but he was brought to touch the corpse, when the head began to bleed ; Phillip was then condemned.

There was a very old and wide-spread belief that there existed men and women who lived in the water. They were called mermen and mermaids, but from the varying descriptions given of these creatures in different ages and localities it is evident that imagination had a pretty free field, and was cultivated according to the fancy of those who described them. The following is from the song of the Niebelungen of the eleventh century:

> " And when he saw the mermaids, he sped him silently;
> But soon they heard his footseps, and quickly did they hie,
> Glad and joyfull in their hearts, that they 'scaped the hero's arm:
> From the ground he took their garments, did them none other harm.
> Up then spake a mermaid, Hilburg was she hight,
> Noble Hero Haghan, your fate will I reed aright,
> At King Etzels' Court what adventures ye shall have,
> If back thou give our garments, thou champion bold and brave.
> Like birds they flew before him upon the watery flood,
> And as they flew the mermaid's form thought him so fair and good,
> That he believed full well what of his fate she spoke;
> But for the hero's boldness she thought to be awroke."

Here we have the mermaids described as wearing garments, but for the time they had laid them aside upon the shore as young maidens did while bathing. Here also they fly naked over the surface of the water as do sea-fowls, and are endowed with power to tell fortunes. In another ballad called " Lady Grimild's Wrack," the hero, who is called Hogen, while walking along the sea-shore, came upon a mermaid sleeping and asked her to tell his fortune:

> " It was the hero Hogen he dauner'd on the strand,
>   And there he found the mer-lady sleeping on the white sand;
>   Heal, heal to thee dear merlady thou art a cunning wife;
>   And I come to Hvenild's Land, it's may I brook my life? "

Her answer not satisfying the hero he was angry :

> " 'Twas then the hero Hogen his swerd swyth he drew,
>   And from the luckless mer-lady her head aff he hew.
>   Sae he has taken the bloody head, and cast it i' the sound,
>   The body's croppen after, and joined it at the ground."

In another ballad, called " Rosmer Hafmand," we find a merman much resembling, in character at least, the dwarf or elf-kings of other ballads. This merman gets possession of a betrothed maiden whom he loves and carries to his abode. Her human lover discovers her place of imprisonment and succeeds in getting to her. She, however, fearing that the merman will kill her lover, concocts a story wherewith to deceive her captor, and tells him that a near relative of hers has come to see her and bespeaks protection for him; the merman grants her request. The lovers then contrive a plan for escaping, and the merman is informed that her relation is prepared to return home. The merman engages to carry him across the water, together with a kist of luggage, the lady's gift to her relative. She herself goes into the kist :

> " He took the man under his arm; the kist on his back took he;
>   Sae he can under the saut-sea gang, sae canny and sae free.
>   Now I hae born thee till the land thou seest baith sun and moon:
>   And I gae thee this kist o' goud, that is nae churlis boon."

When he returned to his abode and found the maiden gone :

> " Now Rosmer waxt sae wroth and grim, when he nae Eline fand,
>   He turn'd into a whinstone gray, sic like he there does stand."

This ballad contains a vast amount of ancient notions concerning mermen and mermaids. But as we come nearer modern times we find great changes have taken place in this particular form of superstition. These changes were without doubt due to the commingling of eastern and northern streams of fable, which joined their currents at an early date, but did not coalesce into a homogeneous flood until a much later date. We must also remember, as I have already said, that Christianity acted as a controlling agent, rejecting what was discordant to its pre-

conceptions, and introducing new material of its own, the product of
a development differing considerably from the early forms, although
the superstitions were about equal in quantity. In the later form
mermen and mermaids have become prognosticators of evil, either of
weather or to some persons, and when they speak, which they had
the gift of doing in any language, it is always to predict evil or decoy
some illfated individual to their destruction. This is illustrated in
several ballads. Take the following, intitled "The Master of Weemys,"
by Motherwell, from *Minstrelsey Ancient and Modern:*

> " They have hoisted sayle and left the land,
>   They have saylit milis throe,
> When up their lap the bonnie mermayd,
>   All in the norland sea.
> ' O whare saile ye,' quo the bonnie mermayd,
>   Upon the saut sea faem,
> It's we are bounde until norroway,
>   God send us scaithless hame.
> Down doukit then the mermayden,
>   Deep intil the middil sea,
> And merry leuch that master bauld
>   With his jolly companie;
> When lo' uplap shee the gude ships side
>   The self same mermayden,
> Shee hild a glass intil her richt hande,
>   In the other shee held a kame,
> And shee kembit her haire and aye shee sang
>   As shee festerit on the faem,
> And shee gliskit about and round about
>   Upon the waters wan.
> O nevir again on land or sea
>   Shall be seen suk a fair woman.
> And shee shed the haire off her milk white bree
>   Wi' her fingers sae sma' and lang,
>   Sae louder was aye her sang.
> And aye shee sang and aye shee sang,
>   As shee rade upon the sea,
> If ye bee men of christian moulde
>   Throwe the master out to mee.
> It's never a word spake the master baulde,
>   But a loud laugh leuch the crewe,
> And in the deep then the mermayden
>   Down drappit frae their viewe.

Good Lord ! there is a scaud o' fire
    Fast coming out owre the sea,
And fast therein that grim mermayden
    Is sayling on to thee.
Shee hailes the ship wi a shrill shrill cry,
    Shee is coming alace more near,
An woe is me now said the master baulde
    For I baith do see and hear."

In a song entitled "The Mermaid," from *Legendary Ballads of England and Scotland*, the mermaid is identified with the Water Kelpie and the Elf. She decoys a knight to his destruction:

" To yon fauso stream, that, near the sea,
    Hides many an elf and plum,
And rives wi fearful din the stanes,
    A witless knicht did come.
Frae neath a rock, sune, sune she raise,
    And stately on she swam ;
Stopped i' the midst, and becked and sang
    To him to stretch his han'.
The smile upon her bonnie cheek
    Was sweeter than the bee,
Her voice excelled the burdies sang
    Upon the birchen tree.
Sae couthie, couthie did she look,
    And meikle had she flecched.
Out shot his hand. Alas ! alas !
    Fast in the swirl he screeched.
The mermaid leuch, her brief was gane,
    And Kilpie's blast was blawin.
Fu' low she duked, ne'er raise again,
    For deep deep was the fawin.
Aboon the stream his wraith was seen,
    Warlocks tirled lang at gloamin,
That e'en was coarse, the blast blew hoarse,
    Ere lang the waves war foamin."

The following is an account of one that was caught in a net in a pool of the sea in Galloway, and her purpose is evident.* We have here more of the elf or the supernatural power of the dwarfs and witches:

" He spread his broad net, where 'tis said in the brine
The mermaidens sport mid the merry moonshine,
He drew it and laugh'd, for he found 'mongst the meshes
A fish and a maiden, with silken eye-lashes ;

* *Historical and Traditional Tales connected with the South of Scotland.*

And she sang with a voice, like May Morley's of Larg,
'A maid and a salmon for young Sandy Harg.'
O white were her arms, and far whiter her neck,
Her long locks in armfuls oerflowed all the deck,
One hand on the rudder she pleasantly laid,
Another on Sandy, she merrily said:
'Thy halve net has wrought thee a gallant days darg,
Thou'rt monarch of Solway, my young Sandy Harg.'
O loud laugh'd young Sandy, and swore by the mass,
I'll never reign king but 'mid gowans and grass;
Oh loud laugh'd young Sandy and swore 'By thy hand,
My May Morley, I'm thine both by water and land:
Twere marvel if mer-woman slimy and slarg,
Could change the true love of young Sandy Harg;'
She knotted one ringlet, syne knotted she twain,
And sang—lo! thick darkness dropp'd down on the main—
She knotted three ringlets, syne knotted she nine,
A tempest stoop'd sudden and sharp on the brine.
And away flew the boat—there's a damsel in Larg
Will wonder what's came of thee, young Sandy Harg.
'The sky's spitting fire,' cried Sandy, 'and see,
Green Criffel reels round and will chocke up the sea,
From their bottles of tempest the fiends draw the corks,
Wild Solway is barmy like ale when it works,
There sits Satan's daughter who works the dread darg
To mar my blythe bridal,' quoth young Sandy Harg.
From his bosom a spell to work wonders he took,
Thrice kiss'd it and smiled, then triumphantly shook
The boat by the rudder, the maid by the hair;
With wailing and shrieks she bewildered the air;
He flung her far seaward, then sailed off to Larg,
There was mirth at the bridal of young Sandy Harg."

Many are the curious details existing in books and coming down to us by tradition of mermaids being seen, of their appearance, and the evil results which attended their appearance. In an Aberdeen almanac for 1488 there occurs the curious statement:

"Near the place where the Dee payeth its tribute to the German Ocean, *if curious observers of wonderful things in nature* will be pleased thither to resort on the 1st, 13th, and 29th of May, and in divers other times in the insueing summer; as also in the harvest time to the 7th and 14th of October *they will undoubtedly see a pretty company of mermaids*, creatures of admirable beauty, and likewise hear their charming sweet melodious voices :

> " In well traced measure and harmonious lays
> Extol their maker and his bounty praise,
> That godly honest men in every thing
> In quiet peace may live. God save the King."

" To the mind of the lower races it seems that all nature is possessed,
pervaded, and crowded with spiritual being." With such a philosophy
of nature as this we need not be surprised that our forefathers believed
that birds and beasts, and even inanimate nature, could at times speak and
carry messages and tell matters they had witnessed in their journeying.
" A bird told it to me " is still a proverbial expression when any one
comes to the knowledge of a secret. The popular Jacobite song "A wee
bird cam to our ha' door," composed within this century, helps to com-
memorate this idea. This song as stated is modern, but at the date to
which it refers, 1745, the notion was not altogether a poetical thought,
but a real belief among the people of the highlands of Scotland, and we
know that it was part of the theology of the old Celtic bards that the
souls of the departed entered into animals, and that at times the spirits
of the living could leave the body to visit, or communicate information,
through animals. In one of the old ballads in *Illustration of Northern
Antiquities* a knight is represented as keeping two nightingales for
the purpose of revealing secrets to him.

> " Two nightingales Sir Samsing has,
>   They ladies ken sae weel,
> And fâs he a may or fâs he nane,
>   Sae soothly they can tell.
> Sir Samsing says to his nightingales,
>   Now sing what luck I hae,
> Hae I a may or hae I nane,
>   I' the bride-bed now wi' me."

The following instance is from the ballad of " Fair Midel and Kirsten
Lyle." Kirsten is seduced and bears twins while Midel is absent
searching for water.

> " And whan to the burn fair Medel he wan,
> A nightingale sat on a twist and sang:
> Little Kirsten she lies i' the green wood dead,
> Twa bairnies are in her oxter laid.
> O' the nightingale's sang sma' reck he's taen,
> And back the lone gait thro' the wood he's gane,
> And when he the hythe sae thick wan to,
> Sae found he the nightingale's sang was true."

Another instance taken from the same work ; it tells its own story.

" The titmouse sang very sweetly, my brother is in the chamber,
　　Go, my little sister, and hear what song the titmouse sings.
　　The titmouse sings this song: Brother must to the wars,
　　Weep not, my little sister, if I return not myself ;
　　Yet, if my charger returns, ask of him, where fell the rider."

In the *Minstrelsy Ancient and Modern*, the young Laird Johnie of
Breadislee goes out with his dogs to hunt, and is attacked by seven
foresters, and left mortally wounded ; he then says :

" O, is there na a bonnie bird, can sing as I can say;
　　Could flee away to my mother's bower, and tell to fetch Johnie away?
　　The starling flew to his mother's window-stane, it whistled and it sang,
　　And aye the ower word o' the tune was—Johnie tarries lang." '

In the ballad of " Earl Richard " from the same volume a young lady
through jealousy murders the young Earl and hides his body in her
bower till the morning, when

" She called her servants ane by ane, she called them twa by twa:
　　I have got a dead man in my bower, I wish he were awa'.
　　The ane has taen him by the hand and the other by the feet,
　　And the've thrown him into a deep draw well, full fifty fathoms deep.
　　Then up bespake a little bird that sat upon a tree,
　　Gae hame, gae hame, ye fause lady, and pay pour maids their fee.
　　Come down, come down, my pretty bird, that sits upon a tree;
　　I have a cage o' beaten gold, I'll gie it unto thee.
　　Gae hame, gae hame, ye fause lady, and pay your maids their fee,
　　As ye have done to Earl Richard, sae would you do to me."

In the ballad of " Sweet William," from the same volume, a father
wishes to force his daughter to marry a man she did not wish: she was
in sore strait.

" She walked up, she walked down, had nane to make her moan.
　　Nothing but a pretty bird sat on the causeway stone.
' If thou could speak, wee bird, she says, as well as thou can flee,
　　I would write a lang letter to Willy ayont the sea.'
' What you want with Will, it says, thou'lt seal it wi' thy ring,
　　Tak a thread o' silk, and another o' twine, and about my neck it hing.
　　　　What she wanted wi' Willie,
　　　　　　She sealed it wi' a ring,
　　　　Took a thread o' silk, another o' twine,
　　　　　　About its neck did hing.
　　　　This bird flew high, this bird flew low,
　　　　　　This bird flew o'er the sea,
　　　　Untill it entered the same chamber
　　　　　　Wherein was sweet Willie."

Our next illustration is from a ballad called "Young Huntin," taken from *Legendary Ballads of England and Scotland* (Chandos Classics); the incidents are the same as in "Earl Richard:" a young lady kills her lover through jealousy, then bribes her maidens to help to dispose of the body, which is taken by them on horseback and flung into the Clyde. Young Huntin being missed, search was being made in the Clyde for his body. The murder having been seen by a popinjay the young lady had, the bird spoke and gave her warning.

> "Then up and spak the popinjay that sat aboon her heid,
> Ladye keep weel your green cleiden frae gude young Huntin's bleid."

While the people were searching for the body, the king, Young Huntin's father, slept in the lady's castle. The following tells the revelation made by the bird:

> "It fell that in that lady's castle the king was boun' to bed,
> And out and spak the popinjay that flew aboon his heid,
> Leave off your douking in the day, and douk upon the nicht,
> And where that snikless knicht lies slain the candles they'll burn bricht.
> They booted him, and sparred him, as he'd been gaun to ride,
> A hunting-horn about his neck, a sharp sword by his side,
> In the deepest pool in Clyde water it's there they flung him in,
> Wi' a turf on his breist bane to haud young Huntin doon."

In a ballad in the same collection called "The King in the North" Earl Percy is warned by a bird of what is before him.

> "Earl Percy is unto his garden gane,
> And after him walks his fair lady,
> I heard a bird sing in mine ear,
> That I must either fight or flee.

In a ballad called "The Maiden and the Hazel" in *Illustrations of Northern Antiquities* we have an instance of a hazel-bush speaking.

> "A lassie gaed out a rose-gathering
> I' the green wood a' her lane,
> And she fand by the gaite a hasel tree
> Was growing fresh and green.
> Gude morrow, gude morrow, my hasel dear,
> How comes that ye're sae green?
> O thank ye, thank ye, maiden gay,
> How comes that ye're sae sheen?
> The lassie that wishes her garland
> To keep maun bide at hame;
> Nor dance o'er late in the gloamin,
> Nor gang to the green wood her lane."

The next quotation is from a ballad called by Sir W. Scott "The

Cruel Sister."* False Helen drowns her sister by pushing her into a milldam. An old harper makes a harp out of-the drowned lady's breast-bone and takes it to her father's hall, where was met the court.

> "He brought the harp to her father's hall,
> And there was the court assembled all.
> He laid his harp upon a stone,
> And straight it began to play alone:
> O, yonder sits my father, the king,
> And yonder sits my mother the queen,
> And yonder stands my brother Hugh,
> And by him my William sweet and true,
> And the last tune that the harp played then
> Was wae to my sister false Helen."

The notion that ghosts or the spirits of the dead at times visit the living is not only very old, but it is still the creed of many. Only the occasion for the visit must have special importance, as for instance where there has been misunderstanding between the dead and living, or in cases of hidden murder, when the buried dead cannot rest in their graves. Of the first case we have an instance in an old ballad, "Young Benjie." Two lovers quarrel, and the young man in a fit of anger and jealousy throws his sweetheart into a pool, and she was drowned. Her brothers by superstitious means try and find the murderers.

> "The night it is her low lykewake, the morn her burial day,
> And we maun watch at mirk midnight, and hear what she will say;
> Wi' door ajar and candle light, and torches burning clear,
> The streiket corps till still midnight they waked but nothing hear.
> About the middle o' the night the cocks began to craw.
> And at the dead hour o' the night the corps began to thraw.
> O whae has done the wrang, sister, or dared the deadly sin ?
> Wha was sae stout and feared nae dout to throw ye o'er the linn?
> Young Benjie was the first ae man I laid my love upon ;
> He was sae stout and proud-hearted he threw me o'er the linn.
> Sall we young Benjie head, sister, sall we young Benjie hang,
> Or sall we pike out his two gray e'en, and punish him ere he gang ?
> Tie a green gravat about his neck, and lead him out and in,
> And the best ae servant about your house to wait young Benjie on.
> And aye at every seven years' end ye'll take him to the linn;
> · For that's the pennance he maun dree, to seng his deadly sin."

The following is from the ballad of the "Jew's Daughter," in Mother-

---

* *Transactions of Archæological Society of Glasgow*, vol. i.; *Minstrelsy of the Scottish Border*, vol. iii.

well's collection. A youth was murdered and his body thrown into a draw-well, and he speaks to his mother from the well :

> " She ran away to the deep draw-well,
>   And she fell down on her knee;
> Saying, bonnie Sir Hugh, o pretty Sir Hugh,
>   I pray ye, speak to me.
> O! the lead it is wondrous heavy, mother,
>   The well it is wondrous deep,
> The little penknife sticks in my throat,
>   And I downa to ye speak.
> But lift me out of this deep draw-well,
>   And bury me in yon church-yard;
> Put a bible at my head, he says,
>   And a testament at my feet,
> And pen and ink at every side;
>   And I will lay still and sleep.
> And go to the back of Maitland town,
>   Bring me my winding sheet;
> For it's at the back of Maitland town,
>   That you and I shall meet."

The ballad of " William's Ghost," is founded upon a superstition as to the interchange of love tokens.

> " There came a ghost to Marjorie's door,
>   Wi' many a grievous maen,
> And aye he tirl'd at the pin,
>   But answer made she nane.
> Oh sweet Marjorie! oh dear Marjorie!
>   For faith and charitie,
> Give me my faith and troth again
>   That I gied once to thee. ·
> Thy faith and troth I'll ne'er gie thee,
>   Nor yet shall our true love twin,
> Till you tak' me to your ain ha'-house,
>   And wed me wi a ring.
> My house is but yon lonesome grave
>   Afar out o'er yon lee,
> And it is but my spirit, Marjorie,
>   That's speaking unto thee."

She followed the spirit to the grave, where it lay down and confessed that William had betrayed three maidens whom he had promised to marry and in consequence of this misdemeanour he could not rest in his grave till she released him of his vows to marry her. On learning this Marjorie at once released him.

> " Then she's taen up her white, white hand,
>   And struck him on the breist
> Saying, have ye again your faith and troth,
>   And I wish your saul good rest."

In " Clerk Sanders " we have another instance of ghost visitation ;
the incidents differ, but the probability is that the ballad quoted and
"Clerk Sanders" are both founded on the same story. Clerk Sanders was
the son of an earl, who courted the king's daughter, Lady Margaret.
They loved each other even in the modern sense of loving too well.
Margaret had seven brothers, who suspected an intrigue, and they came
upon them together in bed and killed Clerk Sanders, whose ghost some
time after came to Margaret's window and said :

> " O, are ye sleeping, Margaret? he says,
>   Or are ye waking presentlie ?
> Give me my faith and troth again,
>   I wot, true love, I gied to thee.
> I canna rest, Margaret, he says,
>   Down in the grave where I must be
> Till ye gie me my faith and troth again,
>   I wot, true love, I gied to thee.
> Thy faith and troth thou shall na get,
>   And our true love shall never twin.
> Untill ye tell what comes o' women,
>   I wot, who die in strong travailing,
> Their beds are made in the heavens high,
>   Down at the foot of our Lord's knee,
> Weel set about wi' gilliflowers,
>   I wot sweet company for to see.
> O, cocks are crowing a merry midnight,
>   I wot the wild fowls are boding day,
> The psalms of heaven will soon be sung,
>   And I, ere now, will be missed away.
> Then she has ta'en a crystall wand,
>   And she has stroken her throth thereon;
> She has given it him out of the shot-window
>   Wi' many a sigh and heavy goan.
> I thank ye, Margaret; I thank ye, Margaret;
>   And aye I thank ye heartilie;
> Gin ever the dead come for the quick,
>   Be sure Margaret, I'll come for thee.
> Then up and crew the milk-white cock,
>   And up and crew the gray;

> Her lover vanished in the air,
>   And she gaed weeping away."

Another instance of ghosts visiting and speaking with the living is found in a song which is more modern than any of the above: in "Mary's Dream" Mary's betrothed is lost at sea, and his ghost visits her.

> "Mary laid her down to sleep,
>   Her thoughts on Sandy, far at sea,
> When soft and slow a voice was heard:
>   Mary, weep no more for me.
> She from her pillow gently raised
>   Her head to ask who there might be,
> She saw young Sandy shiv'ring stand
>   With visage pale and hollow e'e.
> O Mary, dear, cold is my clay,
>   It lies beneath a stormy sea,
> Far, far from thee I sleep in death,
>   So Mary weep no more for me."

The ballad of "Tamlane" is founded upon an ancient superstition. Tamlane, the son of the earl of Murray, was stolen when a boy by the fairies, and kept by them for a while. He was well content to remain, but, hearing that every seven years an inmate was given to the devil as a sort of tax, and having become fat and well-favoured, he was afraid that he might be chosen, and therefore he longed to escape. One day the daughter of the Earl of March went out into the fields, and as she was pulling some roses, a little dwarf stood beside her, and asked her why she did so without his leave. A mutual love soon sprang up between them, but she was anxious to know if he had been baptized.

> "The truth ye'll tell me, Tamlane,
>   A word ye maunna lee,
> Gin ere ye was in haly chapel,
>   Or sained in Christentie.

Then he told her who he was and how he had been stolen away, and what she was to do in order to get him from the fairies, and he promised that, if she succeeded in freeing him from the fairies, he would marry her.

" There cam a wind out of the north,
  A sharp wind and a snell;
A deep sleep came over me,
  And frae my horse I fell.
The Queen o' fairies keppet me,
  In yon green hill to dwell.
And I would not tire, Janet,
  In fairy-land to dwell;
But aye at ilka seven years,
  They pay the teind o' hell ;
And I am sa fat and fair o' flesh,
  I fear t'will be mysell.
The night it is good hallowe'en,
  When fairy folks will ride,
And she that wad her true love win
  At miles cross she maun bide ;
And ye maun gae to the miles cross,
  Between twal hours and one,
Take holy water in your hand,
  And cast a compass roun :
First let pass the black, Janet, and syne let pass the brown,
But grip ye to the milk-white steed, and pu the rider doun ;
They'll turn me in your arms, Janet,
  An adder and a snake,
But haud me fast, let me not pass,
  Gin ye would be my maik (wife);
They'll turn me in your arms, Janet,
  An adder and an aske,
They'll turn me in your arms, Janet,
  A bale that burns fast ;
They'll shape me in your arms, Janet,
  A dove but and a swan:
And last they'll shape me in your arms
  A mother naked man;
Cast your green mantle over me
  I'll be myself again."

The lady obeyed all these instructions and gained her lover from fairie land. Modern instances are recorded of the same means being tried successfully to win stolen people from fairie land.

There was another curious folk-lore belief, that, in cases where lovers had vowed to each other or were betrothed, the one gave the other a love-gift or covenant-token, such as a coin or a ring ; the same also took place in cases where a husband was obliged to leave his wife for some time. If when absent the parties became unfaithfull to their pledges, this covenant-token magically made the fact known. In the ballad of " Lambert Linkin," *Minstrelsy Ancient and Modern,*—

> " The lord sat in England a drinking the wine,
> I wish a' may be weel wi' my lady at hame,
> For the rings o' my fingers they are now burst in twain !
> He saddled his horse and he came riding down:
> But as soon as he viewed Belinkin was in,
> He had na weel stepped twa steps up the stair,
> Till he saw his pretty young son lying dead on the floor.
> He had na weel stepped other two up the stair
> Till he saw his pretty lady lying dead in dispair."

In the ballad of " Hynde Horn " is another instance of lovers' tokens :

> " And she gave me a gay gold ring,
> That was to rule abune a' thing,
> As lang's this ring it keeps the hue,
> You'll know I am a lover true ;
> But when the ring turns pale and wan,
> Ye'll know I love another man.
> He hoist up sails, and awa sailed he
> And sailed into a far countrie,
> And when he looked the ring upon
> He knew she loved another man.
> He hoist up sails and hame cam he,
> Hame unto his ain country ;
> The first he met, on his own land,
> It chanced to be a beggar man.
> What news, what news, my gude auld man,
> What news hae ye by sea or land?
> Nae news, nae news, the puir man did say,
> But this is our queen's wedding day."

He got access to the bride and returned the ring, the old love was re-kindled, and they were married.

In every age a traitor or faithless friend has always been held up to scorn, but in the times when these ballads were composed it was believed that some judgment would soon befall the traitor. In the ballad of " Sir James the Rose " his betrayer is spirited away:

> " Its for your sake Sir James the Rose
>   That my poor hearts a-breaking,
> Cursed be the day I did thee betray,
>   Thou brave knight o' Buleighan.
> Then up she rose and forth she goes,
>   And in that fatal hour,
> She bodily was borne away
>   And never was seen more ;
> But where she went was never kent,
>   And so, to end the matter,
> A traitor's end you may depend
>   Can never be no better."

In a ballad called " Northumberland betrayed by Douglas," Lady Jane Douglas, the sister of the betrayer, possessed a magic ring through which she could see into futurity or witness what was taking place in other parts of the country. In one of the verses, which Bishop Percy believed to be an interpolation, she warns Northumberland of his danger and says:

> " I never was on English ground,
>   Ne never saw it with mine eye,
> But as my book it sheweth mee
>   And through my ring I may descrye.
> My mother shee was a witch ladye,
>   And of her skille she learned mee,
> She wold let me see out of Lough-leven
>   What they did in London citie."

Lady Jane was desirous to show Earl Percy through the ring and convince him of his danger, but he refused to go with her. She then persuaded his chamberlain to look through:

> " James Swynard with that lady went,
>   She showed him through the weme of her ring,
> How many English lords there were,
>   Waiting for his master and him."

A witch lady—for in these times the rich were believed to possess witch power as well as the aged poor—had a son whom she wished to marry to a young lady of her choice, but he refused and married another lady. His mother in revenge planned the young wife's death by magically preventing her confinement. The son, knowing that this was the work of his mother, offered her large gifts to withdraw her spells, but she refused ; he then consulted a wizard, who advised him what to do to find out the spells ; he went to his mother and asked her to congratulate him on the birth of a son. She gets into a rage and says :

> " O, wha has loosed the nine witch knots
> That was among my ladies locks,
> And wha has taen out the kame o' care
> That was among that ladies hair ;
> And wha has killed the master kid
> That ran aneath that ladies bed ;
> And wha has loosed her left foot shee
> And letten that lady lighter be? "

By this strategem he found out his mother's spells and removed them.

> " And now he's gotten a bonny son
> And muckle grace be him upon."

A similar tale to this is told as a fact that took place in Arran within this century. A young man jilted his sweetheart and married another. When the time of the wife's confinement came she was in a great agony. A packman passing suspected the cause, went at once to the house of the old sweetheart, and told that such an one had got a fine bairn ; when up got the jilted fair one in a passion and pulled out a big nail from the beam of the roof, saying to her mother, "Muckle good your craft has done." At the same hour the wife was delivered. This power, which some persons had over others, by the putting in a nail or pin all who passed under it being spell-bound and under the will of the witch, is an old and very common belief in Scotland. There was a noted wizard in Ayrshire, called the Laird of Fail, who had this power, and many stories are current of the amusement he created to his friends by playing tricks upon people. The late Joseph Train, the well-known antiquary, wrote a ballad including all the Laird's acts in witchery, but it may be better given with others of a like nature at another time. The Laird's power was similar to that which is attributed · in the sixteenth century to John Bale.

> " Their wells I can up dry, cause trees and herbs to dye,
> And slae all pulterye. When as men doth me move,
> I cane make stools to dance, and earthen pottes to prance,
> That none shall them enhance, and do but cast my glove.

The following ballad gives a good idea of what was believed respecting witch power and intrigue. It is called the "Witch Lady" in *Traditions of Galloway*.

"Gae, tak' this braide frae 'mang my haire,
 And thae gowde rings aff my hande,
And binde my browe, my burnying browe,
 Wi' a quhyte safte linen bande,
For yestreene I dreamte I was quhair floweres
 Bloomt fayre 'mang the evening dewe,
But the nighte-shade hung over the gilly-flower's head,
 And it withered on my view.
And I saw my William, but a braide riyver
 Row'd him and me betweene,
And a highe-borne dame was by his side,
 Wi' twa dark glancying eyne,
And aye her darke e'e scho fix'd an me
 Till I quail'd beneathe its leme:
Is there ane, amange a' my bour maidens
 Can rede to me my dreame?
Then out and spake scho may Margret,
 Gae saddle your fleetest steede,
And knocke at the pin of the Earlstone yette,
 Let nathing marre your speed,
For lang has the Ladye of Earlstone toure
 Begrudgit ye yere William's love.
And her witch-knottes power in ane evyl houre,
 'Mang his hearte's strings scho has wove,
And scho's coosten the glamoury ower his ee,
 With ane art may nocht withstand,
Till of her wee finger he noo thinks maire,
 Than the haille of his annies hande.
Or wist ye of a wice wazzard
 Could cross the witche's spelle,
But wichte and wice he'd baithe need be
 Quho needes must stryve with helle.
For scho gathered witch-dewe in the Kell's kirk-yard
 In the myrke howe of the moone,
And fed hersell with the wild witch-milke
 With a rede-hotte burnying spoone,
And scho's washit hyselle in the ranke witche dew
 Till her greye eyene shyne like starris,
Till the lip and the cheeke of that ill woman
 The dye of the redde-rose maris,

And sho's bathed hyrsell in the wyld witch-milke,
   That woman voide of drede,
Till the downye swell of her heavying breastis
   Gars the quhyte rose hange its hede.
Then out and spake he, the popinjay,
   Hangs in fayr Annie's bowr—
It's ladye, I'll be your wiche wizzarde,
   Will speede me to Earlstone's towr.
The greene-thorne-tree in the Earlestone lee,
   Its I was nestled there.
But the Ladye of Earlstone herryed the nest
   That cost my dam sic care,
And scho had me to her bowr, that witche Ladye,
   Quhin I conn'd a' her fiend-taught spelles ;
But I sta' the worde quhen I took my leave,
   Quhylk a' her glamour quelles.
I'll sing siecan notes in the Earlstone woodes
   Sall reache that Ladye's boure ;
And I'll weave siecan sang in the Earlstone woods
   Sal twyne her of her powere."

      *   *   *   *

"And alas, and alas ! for that bonnie doo,
   In the shirmars woodes sae greene,
For the greye oulet sits within her nest,
   With her twa big gloweringe eyene.
And its Oh ! and sing Oh ! for that bonnie doo,
   That mournes in the shirmars boure,
For the oulet has reaved her of her mate,
   In ane evyl and luckless houre.
And the lone curdoo of that bonnie doo
   Is herde o'er the braide Loch Ken,
Qwhyle her mate sits under the grey oulet's winge,
   Like the chicken an under the henne.
Then out and spake he, Lord William :
   ' My bonnie bird, tell to me,
Quhair did ye get that waile of woe,
   Or quhac taught it to thee ?'
But up and spake scho, that witche Ladye,
   ' Come, perch on this eglantyne,
And the quhytest brede shall be thy fede,
   And thy drynke of the blude-red wine.'
' But it's nae, and it's nae,' sang the popinjay ;
   ' I've tarryed here owr lange,
Yet before my flychte I tak outrychte,
   Hear the last note of my sange.'

And he minted the worde, the awesome worde,
  Reach'd nae ear butan her ain;
And sterne as death wax'd the ladye's wraithe,
  And loude, loude was her mane.
And scho sprange through the glades, and the deep dark shades,
  Till scho reach'd the boiling linne ;
And there, mid the howle of the wylde turmoile,
  She has buried both schaime and synne."

The following ballad, from *Pedlar's Pack of Ballads*, illustrates a very common piece of folk-lore, yet as old as centuries before the present era :

" There was a ship, and a ship of fame,
  Launched off the stocks, bound to the main,
  With an hundred and fifty brisk young men,
  Well picked and chosen every one.
The first of April we did set sail,
  Blest with a sweet and pleasant gale,
  For we were bound to New Barbary,
  With all our whole ship's company.
One night the captain he did dream
  There came a voice which said to him :
' Prepare you and your company;
  To-morrow night you'll lodge with me.'
This waked the captain in a fright,
  Being the third watch of the night.
Then for his boatswain he did call,
  And told to him his secrets all.
' When I in England did remain,
  The holy Sabbath I did profane.
In drunkenness I took delight.
  Which doth my trembling soul affright;
A squire I slew in Staffordshire,
  All for the sake of a lady dear.'
They had not sailed a league, but three,
  Till raging grew the roaring sea.
There rose a tempest in the skies,
  Which filled our hearts with great surprise.
The sea did wash both fore and aft,
  Till scarce one sail on board was left.
Our yards were split and our riggin tore,
  The like was never seen before.
The boatswain then he did declare
  The captain was a murderer,
Which did enrage the whole ships crew,
  Our captain overboard we threw.

Our treacherous captain being gone,
Immediately there was a calm.
The winds did cease and the raging sea
As we went to New Barbary.
Now seamen all where'er you be
I pray a warning take by me,
As you love your life still have a care,
That you never sail with a murderer.

In a ballad by Ross, the author of "The Fortunate Shepherdess,"
there is reference to an ill e'e making all things disastrous, and the means
to be taken to avert the influence:

" There was an auld wife and a wee pickle tow,
And she would go try the spinning o't,
She louted her down and the rock took alow,
And that was a bad beginning o't ;
She sat, and she grat, and she flate, and she flang,
And she threw, and she blew, and she wriggled and wrang,
And she choaked and boaked and cryed like to mang,
Alas for the dreary beginning o't.
I'll gar my ain Tammie gae down to the howe,
And cut me a rock of a widdershin grow
O' gude Rantry tree for to carry my tow,
And a spindle o' same for the twining o't.
For now when I mind I met Maggie Grim,
That morning just at the beginning o't.
She was never ca'd chancy but canny and slim,
And so it has fared with the spinning o't;
But gin my new rock was anee cutted and dry,
I'll all Maggie Cann and her cantrips defy,
And but any sussie (hesitation) the spinning I'll try,
And ye shall a' hear o' the beginning o't."

From Allan Ramsay we have a fine picture of folk-lore:

" Pictures oft she makes
Of folk she hates and gaur expire,
Wi' slow and racking pain before the fire,
Stuck fu' o' preens the devilish picture melt,
The pain by folk they represent is felt.

The following is an instance of the fairies spiriting away a young
lady into fairieland, and may remind the reader of the story of Bonny
Kelminy in Hogg's " Queen's Wake :"

King Arthur's sons o' merry Carlisle
Were playing at the Ba',

> And there was their sister Burd Ellen
> I' the midst among them a'.
> Child Rowland kicked wi' his foot
> And keppet it wi' his knee,
> And aye as he played out o'er them a'
> O'er the kirk he gar'd it flee.
> Burd Ellen round about the asle
> To seek the Ba' has gane,
> But she bade lang and aye langer,
> And she came na back again.
> They sought her east, they sought her west,
> They sought her up and down,
> And wae were the hearts in merry Carlisle,
> For she was nae gait found."

Her young brother by the aid of a wizard made his way into fairie land, and by virtue of a magic sword overcame the king of elfland and rescued Burd Ellen.

When a company could not agree as to the direction in which they would travel, or when one was in a dilemma as to the road he should take to attain his journey's end, it was customary to let a staff fall without guidance and follow where its head pointed. The practice is very ancient:

> " En' on en' he poised his rung then,
> Watch'd the airt its head did fa',
> Whilk was east; he lapt and sung then,
> For there is dear bade, Meg Macraw."

The following ballad is supposed to be the lamentation of Lady Cassilis, known as the Gipsy Lady, who eloped with an old lover in the garb of a gipsy. Her fall is ascribed to witchcraft or glamour,[*] as in the following verse of a song long popular in Scotland:

> " And she came tripping down the stairs,
> With a' her maids before her,
> As soon as he saw her weel faured face,
> He coost the glamour o'er her."

The lady afterwards sings a lamentation:

> " Quhom suld I warie but my wicked weard,
> Quha span my thriftless thraward fatall threed?
> I was but scantlie entrit in this eard,
> Nor had offendid quhill I felt her feed,

---

[*] See on the word Glamour and the Legend of Glam, a paper by Professor Cowell in *Journal of Philology*, vi.; Conway's *Demonology and Devil-Lore*, i. 244-6.

> In hir unhappy hands she held my heid,
> And straikit backwards woodershins my hair;
> Syne prophecyed I sould aspyre and speid,
> Whilk double sentence was baith suith and sair,
> For I was matchit with my match and mair;
> No worldly woman never was so weill,
> I was accountit countess, but compare,
> Whilk fickle fortune whirld me from her wheel."

The following verses taken from different narratives give snatches of other instances of folk-lore, illustrating an almost universal belief.

A woman took a hatred to her husband for some slight, and in this state of mind the devil appears to her, as she said, and not only suggested the means of revenge but assisted her:

> " The foul thief knotted the tether,
>   She lifted his head on hie,
> Nourice drew the knot,
>   That gar'd Laird Wariston die."

The civil law could not take her plea and beheaded her for murder.

The following, which was written on his magic belt, is the warning and boast of a noted sorcerer in the beginning of the seventeenth century :

> " But, hear ye douce, because ye may meet me
> In many shapes to day, where'er you spy
> This brouded belt with characters : 'tis I.
> A gypsan Lady and a right beldam
> Wraught it by moonlight for me, and starlight,
> Upon your grandam's grave, that very night,
> We earthed her in the shades, when our dame Hecate
> Made it her gaing night, over the kirk yard;
> When all the bark and parish tykes set at her ;
> While I sat whyrland of my brazen spindle,
> At every twisted thred my rock let fly,
> Unto the serveters who did sit me nigh ;
> Under the town turnpike, which ran each spell,
> She stiched in the work and knit it well ;
> See ye take tent o' this."

Were we to take every reference to supernatural agency found in olden time ballads, as the people believed implicitly in the existence of supernatural powers who controlled every event in the lives either of individuals or communities, there would be at hand an ever-ready solution for every thing that occurred which was not understood in these early times. And these beliefs were so fixed in the popular mind that reason was never appealed to; therefore poets or ballad-makers had ample scope for explaining any circumstance. Shakespear's writings, as we all know, are full of folk-lore, and this adds to the truthfulness of his depiction of character. This is what he makes one of his characters, who practised magic, affirm of his powers:

> " I have bedimmed
> The noontide sun, called forth the mutinous winds,
> And twixt the green sea and the azure vault
> Set roaring war : to the dread rattling thunder
> Have I given fire, and rifted Jove's stout oak
> With his own bolt: the strong-based promontory
> Have I made shake, and by the spurs plucked up
> The pine and cedar. Graves at my command
> Have waked their sleepers; oped and let them forth,
> By my so potent art."

And in our own day we find James Hogg in one of his ballads describing the doings of a witch-wife:

> " The second night, when the new moon set,
>   O'er the roaring sea we flew,
> The cockle-shell our trusty bark,
>   Our sails of the green sea-rue.
> And the bauld winds blew, and the fire flauchtis flew,
>   And the sea ran to the sky,
> And the thunder it growlit, and the sea-dogs howlit,
>   As we gaed scouring by.
> And aye we mounted the sea-green hills,
>   Quhilk we brushed thro' the cluds of the hevin,
> Then sonsit downright, like the stern-shot light,
>   Frae the lifts blue casement driven."

Coming to modern times, we have songs in which folk-lore is referred to as of common knowledge; thus in Burns's song of "Tam Glen" a young girl is in a great dilemma and is seeking advice from her sister. She is courted by a rich man who trusts to his riches to gain her hand, but love has been before him in the person of a youth of her own order, and she is desirous to obtain direction from Providence to enable her to decide between the two, and she puts into practice the usual means to gain this end. On Hallowe'en she went to a south-running burn at a point where three lairds' lands met, and dipped the left sleeve of her shirt, taking care that no person saw her, and retired to her bed, first hanging up the shirt before the fire; she then lay awake till midnight; then she saw her future husband or his wraith come and turn over the shirt. Not content with this, she along with a number of others, as was usual on Valentine eve, met together, wrote down the names of a number of young men, put them into a hat, and each girl drew out a name, which, being repeated three times, if the same girl drew the same name every time, it was a decisive indication of the will of Providence.

> " The last Hallowe'en I was waukin
>   My drouket sark sleeve as ye ken,
> His likeness came up the house staukin,
>   And the very gray breeks o' Tam Glen.

> " Yestreen, at the Valentine's dealing
>   My heart to my mou' gied a sten,
> For thrice I drew ane without failing,
>   And thrice it was written Tam Glen."

In another modern ballad by Tannahill the poet makes a lover endeavour to excite compassion in the heart of his lady-love by drawing upon old superstitious freets in order to gain admission to her house.

> " Fearful souchs the Bourtree Bank,
>   The rifted wood roars wild and dreary,
> Loud the iron yetts do clank,
>   The cry o' howlets maks me eery.
> O, are ye sleeping, Maggie,
> O, are ye sleeping, Maggie,
> Let me in, for loud the linn
> Is roaring o'er the Warlock Craigie."

A beautiful description of a dark stormy night, but the effect is greatly increased by the belief that all is the work of the spirit of evil. The Bourtree Bank is a haunted place. The loud noise of the linn is the roaring of the water kelpie, and it is dangerous to go near. And the weirdness of the occasion is heightened by the addition of a wizard-haunted rock over which the water falls. The " Warlock Craigie " is the wizard rock. Indeed, everything is suggestive of danger from evil spirits, and seems well calculated to excite sympathy in the heart of the sweetheart who was a believer in all these freets.

The beliefs referred to were the theology of the day, and formed the practical creed of the people, of the educated as well as the ignorant. The present paper is, of course, meant to be suggestive rather than exhaustive—the initial contribution, it is hoped, to some further study of the subject that would make a valuable chapter of Folk-Lore. Writers on history and on the social condition of by-gone times too often overlook the character of the beliefs that really ruled and guided the people, and so their readers are left in ignorance of the true cause of much which occurred, and fail to explain the natural growth of civilization and the progress of man's mind. The old ballad, says Mr. Wheatley, in his Introduction to Bishop Percy's *Reliques*, filled the place of the modern newspaper, and history can be read in ballads by those who try to understand them.

JAMES NAPIER.

A NOTE ON THE "WHITE PATERNOSTER."

MR. THOMS, in his valuable Paper on Chaucer's *Night Spell* (Folk-lore Record, 1878, p. 145), makes mention of the *Paternostre Blanche*, preserved in the *Enchiridion Papæ Leonis*. It is, perhaps, not generally known that one paragraph of this curious formula survives to the present day as a part of the living traditional matter of at least five European countries. The variants that I have collected in the course of some years' studies in folk-song might probably be added to almost *ad libitum*, but even by themselves they furnish a striking illustration of the universality of certain forms of popular lore.

The paragraph I allude to runs as follows :—"Au soir m'allant coucher, je trouvis trois anges à mon lit couchés, un aux pied, deux au chevet, la bonne Vierge Marie au milieu, qui me dit que je me couchis, que rien ne doutis."

Most persons are familiar with the English version of this :—

> " Four corners to my bed,
> Four angels round my head,
> One to watch, one to pray,
> And two to bear my soul away."

A second variant was set on record by Aubrey, and may also be read in Ady's *Candle in the Dark* (1655) :—

> " Matthew, Mark, Luke, John,
> Bless the bed that I lye on ;
> And blessed guardian angel keep
> Me safe from danger while I sleep."

Halliwell suggests that the two last lines were imitated from the following in Bishop Kerr's Evening Hymn :—

> " Let my blest guardian, while I sleep,
> His watchful station near me keep."

But, if there was any imitation in the case, it was the bishop who copied from the folk-rhymer, not the folk-rhymer who copied from the bishop.

Somewhat analogous with the above is a quatrain I have known since my childhood, but which I do not remember to have seen in print :—

> " I lay me down to rest me,
> And pray the Lord to bless me.
> If I should sleep no more to wake,
> I pray the Lord my soul to take."

The Petite Patenôtre Blanche still lingers in France under a variety of shapes. One version was written down as late as 1872 from the mouth of an old woman named Cathérine Bastien, an inhabitant of the department of the Loire. It was afterwards communicated to *Mélusine*, from which interesting publication I borrow it :—

> " Jésus m'endort,
> Si je trépasse, mande mon corps,
> Si je trépasse, mande mon âme,
> Si je vis, mande mon esprit.
> (Je) prends les anges pour mes amis,
> Le bon dieu pour mon père,
> La Sainte Vierge pour ma mère ;
> Saint Louis de Gonzaque,
> Aux quatre coins de ma chambre,
> Aux quatre coins de mon lit ;
> Preservez moi de l'ennemi,
> Seigneur, à l'heure de ma mort."

Quenot, in his " *Statisque de la Charente* " (1818), gives the subjoined :—

> "Dieu l'a faite, je la dit ;
> J'ai trouvé quatre anges couchés dans mon lit ;
> Deux á la tête, deux aux pieds.
> Et le bon Dieu au milieu.

> De quoi puis-je avoir peur ?
> Le bon Dieu est mon père,
> La Vierge ma mère,
> Les Saints mes frères,
> Les Saintes mes sœurs.
> Le bon Dieu m'a dit :
> Lève-toi, couche-toi,
> Ne crains rien ; le feu, l'orage, et la tempête
> Ne peuvent rien contre toi.
> Saint Jean, Saint Marc, Saint Luc, et Saint Matthieu,
> Qui mettez les âmes en repos,
> Mettez-y la mienne si Dieu veut."

In Provence many a worthy countrywoman repeats each night this *priero doou soir :—*

> Au liech de diou
> Me couche iou,
> Sept angis n'en trouve iou,
> Tres es peds,
> Quatre au capet ; (caput,=tête,
> La Boueno Mero es au mitan
> Uno roso blanco à la mau."

The white rose borne by the Good Mother is a pretty and characteristic interpolation peculiar to flowery Provence. In the conclusion of the prayer the *Boueno Mero* tells whosoever recites it, to have no fear of dog or wolf, or wandering storm, or running water, or shining fire, or any evil folk. M. Damase Arbaud, the late collector of Provençal songs, got together a number of other devotional fragments that may be regarded as offshoots from the parent stem. St. Joseph, " Nourricier de diou," is asked to preserve the supplicant from sudden death, " et de l'infer et de ses flammos." St. Ann, " mero-grand de Jesus-Christ," is prayed to teach the way to Paradise. To St. Denis a very practical petition is addressed :—

> Grand Sant Danis de Franço,
> Gardetz me moun bouen sens, ma boueno remembranço.

Another verse points distinctly to a desire for protection against witchcraft. The Provençaux, by-the-by, are of opinion that the Angelus was instituted to scare away any ill-conditioned sprites that may be tempted out by the approach of night-fall.

In Germany the guardian saints are dispensed with, but the angels are retained in force. I am indebted to my friend Mr. C. G. Leland ("Hans Breitmann") for a translation of the most popular German even-song :—

> " Fourteen angels in a band
> Every night around me stand.
> Two to my left hand,
> Two to my right,
> Who watch me ever
> By day and night ;
> Two at my head,
> Two at my feet,
> To guard my slumber,
> Soft and sweet ;
> Two to wake me
> At break of day,
> When night and darkness
> Pass away ;
> Two to cover me
> Warm and nice,
> And two to lead me
> To Paradise."

Passing on to Italy, we find an embarrassing abundance of folk-prayers framed after the self-same model. The repose of the Venetian is under the charge of the Perfect Angel, the Angel of God, St. Bartholomew, the Blessed Mother, St. Elizabeth, the four Evangelists, and St. John the Baptist. Venetian children are taught to say : "I go to bed ; I know not if I shall arise. Thou Lord, who knowest, keep good watch over me. Before my soul separates from my body, give me help and good comfort. In the Name of the Father, the Son, and the Holy Ghost: so be it. Bless my heart and my soul ! " The Venetians also have a " Paternoster pichenin " and a " Paternoster grande," both of which are, in their existing form, little else than nonsense verses. The native of the Marches goes to his rest accompanied by our Lord, the Madonna, the four Evangelists, *l'angelo perfetto*, four greater angels, and three others—one at the foot, one at the head, one in the middle. The Tuscan, like the German, has only angels around him : of these he has seven—one at the head, one at the foot, two at the sides, one to cover him, one to watch him, and one to bear him to Paradise. The Sicilian says : " I lay me down in this bed, with Jesus on my breast. I sleep and He watches. In this bed where I am laid, five saints I find ; two at the head, two at the feet, in the middle is St. Michael." Among the Greek-speaking populations of South Italy the well-worn theme is treated with tender grace in a little song that serves either for lullaby or child's prayer—prayer in the popular sense, meaning any devotional thought or act, and not necessarily a supplication.

> " In my little bed I lie down to sleep,
> I lie down with my mother Mary ;
> The mother Mary goes away,
> And she leaves me Christ for company."

But perhaps the best expression of the belief in the divine guardians of sleep is that given to it by an ancient Sardinian poet :—

> " Su letto meo est de bàttor cantones,
> Et battor anghelos si bie ponen ;
> Duos in pes, et duos in cabitta,
> Nostra Segnora a costazu m'ista.
> E a me narat : Dormi e reposa,
> No hapas paura de mala cosa,
> No hapas paura de mala fine.
> S. Anghelu Serafine,
> S. Anghelu Biancu,
> S. Ispiridu Santu,
> Sa Vigine Maria
> Tote Siant in cumpagnia mea.
> Anghelu de Deu,
> Custodia meo,
> Custa nott' illuminame !
> Guarda e difende a me
> Ca eo mi incommando a Tie."

" My bed has four corners, and four angels stand by it. Two at the foot, and two at the head ; Our Lady is beside me. And to me she says : Sleep and repose. Have no fear of evil things, have no fear of an evil end. The angel Serafine, the angel Blanche, the Holy Spirit, the Virgin Mary—all are here to keep me company. Angel of God, Thou my Guardian, illuminate me this night. Watch and defend me, for I commend myself to Thee."—(Quoted from Dr. Corbetta's " Sardegna e Corsica."

I come now to my last specimen—a Spanish verse, so like the above that it would be superfluous to give it a separate translation. It was sent to me a year ago by a friend who was at that time in the Royal College of Santa Ysabel, at Madrid.

> " Quatro pirondelitas
>   Tiene mi cama ;
> Quatro angelitos
>   Me la acompâna.
> La Madre de Dios
>   Esta enmedio
> Dicendome :
>   Duerme y reposa
> Que no te sucedera
>   Ninguna mala cosa.
>
> Amen.

It seems likely that not a few of the variants cited in this note have been handed down orally from a date much earlier than that of the publication of the Enchiridion. The Paternostre Blanche is apparently a sort of magic-working parody of an older Latin prayer, of which the original tale may yet be brought to light. Till then, we cannot say which of the surviving versions may lay claim to seniority. What is plain is, that the people have clung to their common *motif* with a tenacity that proves them to have found in it an inexhaustible source of consolation and re-assurance.

It is worth remarking how certain English lettered compositions have become truly popular in consequence of their introducing the same leading idea. A dignitary of the Church of England once asked an old woman—who dwelt alone without chick or child—whether she said her prayers. " Oh ! yes," was the reply. " I say every night of my life :

> " Hush, my babe, lie still in slumber,
> Holy Angels guard thy bed," &c.

Since writing the above, my attention has been called to a popular story which, though it treats of the veritable Paternoster, and not of the " White " one, may still be mentioned here as affording another instance of the important class of folk-songs and tales that bear evidence of a semi-ecclesiastical origin. The story relates to the method by which a well-to-do, somewhat avaricious, and not too intelligent, countryman is taught to say the Lord's Prayer. The man confesses to the parish priest his inability to get the words by heart, and, on hearing the very serious consequences that will result upon his failing to do so, he offers any recompense provided they are fixed in his memory. The priest answers that he will do what is required of him, but that first of all the countryman must agree to lend forty poor neighbours as much corn as they can carry away, on the condition that he will be paid back twice its value at harvest time. The countryman thinks that the speculation promises well, and readily consents to the terms. Thereupon the priest goes out into the highway and assembles forty poor men—he has no difficulty in finding them, for there is a scarcity throughout all the land. Then he warns them what they shall say, and sends them to the house of the countryman. The latter asks their names, and the first (following the priest's instructions) says, he is called *Pater*, the second *Noster*, the third *Qui es in celis*, the fourth and fifth *Sanctificetur* and *Nomen Tuum*, and so on right down to *Amen*. By-and-bye the day of payment comes round, but the priest absolutely declines to refund a farthing of what is owing. The indignant creditor takes the case before the magistrate, to whom the priest, when put on his defence, simply says, " This man could not get by heart his *Paternoster*, and offered to give me anything so that he might learn it; now let him repeat the names of the persons who borrowed his corn." The countryman forthwith repeats the names one by one, and each in its proper order. He is then triumphantly informed that he has said the whole prayer, and the magistrate bids him go home and be thankful. He does go home, but apparently is the reverse of thankful, as he assures his wife that while he lives he will " never trust priest again." Such is an outline of the story, of which an English rhymed transcript is preserved, (printed in black letter by Wynkyn de Worde), in the public library at Cambridge.* Dr. Reinhold Köhler has recently collected proofs that this tale was current in the fifteenth and sixteenth centuries over a great part of the continent. St. Bernardino, of Siena, told it at full length in a sermon delivered at Santa Croce in the year 1424. Whether it survives among the extant folk-lore of any country has yet to be ascertained.

EVELYN CARRINGTON.

* Wright and Halliwell have reprinted this in *Reliquæ Antiquæ*, i. 43-47.

SOME FOLK-LORE FROM CHAUCER.

THESE extracts from a larger unpublished paper on the subject have no pretensions to literary merit or artistic arrangement. I thought the most useful plan in such a matter would be to carefully extract and arrange in as easy a shape for reference as might be such material as I could find available for the purposes of the Folk-Lore Society; leaving any comparisons, inferences, or historical allusions that it might suggest to an after-period, when the principal poets of our early literature shall have been thoroughly examined. The arrangement is tentative, and suggested by the character of the matter taken out of Chaucer's writings rather than by any scientific motive. I firstly extract the proverbs which I find in him; next the notices of dreams and omens; thirdly, I notice the passages that concern astrology and alchemy, under which head I found nearly all the work efficiently done to my hand by Mr. Brae; fourthly, I extract all mentions of Saints even down to petty oaths: these have been hitherto neglected, but are often useful in determining the nationality of the version followed by Chaucer in his tales; fifthly, I quote from my larger MS. such notices of Folk-Lore matters miscellaneous as the limits prescribed me will allow; and finally, I give a short explanation of my reasons for adopting a peculiar order in quoting from the poems. I may mention as collateral discoveries made in consequence of these researches: 1. The explanation of the celebrated crux of "the dry sea;" 2. A probable emendation of "Eelympastere;" 3. The assignment of Chaucer's Dream (whether genuine or not) to its proper date and occasion. 4. Various rectifications of my previous chronological arrangements of the poems. Of course I have here confined myself to folk-lore; but it will I trust be gratifying to the members of the Society to learn that work done for them does not necessarily end with them. I should add that all references are made to volume and page of Bell's edition, 8 vols. as issued by Griffin and Co. This is not because I regard it as the best, but because all my MS. notes on Chaucer are made with reference to it, for it was the best when most of my work was done, years before Dr. Morris's edition appeared, and it does not seem worth while to alter all these references until an edition appears with the tales in a proper arrangement and the poems in chronological order. Nevertheless, wherever I had references to book and line at hand at the moment, I have inserted them in addition between parentheses.

PROVERBS.

It is hard to draw a line as to these, so as to determine what are pithy sayings of Chaucer's own and what are genuine folk-words which ought to be extracted here. I have tried to err on the side of omission rather than risk inserting what might mislead future investigators.

Hyt is not al golde that glareth.
> *House of Fame* (lib. i. l. 272), vi. 202.

Loo, ryght as she hath done, now she
Wol do eftsoones hardely.
[From the Latin
Cras poterunt fieri turpia, sicut heri.]
> *Ibid.* (l. 359), vi. 205.

To make the beard=deceive.
> *Ibid.* (lib. ii. l. 181), vi. 215.
> *Reeves Tale*, i. 226.
> *Wife of Baths Prologue*, ii. 55.

For ye be lyke the swynt catte
That wolde have fissh: but wostow whatte ?
He wolde nothing wete his clowes.
> *Ibid.* (lib. iii. l. 693), vi. 251.

For alle mote oute other late or rathe,
Alle the sheves in the lathe.
> *Ibid.* (lib. iii. l. 1050), vi. 262.

For hyt is seyd men makyn oft a yerd
With which the maker is himself ybetyn,
In sundry maner us thes wise men tretyn.

> *Troylus and Cryseyde* (lib. i. st. 106), v. 43.

The wrecche is dede, the devil have his bonis.

> *Ibid.* (st. 115), v. 45.

A blynd man cannot juggyn wele in hewis.

> *Ibid.* (proem to lib. ii. st. 3), v. 55.

For every wighte that to Rome went
Holt not o pathe, ne alwey o manere.

> *Ibid.* (st. 6), v. 56.

For thus men seyn eche cuntre hath his lawis.

> *Ibid.* (lib. ii. st. 6), v. 56.

Let this proverbe a lore unto yow be,
"To late I was ware," quod bewte, "whan it past,
And eld dauntith daunger at the last."

> *Ibid.* (lib. ii. st. 50), v. 69.

Ho that nothing undirtakith
Nothing acheveth, be hit leve or dere.

> *Ibid.* (lib. ii. st. 109), v. 84.

Thei spekyn mych but thei bent never his bow.

> *Ibid.* (lib. ii. st. 116), v. 86.

And forthi, who that hath an hede of verre,
Fro caste of stonys ware hym in the werre.

> *Ibid.* (lib. ii. st. 117), v. 86.

Forwhy men seyn impressions lyght
Full redy bene ay lightly to the flight.

> *Ibid.* (lib. ii. st. 172), v. 99.

Felt the iryn hote, and he gan to smyte.

> *Ibid.* (lib. ii. st. 178), v. 101.

For hym men demeth hoot that men se swete.

> *Ibid.* (lib. ii. st. 214), v. 109.

These wise clerkis that ben dede
Han ever this proverbid to us yonge,
The first vertu to kepe wel the tonge.

> *Ibid.* (lib. iii. st. 36), v. 126.

Or caste al the grewel in the fire.

> *Ibid.* (lib. iii. st. 95), v. 140.

And makyn him a howe above a calle.

> *Ibid.* (lib. iii. st. 104), v. 143.

The harme is don, and farewel feldyfare.

> *Ibid*. (lib. iii. st. 116), v. 145.

Ye, hasyl wodis shakyn.

> *Ibid*. (lib. iii. st. 121), v. 146; *cf.* (lib. v. st.
> 73), v. 254.

Thus seyde here and howne.

> *Ibid* (lib. iv. st. 26), v. 187.

Nettle in dokke out.

> [This is usually 'dock in nettle out.']
> *Ibid*. (lib. iv. st. 62), v. 196.

Ek wonder last but nine nyght nevere in towne.

> *Ibid*. (lib. iv. st. 80), v. 200.

Ful ofte a byworde here I seye,
That rooteles mot grene soone deye.

> *Ibid*. (lib. iv. st. 106), v. 206.

Men seyne that ful harde it is
The wolfe ful and the wether hoole to have.
This is to seyn, that men ful oft, ywis,
Moot spenden parte the remenaunte for to save.

> *Ibid*. (lib. iv. st. 193), v. 225.

For thus men seith that oon thynketh the bere,
But al another thynketh the ledere ;
Your sire is wis, and seyde is, out of drede,
Men may the wise outrenne and nought outrede.
It is ful hard to halten unespied,
Bifor a crepul, for he kan the craft.

> *Ibid*. (lib. iv. st. 206), v. 228.

For hastif man ne wantethe never care.

> *Ibid*. (lib. iv. st. 220), v. 232.

As he that kouthe moore than the crede.

> *Ibid*. (lib. v. st. 13), v. 240; cf. *Millers*
> *Tale*, p. 202.

I have herde seyde ek, tymes twyes twelve,
He is a foole that wol foryete hyme selve.

> *Ibid*. (lib. v. st. 14), v. 240.

But al to late cometh the latuarye,
When men the cors unto the grave carye.

> *Ibid*. (lib. v. st. 106), vi. 13.

He that nought nassayeth nought nacheveth.

> *Ibid*. (lib. v. st. 112), vi. 14.

Swich as men clepe 'a word with two visages.'

> *Ibid*. (lib. v. st. 129), vi. 18.

From hasel woode ther jolye Robin pleyde,
Shal come al that thow abydest here !
Ye, farwel al the snowgh of ferne yere.

Ibid. (lib. v. st. 168), vi. 28 ; cf. (lib.
v. st. 73), vi. 254.

A trewe man, withouten drede,
Hath nat to parten with a theves dede.

Good Women.   Prol. (l. 444), viii. 60.

Pite renneth soone in gentil herte.

Ibid. Prol. (l. 482), viii. 61 ; *Knights Tale,*
i. 145; *Squires Tale,* ii. 217.

[Compare : Gentil hert is fulfild of pite.

Man of Lawes Tale, ii. 28.]

Wrie the glede and hotter is the fire.

Ibid. Thisbe, (l. 30), viii. 68.

Bele chere flourith, but it wil not seede.

Ibid. Anelyda, vi. 189.

He that dronke is as a mows.

Knightes Tale, i. 129.

For soth is seyde, goon ful many yeres,
That feld hath eyen and the woode hath eeres.

[Compare : Campus habet lumen, et habet nemus auris acumen.]

Ibid. i. 137.

Shapen was my deth erst than my scherte.

Ibid. i. 138.

[Compare : Syn firste day that shapen was my sherte,
          Or by the fatale sustren hadde my dome.

Good Women. Ypermystre (l. 68), viii. 123.]

He may go pypen in an ivy leef.

Ibid. i. 147; *Troylus,* (lib. v. l. 205), vi. 37.

Men may the celde at-ren, but nat at-rede.

Ibid. i. 168.

Therfor bihoveth him a ful long spoon
That schal ete with a feend.

Squires Tale, ii. 221.

He hastith wel that wisely can abyde; and in wikked haste is no profyt.

Melibeus, iii. 136.

He that alle dispyseth, saith the book, alle displeseth.

Ibid. 137.

The proverbe saith he that moche embrasith destreineth litel.

Ibid. 147.

The proverbe saith, that for to do synne is mannyseh, but certes for to perse-
vere longe in synne is werk of the devyl.

Melibeus, iii. 150.

Ther is an olde proverbe that saith, the goodnesse that thou maist do this
day abyde not ne delaye it nought unto to morwe.

Ibid. iii. 177.

And what man hath of frendes the fortune,
Mishap wil make hem enemyes, I gesse;
This proverbe is ful sothe and ful comune.

Monkes tale, iii. 195.

His purchace was bettur than his rente.

General Prologue (Friar), i. 89.

To set a man's cap or howe=to cheat; [cf. to glaze his howe.

Troylus (lib. iv. st. 67, v. 253;] *Ibid* (Manciple), i. 101;
Millers Prologue, i. 189; *Reeves Prologue*, i. 218.

Schal beren him on hond the cow is wood.

Prologue to Wyf of Bathe, ii. 51.

Ne noon so gray a goos goth in the lake,
As sayest thou, wol be withouten make.

Ibid. ii. 53.

Deceipt, wepyng, spynnyng, God hath give
To wymmen kyndely whil thay may lyve.
[Compare : Fallere, flere, nere, dedit Deus in muliere.]

Ibid. ii. 56.

Who so first cometh to the mylle, first grynt.
[Compare : Qui premier vient au moulin premier doit mouldre.]

Ibid. ii. 56.

For al so siker as cold engendrith hayl,
A likorous mouth most have a licorous tail.

Ibid. ii. 58.

The flour is goon, ther nis no more to telle,
The bran, as I best can, now mot I selle.

Ibid. ii. 59.

I made him of the same woode a croce.

Ibid. ii. 59.

In his owne grees I made him frie.

Ibid. ii. 59.

Greet pres at market makith deer chaffare,
And too greet chep is holden at litel pris.

Ibid, ii. 60.

Who that buyldeth his hous al of salwes,
And priketh his blynde hors over the falwes,

And suffrith his wyf to go seken halwes,
Is worthy to be honged on the galwes.
Ibid. ii. 65.

To put an ape in ones hood=to cheat.
Prioresses Prologue, iii. 106.

I woot best wher wryngith me my scho.
Marchaundes Tale, ii. 171.

Passe over is an ease.
Ibid. ii. 189.

Unbokeled is the male.
Millers Prologue, i. 188.

Ful soth is this proverbe, it is no lye,
Men seyn right thus alway, the ney slye
Maketh the ferre leef to be loth.

[Compare : An olde sawe is who that slyghe,
In place wher he may be nyghe,
He maketh the feere leef loth.
Gower, Conf. Amant. iii. 58.]
Millers Tale, i. 201.

He fond nowthir to selle,
No breed ne ale.
Ibid. i. 215.

Of a sowter a schipman or a leche.

[Compare : Ex sutore medicus (Phœdrus)
Ex sutore nauclerus (Pynson).]
Reeves Prologue, i. 218.

Sche was as deyne as water in a dich.
Reeves Tale, i. 221.

Unhardy is unsely, as men saith.
Ibid. i. 231.

And thereto this proverbe is seyd ful soth,
He thar nat weene wel that evyl doth.
Ibid. i. 234.

Soth play quad play as the Flemyng saith.
[Compare : Soth bourde is no bourde.
Sir John Harrington.]
Cokes Prologue, i. 236.

A proverbe that saith this same word,
Wel bette is roten appul out of hord,
Than that it rote al the remenaunt.
Cokes Tale, i. 237.

Thing that is overdon it wil nought preve
Aright, as clerkes sein, it is a vice.

Comp are : Ne quid nimis.]

Chanounes Yemannes Prologue, iii. 27.

Profred servise Stynketh, as witnessen these olde wise.

Ibid. iii. 42.

Ye ben as bolde as is Bayard the blynde,
That blundreth forth, and peril casteth noon.

Ibid. iii. 53.

Bet than never is late.

Ibid.

Dun is in the myre.

Manciples Prologue, iii. 236; *Manciples Tale*, iii. 246.

The Flemyng saith, and lere it if the lest,
That litil jangling causeth mochil rest..

Manciples Tale, iii. 248.

Neither knew I kirke ne seynt.

Chauceres Dream (l. i. 305), vi. 93.

Brent child of fier hath mych drede.

Rose, vii. 72.

This have I herd ofte in seiyng,
That man may for no dauntyng
Make a sperhauke of a bosarde.

Ibid. vii. 137

For tweyne in nombre is bet than thre,
In every counselle and secre.

Ibid. vii. 178

A fooles belle is soon range.

Ibid. vii. 178.

Go, farewell feldfare.

Ibid. vii. 186.

For freend in court ay better is
Then peny in purs, certis.

[Compare: 2 Hen. IV. Act. v. Sc. 1. l. 84.]

Ibid. vii. 187.

Habite ne makith neithir monk ne frere.

[Compare : Cucullus non facit monachum.]

Ibid. vii. 209.

DREAMS.

Dreams play so important a part in Chaucer's writings as to demand a separate notice. Nearly every poem of his which has a personal reference to himself or his patrons is written under the form of a dream. 1. The Romaunt of the Rose; 2. Chaucer's dream; 3. The death of the Duchess; 4. The House of Fame; 5. The Assembly of Birds;

6. The Legend of Good Women—are all dreams. In the Rose [? written in 1363], he says, " Many say dreams are deceitful, but some dreams are true ; witness the dream of Scipio in Macrobius (on Cicero). You may call me a fool for it, but I believe some dreams are prophetic, especially this which I am going to tell you of the Kissing of the Rose, or the Art of Love, which I dreamed one May when I was in my 20th year, five years ago " [? 1358]. In the Ile of Ladies he says: " One May thinking on my lady I lay in a lodge in a forest after hunting [at Windsor], and dreamed ' with mind of knowledge-like making.' I believe I really saw what I dreamed, and that I was taken to the place by some good spirit. It was no dream, but a sign or signification of facts." In The Duchess Chaucer falls asleep in May after reading the story of Ceyx and Alcyone. Here, too, he refers to Scipio's dream as told by Macrobius ; he also dreams of birds that sing solemn service, and mentions Pharaoh's dream. In the House of Fame he gives a fuller statement of his views. Some are oracles and revelations, others are phantoms and " never come." The causes may be the " complexion " of the dreamer, weakness of brain from fasting, illness, distress, study, melancholy, love, inspiration by spirits, or prophetic power of the soul, when not darkened by the flesh as in waking hours. This dream, un- like the preceding, as happening in the winter on 10 December, is like the preceding, in mentioning (vi. 210) Pharaoh, Scipio, &c. In the Parlement of Fowls Chaucer falls asleep reading a book, as in the Duchess; the book is " Tullius of the dream of Scipio," so often men- tioned by him. In his dream Scipio guides him as Virgil does Dante; he dreams of birds that sing on Valentine's day. In the Good Women Chaucer hears the birds sing praises of St. Valentine in May while he is awake; he sleeps in a " harbour," and dreams of Alceste, &c. This must be in May 1386. In this poem Dido's dream is referred to (viii. 86); also the ominous owl, the prophet of woe (viii. 112); and in the legend of Hypermnestra, the dream of Egisthus (viii. 124). In all these poems a regular sequence can be traced if they be read chronologically; in the references to May, to Scipio's dream, to Valentine's day, to the song of birds, to the causes of dreaming, &c. &c. But this could only be properly displayed in a commentary on the passages referred to.

In Troylus there are many references to dreams. Cryseide has
dreamed thrice of Pandarus (v. 58). "May it turn to good !" says
she. Again (v. 88) she dreams that a white eagle exchanges hearts
with her. Troylus too has dreams and omens—the owl Ascaphilo shrieks
after him two nights. And Pandarus gives his opinions on the matter
as Chaucer does in the House of Fame. "They mean nothing,"
says he, "they proceed of melancholy. Priests say they are revelations;
doctors say, they are caused by complexions or fasting; others say, they
arise from contemplation, or seasons, or the time of the moon, but
dreams and augury are merely old wives' tales" (v. 249). Nevertheless
Troylus has true dreams of the boar Diomed (vi. 40, 47), and Chaucer
had not yet adopted Pandar's scepticism. In the Canterbury Tales the
notices of dreams are much fewer. In the Squire's Tale Canace has
a vision (ii. 214); in the Monk's (iii. 212) Cresus' dream is given:
but in the Nun's Priest's we have Chaucer's fullest statement on the
matter. Chanticleer dreams of the fox, but Partelet tells him dreams
are vanity engendered of repletions, complexions, abundant humours; the
red fox, for instance, by abundance of red choler, black boars by abundance of melancholy, and bids him "take a laxative" and believe in Cato.
But Chanticleer answers with the well-known case, given by Cicero,
the dreams of Kenelm, Scipio, Daniel, Joseph, Pharaoh, Cresus,
Andromache, and gets the best of the argument. His own dream is a
true one. In the Miller's Tale (i. 211) Absolon's mouth itches (a
sign of kissing at least) and he dreams of feasting. In the Sumner's
tale the Friar says (falsely) that he saw the wife's child borne to bliss
in a vision (ii. 109). In the Prologue to the same tale the vision of a
friar is given (taken from Romaunt of the Rose) as to the abode of
friary in hell (ii. 102); and finally in the Prologue to the Wife of Bath
we find that she too tells lies as to her dream, telling her suitor she
had dreamed of him and of blood, which betokened gold, when she had
not. On the whole it seems that Chaucer believed in prophetic dreams
granted by special revelation, but not in oneiromancy as applied to
ordinary dreams.

ASTROLOGY AND ALCHEMY.

For there nys planete in firmament
Ne in ayre ne in erthe noon element
That they ne yive me a yift echone
Of wepynge whanne I am alone.

Book of the Duchess, vi. 158.

This is the earliest allusion to astrology in Chaucer. [1369].

The nine speris.—*Assembly of Foules* (st. 9) iv. 190.

These are:—

Primum Mobile 9
Fixt stars 8
1 Saturn 7
2 Jupiter 6
3 Mars 5
4 Sun 4
5 Venus 3
6 Mercury 2
7 Moon 1

Chaucer uses the reckoning on the right hand in Troylus and Cryseyde (Proem to lib. iii. st. 1), v. 116.

O blisfull light of which the bemes clere
Adornith all the thrid hevyn faire !
O Sonnys leef, o Jovis doghtir dere.

Venus is here in the third sphere. So in (lib. v. st. 259) vi. 50,

His light gost ful blisfully is wente
Up to the holughnesse of the seventhe spere.

Saturn's sphere is indicated as furthest from the earth; and in the Good Women (Philomene) viii. 112, the innermost circle is called " the firste heven;" but in the Complaint of Mars (st. 5) viii. 30, Mars is called " the thridde heven's lord; " and in L'Envoy a Scogan (st. 2) viii. 146, the sphere of Venus is called " the fyft sercle." In these instances Chaucer uses the order given on the left in the list above. This shows that Chaucer changed his reckoning after writing the Legend of Good Women.

> Whan Phœbus dothe his righte bemys sprede
> Right in the white Bulle, so it bytyd
> As I shall syng: on Mayes day the thrid.
>
> *Troylus* (lib. ii. st. 1) v. 57.

The sun was then in the 22nd degree of Taurus.

> And cast, and knew in good plyte was the Mone
> To do viage.
>
> *Ibid.* (lib. ii. st. 4), v. 57.

> And also blisful Venus, wel arayed,
> Sate in her seventh hous of Hevyn tho,
> Disposyd wele, and with aspact purvayed
> To helpe soly Troylus of his wo:
> And soth to seye, she nas not his fo
> To Troylus, in his nativyte.
>
> *Ibid.* (lib. ii. st. 91) v. 79.

The seventh house is Libra.   A planet was stronger in its own house than in any other.

> The bente Mone with her hornys pale,
> Saturn and Jovis in Cancro joyned were,
> That madyn such a reyne fro hevyn avail, &c.
>
> *Ibid.* v. 137.

The Moon is an airy sign, her own mansion: Saturn and Jupiter, whose mansions are watery, are in conjunction with her. Hence there will be rain. Planets in conjunction are most powerful.

> And if I had, O Venus ful of mirthe!
> Aspectes bad of Mars or of Saturne,
> Or thou cumbrid, or let were in my birthe, &c.
>
> *Ibid.* v. 140.

Explained by Astrolabie, part ii. sect. 4. " Yit sein these Astrologiens that the assendent and eke the lord of the assendent may be shapen for to be fortunat or infortunat, as thus a fortunat assendent clepen they whan that no wykked planet, as Saturne or Mars, or elles the tail of the dragoun is in hows of the assendent, ne that no wikked planet have non aspecte of enemyte upon the assendent, but they wol easte that thei have a fortunat planete in hir assendent and yit in his felicite, and than sey they that it is wel; fortherover, they seyn that the infortunyng of an assendent is the contrarie of thise forseide thinges; the lord of the assendent sey they that he is fortunat whan he is in god place fro the assendent, as in angle, or in a succedent whereas he is in his dignite and consorted with frendly aspectys of planetes and [wel] resceived, and ek that he may sen the assendent, and that he be not retrograd ne combust ne ioigned with no shrewe in the same signe, ne that he be nat is his desencioun, ne joigned with no planete on his discencioun, ne have upon him non aspecte infortunat, and than sey they that he is wel. Natheles theise ben observauneez of iudicial matiere and rytes of paiens, in which my spirit ne hath no faith, ne no knowyng of hir *horoscopum*."—Compare Troylus (lib. iv. st. 103), v. 205.

> Estward roos to hym that cowde it knowe,
> Fortuna maior.
> > *Ibid.* (lib. iii. st. 196), v. 165.

Fortuna major is Jupiter.   Speght.

> For though that Venus yaf hire grete beaute,
> With Jubiter compouned so was she,
> That conscience, trouthe, and drede of shame,
> And of hire wyfhode for to kepe hire name,
> This thoghte hire was felicite as here.
> And rede Mars was that tyme of the yere
> So feble that his malice ys him rafte;
> Repressed hath Venus hys cruel licrafte.
> And what with Venus and other oppressyoun
> Of houses, Mars his venyme ys adoun,
> That Ypermystre dar not handel a knyf
> In malyce, though she shulde lese hire lyf.
> But natheles, as heven gan thoo turne,
> To badde aspectes hath she of Saturne,
> That made hire to dye in prisoun.
> > *Good Women.* *Ypermystre* (l. 23), viii. 120.

The aspects were distances of 0° conjunction, 60° sextile, 90° quartile, 120° trine, 180° opposition.   Quartile and opposition were malign;

trine and sextile, benign; conjunction, indifferent. Mars has influence on imprisonment, not Saturn; but Saturn has rule on life and buildings, which is near enough for astrology. Venus, of course, rules love; Jupiter, wishes and dress; Mars, war and hatred.

> O firste meving cruel firmament,
> With thi diurnal swough that crowdest ay,
> And hurlest al fro est to occident.
> That naturelly wold hold another way;
> Thyn crowdyng sette the heven in such array
> At the bygynnyng of this fiers viage,
> That cruel Martz hath slayn this marriage.
>   Infortunat ascendent tortuous,
> Of which the lordes helpless falle, allas!
> Out of his angle into the derkest hous.
> O! Mariz Attezere! as in this caas;
> O! feble Moone! unhappy been thi paas.
> Thou knettest ther thou art not receyved;
> Ther thon were wel, for thennes artow weyved.
>   *Man of Law* (l. 197), ii. 16.

"First moving" is the *primum mobile* which resolved from west to east, carrying all the inner spheres with it; the "natural" motion of all the interior spheres being from east to west.

The "tortuous" signs rise in less than two houses; they are obedient to the other signs. Of them Aries is the mansion of Mars. The "angle" is the first house, of which Mars was lord: he had passed from this into the seventh house, which is a cadent, or "derkest" house; in other words, Mars had just set. Atazir is Spanish-Arabic for influence. The last two lines mean, Thou goest into a conjunction where thou hast no benign aspect, and leavest thy former friendly position.

> Of viage is ther noon eleccioun,
> Nought whan a roote is of a birthe i-knowe?
>   *Ibid.* (l. 214), ii. 17.

The time for travelling was when the moon was in a mobile sign. A roote of a birthe is a primary datum from which a horoscope can be calculated—*i. e.*, the exact time (and place) at which birth took place.

Chaucer in this same tale says that "the death of every man is written in the stars clearer than glass," if we could but read it.

Som wikke aspect or disposicioun
Of Saturne, by sum constellacioun
Hath geven us this, although we hadde it sworn;
So stood the heven whan that we were born.

Knight (l. 229), i. 123.

Saturn, a baleful planet, was in power at my birth;

But I moste be in prisoun through Saturne, . . .
And Venus sleeth me on that other syde.

Ibid. (l. 470), i. 131.

See above for Saturn as causing imprisonment.

That oon Puella, that othur Rubius.

Ibid. i. 155.

Mars retrograde and Mars direct.

Venus' hour, &c.

Ibid. i. 161, 162, 165.

The following rule is simple. To find to what planet any hour of a given day of the week is consecrated, divide the hour-number by seven and count the remainder, beginning with the planet to whom the day belongs, in the following order (that of the spheres): 1, Saturn; 2, Jupiter; 3, Mars; 4, Sun; 5, Venus; 6, Mercury; 7, Moon. Thus the 23rd hour of Sunday is sacred to Venus, for 23÷7 gives 2 remainder —*i.e.*, 1, Sol; 2, Venus. Palamon reaches the temple of Venus in the 23rd hour, but starts in the 22nd. In the third hour from his *starting* —*i.e.*, on the first hour on Monday—Emily goes to Diana's temple in a Moon-hour; and in the next hour of Mars—*i.e.*, in the fourth hour on Monday—Arcite visits the temple of Mars.

In the Knight's tale, i. 168, we have a fuller list of Saturn's influences than Chaucer has given us for any other planet. I do not quote the passage. I want to send readers to Chaucer, not to take his place; but I give a list of them. 1, Drowning; 2, Prison; 3, Strangulation; 4, Rebellion; 5, Discontent; 6, Poisoning; 7, Vengeance (when in Leo); 8, Ruin of buildings; 9, Cold maladies (ague, &c); 10, Treason; 11, Deceit; 12, Pestilence.

The connection of Venus and Saturn in this poem is most unusual astrologically: they are commonly connected only when they are not powerful, the fall of Venus (in Aries) being the dejection of Saturn. The pestilence is due to Saturn, but the rain (the fruitful rain) to Venus. Chaucer again uses his conceit of rain being "Venus' tears" in his "*Envoy a Scogan.*"

The astrological allusions in the Squire's Tale have been accurately and clearly explained by Mr. Skeat. It will be sufficient here to refer to them. In (part i. l. 264) ii. 211, we read that lovers (not "men and women," as Mr. Skeat says), exult, for Venus is exalted in the fish. The exaltation of Venus is in Pisces. In (i. 39) ii. 203, the Sun is in Aries, the mansion of Mars, and in the face of Mars—*i. e.*, in the first third of Aries, 0° to 10°. Aries is a hot choleric sign. The "last Idus" of March is a curious expression for the Ides (15th). The Sun entered Aries on the 12th, and was on the 15th in 4° Aries (ii. 39), ii. 214, where read "foure," not "ten." In (i. 255) ii. 210, the angle meridional is the 10th house; the angles were the 1st, 4th, 7th, 10th houses, corresponding to east, south, west, north. The 10th house is the northern (not the southern) angle. The Sun leaves the 10th house at noon. Leo and his Aldryan (Aldiran) were just rising at noon on the 15th March. Chaucer is accurate as usual.

In the Franklin's tale we find a good deal of astrology. Passing over such slight matters as the Moon's opposition in Leo (l. 178, &c.) ii. 237, the Sun on May 6 being in Taurus, the Sun being in Capricorn in December (l. 509;) ii. 243, we come to the 28 mansions of the Moon (l. 401), ii. 236. These Moon-stations, as the Arabians called them, are given with their Arabic names, their characteristic stars, &c. by Ideler (see Mr. Brae in his edition of Chaucer's Astrolabic), and the influences of the Moon in each mansion can be found in any of the astrological books. They do not, however, illustrate Chaucer. It is more to the purpose that here we find the earliest intimation of Chaucer's growing disbelief in astrology so far as any influence on man's actions is concerned. He makes the Franklin say it is folly and not worth a fly in our days. This I attribute to his taking up the study of astronomy proper about this date (1387-8) in preparation for his Astrolabic (1391); for, although the Franklin says (1. 530), ii. 245 that he "can no termes of astrology," he straight proceeds to give forth a string of them from his Alphonsine tables, which demand a mention here. "Collect years" are round numbers of years, say 20, 40, &c. "Expanse years" are smaller numbers: thus the position of a planet would be given first in tables for periods of 20 years, and those for any remaining shorter period would be calculated and tabulated separately. An "argument" is the angle under which other angles thereto corresponding are tabulated. A "root" is a quantity tabulated for any fixed date from which corresponding quantities at other dates can be derived. "Proportionals convenientes" are tables of proportional parts. As to the spheres, Tyrwhitt and Brae give the reading "eighte sphere" for the fixed stars with Alnath and ninth for the *primum mobile* with the true equinoxial point in it. But they do not seem to have noted that Chaucer at this date counted his spheres from the outside planet inward (see above, p. 11), and, having called Saturn the first sphere, would be in a difficulty about the outer starry spheres; hence the muddle. "Faces" are equal third-parts of signs: each face has its planetary lord. See Mr. Skeat's table in his edition of the Astrolabie. "Terms" are similar divisions, but unequal.

In the Nun's Priest's tale (1. 37), iii. 217 we learn that the world was created in March, and that on the 3rd May the Sun was in 21° of Taurus, and at prime his altitude was 41° or 21° according to various readings: if 41°, then prime means 9 A.M. As Mr. Skeat says, prime is either the beginning or the ending of a period, the period being either an hour or a quarter of the day. I believe that prime was from 3 to 6 A.M., and that 21° is the right reading.*

In the Merchant's tale, ii. 183, (1. 642), the marriage takes place when the moon is in 2° Taurus, 4 days after she enters Cancer. In ii. 90, (1. 888), the date is 8 June (Mr. Brae's emendation Juin for Jnil), and in ii. 192, (1. 978), the sun is in Gemini near his maximum northern declination in Cancer. In ii. 185 we have also allusions to the influences of the constellations.

* Prime. This word occurs so often, and the commentators disagree so about it, that I think it desirable to note my own opinion, though the question is still an open one. The canonical hours were:

In the Miller's tale the poor scholar knew "a certain of conclusions," the very phrase that Chaucer uses in his Astrolabic when he says what he purposes to teach little Lewis; hence the tale is probably not far from 1391 in date. The scholar uses his almagest (Ptolemy's $\mu\epsilon\gamma\alpha\lambda\eta$ $\sigma\nu\nu\tau\alpha\xi\iota s$), his astrolabic, on which instrument Chaucer wrote a treatise, and his augrim (algorithm) stones for numeration. He prophecies that there shall be rain on Monday at quarter night (16th hour beginning, Saturn's hour), but the rain does not come; and here we have positive proof that Chaucer had given up whatever faith in astrology he had in earlier life. This is confirmed by his own statement in his Astrolabie, ii. 4, 36, and I have little doubt that his study in preparing that treatise was the cause of his change of belief.

In the Man of Law's Prologue we find Chaucer's astronomical knowledge clearly displayed; he knows how to calculate the hour from the length of shadows, and finds it 10 a.m. on 18 April, 1388, when the sun's altitude is 45°. All this is clearly explained by Mr. Brac. But the explanation he gives as to how "the host saw that the bright sun had run the arc of his artificial day the fourth part, of half-an-hour and more" is not so clear. He says Chaucer confused the sun's azimuthal arc with his altitude. Surely a very strange mistake for the host to make. It seems to me more likely that Chaucer un-thinkingly took the sun's total arc from his rising to his highest altitude to be 90°, as if the sun passed through the zenith, and 45°

1 Matins	Midnight	_i.e._ 9—12 P.M.
[Lauds	after Matins	12—3 A.M.]
2 Prime	6 A.M.	_i.e._ 3—6 A.M.
3 Tierce	9 A.M.	_i.e._ 6—9 A.M.
4 Sext	12 A.M.	_i.e._ 9—12 A.M.
5 None (noon)	3 P.M.	_i.e._ 12—3 P.M.
6 Vespers	6 P.M.	_i.e._ 3—6 PM.
7 Compline	9 P.M.	_i.e._ 6—9 PM.

The fact that noon is at 12 fixes the three hours of noon at 12 to 3 P.M. and not 3 to 6 P.M. By parity of reasoning, the three hours of prime are 3 to 6 A.M., not 6 to 9 A.M, as Mr. Skeat takes them to be. The exact hours are those at which the canonical services begin. The periods are those preceding, not following, the exact hours. The ecclesiastics naturally reckoned the time by the next service they would have to attend, not by the one that was done with.

to be half this or a quarter of the day. In any case he is wrong, as the quarter day was over at 8h. 22m.

In the description of the Doctor the astrological nature of the mediæval medical practice is well brought out. He is grounded in astronomy, keeps by natural magic his patient in order, and makes him do all things in the houses that are favourable; he can calculate the aspects of the constellations (fortune the ascendent of his images), and understands the humours : viz. the white phlegm, the red blood, the yellow gall, the black gall; phlegmatic, sanguine, choleric, melancholic ; he knows the temperatures, hot, cold, moist, and dry. He knows how the phlegm produces quotidian fevers, the blood continual fevers, choler tertian fevers, and melancholy quartan fevers. He knows the seats of these, phlegmatic in the stomach, sanguine in the blood, choleric in the gall, melancholic in the spleen. This description is taken by the commentators to be ironical. They give no reason for their supposition. Chaucer in 1388 certainly believed in astrology as far as the Doctor does, and the rest of the description is merely a syllabus of a first medical lecture and quite simply earnest.

From the Wife of Bath's Prologue we learn that she derived her hardiness from Mars, her lust from Venus.

Myn as[cend]ent was Taur and Mars therinne, ii. 64.

Taurus was Venus' mansion.

The Canon Yeoman's Prologue treats of alchemy, which is so closely allied to astrology that this seems the fittest place to notice it. I give a list of the Materials :

* Orpiment, yellow Arsenium-Sulphide,
Burnt bones, for Calcium-Phosphate,
Iron squames (filings).
Salt, Sodium-Chloride.
Pauperc ?
Mercury crude, Quicksilver.
* 	„ 		„ 		sublimed.
Litharge, yellow Plumbum-Sesquioxide.

Bole armoniac, a magnesian clay.

Verdigris, Copper-Acetate.

Borax, Sodium-Borate.

Lime unslacked, Calcium-Oxide.

Clay, an Aluminum-Silicate.

Saltpetre, Potassium-Nitrate.

Vitriol, white, Zinc-Sulphate.

     „   green, Iron   „   (of Mars).

     „   blue, Copper „

Copper and Silver Nitrates were also termed vitriols of Venus and the Moon.

Arsenic, Arsenium-Sesquioxide.

* Sal ammoniac, Ammonium-Chloride.

* Brimstone, Sulphur.

Salt tartar, Hydrogen-Potassium-Tartrate.

Alkali, Potassium-Carbonate, from wood-ashes.

Salt preparate, ? artificially made, not found native.

Oil of Tartar, a purified Potassium-Tartrate made from crude Tartar by exposure to the air in a moist place.

Alum, Aluminum-Potassium-Sulphate.

Argil, clay.

Realgar, Red Arsenium-Sulphide.

Metal fusible, Fusible Alloy.

Of these the four asterised substances are the four "spirits." Chaucer also gives the 7 planatary metals : Sun, gold; Moon, silver; Mars, iron; Mercury, quicksilver; Saturn, lead ; Jupiter, tin; Venus, copper.

Organic substances were also used. Chaucer mentions bull's gall (for the acid), glaire of ey (albumen), ashes (for tartar), dung, urine (for ammonia), hair (for magical incantations and for binding clay), barm (yeast), and wort (for fermentation). Of herbs, Chaucer mentions agrimony (*eupatorium cannabinum*), valerian (*valeriana officinalis*), and lunarie (*botrychium lunaria*). This last, a fern, was that used by witches (see Gerard's Herbal). Chaucer calls this alchemy " elfish lore."

HAGIOLOGY.

I have under this head collected the allusions to Saints that occur in Chaucer's works, independently of the Fathers, allusions to whose writings I have collected in MS. not here printed.

1. Chaucer's Dream.—The phrase, " S. John to borrow," S. John be my security, occurs, vi. 118.

2. Duchess.—" By S. John;" vi. 178. The oaths " by the mass," vi. 165, and " by the rood," 1, 917, also occur.

3. Fame.—" The corseint Leonard," patron of captives, vi. 197; " S. Mary," vi. 211; " by S. Jame," vi. 221; " S. Julian, lo, bon hostele," patron of hospitality," vi. 226; " Peter," vi. 226, 258; " by S. Clare," vi. 228; " by S. Thomas of Kent," vi. 230; " by S. Gile," vi. 232.

4. Birds.—" By S. John," iv. 208; S. Valentine, *passim.*

5. Orison.—Mary and John, *passim.*

6. Mars.—" S. John to borwe," viii. 29; cf. Dream; S. Valentine, *passim.*

7. Good Women.—Bernardus monachus non vidit omnia, viii. 44; " Blessed be S. Valentine!" viii. 49.

8. Nun's Tale.—S. Urban, S. Cecile, Virgin, *passim.*

9. Prioress.—" S. Nicholas, so young, to Christ did reverence." This saint, though not abstinent by any means on other days, would only take the breast on evenings, and that not more than once on Wednesdays and Fridays in the evening.

10. Man of Law.—Virgin Mary, *passim.* " By S. John," ii. 39.

11. Squire.—" S. John to borwe," ii. 221, as before.

12. Nun's Priest.—S. Kenelm. See under Dreams.

13. Shipman.— " By S. Martin," " by S. Denis," iii. 97; " Peter !" iii. 99; " by that lord that cleped is S. Ive", iii. 99; S. Ive was of Lantriguier, in Bretagne; " S. Austin speed you," iii. 101; " by S. Jame," iii. 103. All these are of French origin.

14. Merchant.—" S. Mary," ii. 183, 198.

15. Miller.—" By S. Thomas of Kent," i. 196; cf. Fame; " Help us, S. Frideswide !" i. 202 : she was patroness of an Oxford priory.

"S. Benedight," i. 204, in the White Paternoster; "By S. Noet" (Neot), a Saxon saint, i. 213.

16. Reeve.—"Help, holy cross of Bromholme!" i. 233. This reliquary, containing a piece of the true cross, was brought to Bromholme Priory, in Norfolk, in 1223. "By S. Cutberd," i. 227, of Linsisfarne; see *Marmion.* "By that lord that cleped is S. Jame," i. 232. Cf. S. Ive, in Shipman.

17. Friar.—"By S. Jame," ii. 94; "S. Dunstan," ii. 96, who ruled the Devil; "Lady S. Mary, help me!" ii. 100; "by the sweet S. Anne," ii. 100; "S. Loy save thy body," ii. 99; S. Eligius was a worker in metals.

18. Sumner.—"For Christ's moder deere," ii. 106; "God's moder," ii. 120; "by S. John," ii. 107, 122; " by that lord that cleped is S. Ive," ii. 112: cf. Shipman; "Thomas of Ind," ii. 113; "by S. Simon," ii. 117.

19. Pardoner.—"By S. Mary," iii. 81; "by S. John," iii. 83; "the cross which that S. Helen found," iii. 89.

20. Canon's Yeoman.—"By S. Gile," iii. 46. His hermitage was near Arles.

21. General Prologue.—S. Thomas of Kent, "the holy blissful martyr," *passim;* "a Christopher of silver," with the saint carrying Jesus Christ," i. 81; S. Loy (qy. S. Eligius or S. Louis?) i. 81, the Prioress's oath; "S. Julian," the hospitable, i. 92; "the sail that S. Peter had," i. 106.

22. Prioress Prologue.—"By S. Austin," iii. 106.

23. Man of Law Prologue.—"For the love of S. John," ii. 5.

24. Monk Prologue.—"By the precious corpus Madryan," ii. 181; ? the corseint of S. Maternus of Treves.

25. Wife of Bath Prologue.—"By S. John," ii. 49; "by that lord that cleped is S. Jame," ii. 54; "Peter!" ii. 58; "by S. Joce," ii. 59. S. Judocus was of Ponthieu.

26. Pardoner Prologue.—"Our lady S. Mary bless hem," iii. 67; "by S. Runyan," iii. 67.

27.—Canon Yeoman's Prologue.—"Peter!" iii. 28.

HOUSE OF FAME.

The old custom of appointing days for amicably settling differences
(vi. 215) at which the friars were conspicuous (General Prologue,
i. 89), requires here only a passing mention; see Bracton, lib. v.
fol. 369.

The minstrels at bride-feasts are spoken of in vi, 233, and elsewhere.
But the well-known passage on magic must be given in full.

> There saugh I pleyen jugelours,
> Magiciens, and tregetours,
> And phitonisses, charmeresses,
> Olde witches, sorceresses,
> That use exorsisaciouns,
> And eke thes fumigaciouns;
> And clerkes eke, which konne wel
> Alle this magike naturel,
> That craftely doon her ententes,
> To make in certeyn ascendentes,
> Ymages, lo, thurgh which magike,
> To make a man ben hool or syke.
> Ther saugh I the quene Medea,
> And Circes eke and Calipsa.
> Ther saugh I Hermes Ballenus,
> Lymeote, and eke Symon Magus.
> Ther saugh I Colle Tregetour
> Upon a table of sygamour.
> Pleye an uncouthe thynge to telle;
> I saugh him carien a wynd-melle
> Under a wal-note shale.

vi. 233.

Tyrwhitt rightly compares Maundeville's account of the jugglers at
the Court of the great Cham, who produce visions of sun and moon,
dancings, jousts and huntings (in other words exhibit magic lantern
slides) with the illusions in the Franklin's tale. Pythonesses are mentioned afterwards in the Friar's tale. Hermes Ballenus, Lymeote, and
Colle wait for elucidation; but the use of waxen images and the astrological times for taking medicine are well known. The cry of "largess"
may be found in l. 219, vi. 237, and the laudes of rich folk announced
by pursuivants and heralds a few lines further on (l. 230).

TROYLUS AND CRESSEYDE.

I cannot omit a passing mention of the puns (most unusual in Chaucer), "Troy distroyed; Calkas Calkelyng," in (i. 10, 11), v. 19, 20. I must also notice the blaunch fevere of (i. 131), v. 49. It is a quotidian fever. Fevers were divided into red (Mars), black (Saturn), yellow (Sun), white (Moon), according as they showed inflammation, mortification, jaundice, or pallor. White fever does not mean fasting, as the commentators tell us.

In the second book we come on the observance of the month of May, which is repeated afterwards in the Knight's Tale; in neither instance is it the first of May that is observed. Yet I can find no trace of any English custom connected with the third day; and Shakespeare, who almost repeats Chaucer's words, certainly, as I have shown elsewhere, refers to the first of May. Compare:

> And let us do to May some observance. (May 3rd.)
> > *Troylus*, v. 59 (ii. 9).

> And for to done his observance to May. (May 4th.)
> > *Knight's Tale*, i. 136.

> > in a morrow of May.........
> Arise and do thine observance............
> > > *Ibid*, i. 121.
> To do honour to May.
> Do observance to a morn of May.
> > > *Midsummer Night's Dream*, i. 1.
> To observe the rite of May.
> > > *Ibid*. iv. 1.

Mr. Brae takes the 3rd May to mean the last day of the Floralia. I cannot agree with him; I feel sure that an English or Italian custom is alluded to. Is there any notice of the 3rd May in Boccaccio? Both the Chaucerian passages occur in works founded on that author's poems. In (i. 147), v. 52, we meet with a notice of the Man in the Moon:

> Thou hast ful grete care
> Lest the cherl may fal out of the Mone.

In (ii. 5), v. 58, a maiden is employed to read romances to Cressida for her amusement. In Sir Thopas (iii. 122) gestours (readers of

gesta) amuse him in the same way. This poem of Chaucer's appears
from several passages to have been written for the same end (see my
Guide to Chaucer). It was probably made at the request of John
of Gaunt to be read in his family, and the similarity of some incidents
in it to the connection between Gaunt and the widow Katherine Swyn-
ford would naturally annoy the Duchess Constance.

In (ii. 86), v. 77, the giving of love potions is alluded to, and in
(ii. 141), v. 91, the belief that when your ears glow there is somebody
talking of you.

In (ii. 126), v. 89, Troylus is represented by a white eagle; in the
Knight's Tale (i. 159), Emetrius bears a white eagle on his head.
As there is no white eagle in nature, this looks like an allusion to a
heraldic bearing, which may aid in deciphering the story. Or does
the white eagle come from Boccaccio ?

In (ii. 221), v. 110, the use of charms in medicine is alluded to.

In (iii. 20), v. 122, the custom of ringing the bells when a miracle
had been performed is mentioned; in (iii. 72), v. 134, the notion that
weather changes at the change of the moon.

In (iii. 81), v. 136, "the Tale of Wade," the Scandinavian Ulysses,
is mentioned: his boat (Guingelot) occurs again in the Merchant's
Tale (ii. 168).

In (iii. 98), v. 141, we meet with an expression repeated frequently
in Chaucer, but the origin of which still awaits some elucidation:

> O fatale sustrin which, or eny cloth
> Me shapyn was, my destiny me sponne.

Compare Good Women (viii. 122):

> Sens first that day that shapen was my sherte,
> Or by the fatal suster had my dome.

And Knight's Tale (i. 138):

> That schapen was my deth erst than my scherte.

In (iii. 196), v. 165, note the use of the term astrologer as equivalent to horologer, showing that the science of astronomy had not yet
been separated from its practical applications. This occurs again in
the Priest's Tale. So in (iv. 13), v. 184, Calchas groups astronomy

(astrology), sort (divination by lot), and augury (divination by birds) in the same category. In (iv. 197), v. 226, Cressid laughs at "sort," and says the gods speak "amphibologies." In (iv. 174), v. 221, the wax night-light called a mortar is mentioned as a rough time-measurer by night.

The wake-vigils and wake-plays, only recently extinct in North Britain, are mentioned in (v. 44), v. 247:

> of the feste and pleyes pastoral
> At my vigil.

Compare Knight's Tale (i. 183):

> Ne how the liche wake was y-holde,
> Al thilke night, ne how the Grekes play
> The wake pleyes.

In (v. 259), vi. 50, we meet with the notion that the planets partook of the nature of the four elements in proportion to their distance from the fiery sun in this order:

Fire	Air	Water	Earth
Sun	Venus	Mercury	Moon.
Mars	Jupiter	Saturn	

So that Troylus' soul in going to the sphere of Saturn through the spheres of — 1 Moon, 2 Mercury, 3 Venus, 4 Sun, 5 Mars, 6 Jupiter, 7 Saturn, would pass through earth, water, air, fire, and then conversely through fire, air, water:

> In convers letyng everych element.

I have not seen this explained heretofore. A good account of the "natures" of the planets is contained in Primaudaye's French Academie.

NOTES.

As the order in which the poems are quoted is neither that of the editions nor that put forth by the Director of the Chaucer Society, I think it necessary to state here the chronological order that I have followed. It differs in one or two minor points from that given by me elsewhere, in consequence of recent investigations by myself and others.

1338. Chaucer born.

1361. Chaucer's Dream, written for the marriage of the Black Prince—not for that of John of Gaunt.

1363. Romaunt of the Rose begun. Chaucer 25 years old: one year after his marriage.

1369. Book of the Duchess (John of Gaunt's wife, Blanche).

c. 1376. Translation of Boethius.

c. 1380. House of Fame.

1381-2. Parliament of Birds.

c. 1382. Orison to the Virgin.

c. 1382-5. Troylus and Cryseyde (with lines to Adam Scrivener).

c. 1385. Complaint of Pity.

1386 (before May) Palamon and Arcite.

1386 (May) Legend of Good Women begun.

1388-9 L'Envoy a Bukton.

    „   Former Age.

    „   A. B. C.

1391 Astrolabie.

1393 L'Envoy a Scogan.

c. 1394 Complaint of Annelida.

c. 1394 Complaint of Mars.

1394 Second Version of Good Women (called Earlier Version by Mr. Furnivall.)

c. 1397 Flee from the press.

    „   Stedfastness.

    „   Gentleness.

c. 1398 Complaint of Venus.

    „   Fortune.

1399 Complaint to his Purse.

The following table gives the Canterbury tales (with the order in which I believe them to have been written, indicated by numerals postfixed), arranged in the order in which they should be printed, as told in a Two-Days' Journey to Canterbury.

GENERAL PROLOGUE—(1388.)

[The Braces on the right side indicate Mr. Bradshaw's groups.]

First day before breakfast	Knight (1386)	5
	Miller	16
	Reeve	17
	Cook	18
	Doctor	9
	Pardoner	21
First day after breakfast	Man of Law	3
	Shipman	14
	Prioress	2
	Sir Thopas	10
	Melibœus	11
	Monk	12
	Nun's Priest	13
Second day before breakfast	Squire	6
	Franklin	7
	Wife of Bath	8
	Friar	19
	Sumner	20
	Clerk	4
	Merchant	15
Second day after breakfast	Nun (? 1373 or 1381)	1
	Canon's Yeoman	22
	Manciple (c. 1391)	23
	Parson	24

I have not included any poem that has been shown on good evidence to be spurious. The Romaunt of the Rose and Chaucer's Dream, which are only suspected on the uncertain ground of sundry imperfect rhymes, I retain until it is shown that Chaucer at the age of twenty-five must have followed the same accurate rules as he did when past thirty. He says himself, I think, that he wrote these two books (the latter being probably the Book of the Leo mentioned in the prayer at the end of the Parson's tale.) I have, however, marked the doubt thrown on their authenticity by giving them a position apart, generally at the end of the poems.

F. G. FLEAY.

REPRINTS.

FOUR TRANSCRIPTS

BY THE LATE THOMAS WRIGHT, F.S.A.

THE following ballad of " Thomas and the Elf Queen," transcribed from the Cambridge MS., and the three tales
which follow it, were given to me five and forty years ago
by that varied scholar, the late Thomas Wright.   They were intended
to appear in that part of my little book, *Lays and Legends of Various
Nations*, devoted to England.   But before that Part was given to the
press the work came to an untimely end.   I have not seen Mr.
Wright's beautifully written MSS. from 1834 until a few weeks since,
but, having then found them, I think they might be very appropriately
included in our RECORD as a memorial of one who has in his numerous
publications done so much to illustrate the folk-lore and early
literature of England.

WILLIAM J. THOMS.

THOMAS AND THE ELF QUEEN.

Carefully transcribed from the MS. in the Public Library of the
University of Cambridge, ff. v. 48.   Mr. Jamieson, who has printed
it very incorrectly in his *Ancient Ballads*, supposes the MS. to be of
the fifteenth century, but from internal evidence it would seem to be
older, probably of a not much later period than the middle of the
fourteenth century.   From the manner in which the scribe has in
several instances erased what he had first written and from the kind of
alterations he has made, we might almost suppose he was the author
of the ballad; and, from the quotations which Mr. Jamieson has made

from the MSS. of the same ballad in the Cotton and Lincoln libraries,
those would seem to be later copies in which all our scribe's alterations
are adopted. Sir Walter Scott has printed an imperfect copy in his
Border Minstrelsy, but has not told us whence he took it. The very
variations, however, are quite sufficient to show that it is a later copy,
by a ruder and more illiterate scribe, either from our MS. or from a
common original. Thus, in the 29th stanza, the scribe who wrote Sir
Walter's copy, not understanding the word *beteche*, altered " my soule
beteche I the" into " my sole tak to the; " and shortly after he has
turned "drye ther payne " into " derayed their payne," which is
nonsense. It need hardly be observed, that from the language of all
the copies known, and from the manuscripts in which they occur, as
well as from the tone of the second and third cantoes, which consist of
prophecies relating principally to the Scotch Wars of Edward III.,
the following is clearly not a Scotch, but an English, ballad.

> As I me went this andyrs [a] day
>   ffast on my way, makyng my mone,
> In a mery mornyng of may,
>   Be Huntley banks my self alone,
>
> I herde the iay and the throstell,
>   The mavys menyd [b] in hir song,
> The wodewale farde [c] as a bell,
>   That the wode abonte me rong.
>
> Alle in a longyng as I lay
>   Vnderneth a cumly tre,
> Saw I wher a lady gay
>   Came ridand oner a lonely le.
>
> ʒif [d] I shuld sitte till domesday,
>   Alle with my tonge to know and se,
> Sertenly alle hir aray
>   Shalle hit neuer be seryed [e] for me.
>
> Hir palfray was of dappull gray,
>   Like on [f] se I neuer non:
> As dose [g] the sune on somers day,
>   The cumly lady hir selfe schon. [h]

[a] St. Andrew's day. [b] the thrush. [c] went on. [d] if.
[e] described. [f] snch one. [g] does. [h] shone.

Hir sadill was of reuyll bon,
   Semely was that sight to se,
Stifly sette with precious ston,
   Compaste aboute with crapste.

Stonys of oryons [a] gret plente;
   Hir here [b] aboute hir hed hit [c] hong.
She rode out ouer that lonely le,
   A while she blew, a while she song.

Hir garthis of nobull silke thai were.
   Hir boenls thei were of barys [d] ston,
Hir stiroppis thei were of cristall clere,
   And alle with perry [e] aboute be gon.

Hir paytrell [f] was of a riall fyne,
   Hir cropur [g] was of arafe,
Hir bridull was of golde fyne,
   On euery side hong bellis thre.

She led iij grehoundis in a leesshe,[h]
   viij rachis [i] be hir fote ran.
To speke with hir wold I not seesse.[j]
   Hir lire [k] was white as any swan.

She bare a horne about hir halee,[l]
   And vnder hir gyrdill meny flonne.[m]
Ffor sothe,[n] lordyngs, as I you tell,
   Thus was this lady fayre be gon.

Thomas lay and saw that sight
   Vnderneth a semely tre;
He seid, "yonde is Mary of myght
   That bare the childe that died for me.

But I speke with that lady bright
   I hope my hert wille breke in thre;
But I woll go with alle my myght
   Hir to mete at eldryn tre."

[a] the east (*orient*).   [b] hair.

[c] it, the neuter of the pronoun *he, heo, hit*—we now use for the fem. an older form *she*, and in the neuter we drop the *h*.

[d] beryl.   [e] pearl.   [f] the breast leather of the horse.

[g] crupper.   [h] leash.   [i] hounds.

[j] cease.   [k] complexion.   [l] neck.

[m] arrows.   [n] truth.

Thomas radly ^a vp he rase,^b
  And ran ouer that mownteyne hye,
And certanly, as the story sayes,
  He hir mette at eldryn tre.

He knelid down vpon his knie
  Vnderneth the grene wode spray;
"Louely lady, thu rew ^c on me,
  Qwene of heuen, as thu well may."

Than seid that lady bright,
  "Thomas let such wordis be:
Ffor quen of heuen am I noyght;
  I toke neuer so hye degre.

But I am a lady of a nother cuntre,
  If I be parellid moost of price,^d
I ride after the wilde fee,^e
  My raches rannen at deuyse."

"If thu be pareld ^f most of price,
  And ridis here in thi balye,^g
Lufly lady, as thu art wyse,
  To gif me leve to lye the by."

"Do way! Thomas, that were foly,
  I pray the hertely, let me be,
Ffor I say the securly,^h
  That wolde fordo ⁱ my bewte."

"Lufly lady, thu rew on me,
  And I shall euer more with the dwell,
Here my trouth I plight to the,
  Wheder thu wilt to heuen or hell."

"Man of molde thu wilt me marre:
  But ʒet thu shalt haue thy wille;
But trow thu well thu thryuist the warre,
  Ffor alle my beute thu wille spille." ^k

Down then light that lady bright
  Vnderneth a grene wode spray,
And, as the story tellus ful right,
  vij tymes be hir he lay.

^a quickly	^b rose.	^c rue, have pity.
^d apparelled most costly.	^e cattle (*A. Sax.* feoh.)	^f apparelled.
^g dominion.	^h certainly.	ⁱ destroy.
^j worse.	^k spoil, destroy.	

She seid, " Thomas, thu likes thi play:
 What byrde^a in boure^b may dwel with the?
Thu marris^c me here the lefe long day:
 I pray the, Thomas, let me be."

Thomas standand in that stid,^d
 And beheld that lady gay:
Hir here that hong vpon her hed,
 Hir eien semyd out that were so gray;

And alle hir clothis were a way,
 That he before saw in that stede.^e
The tother black, the tother gray;
 The body blee^f as beten leed.^g

Thomas seid, " Alas! alas!
 In feith that is a dolfull sight,
That thu art so fadut^h in the face,
 That be fore schone as sunne bright."

" Take thi leve, Thomas, at sune and mone,
 And also at levys of eldryn tre,
This twelmond shall thu with me gone,
 That mydul erth thu shalt not se."

He knelyd down vpon his kne,
 To Mary mylde he made his mone,
" Lady, but thu rew on me,
 Alle my games fro me ar gone.

" Alas ! " he seyd, " wooⁱ is me,
 I trow my dedis wil wyrk me woo,
Ih'u my soule be teche^j I the,
 Wher so euer my bonys shall goo."

She led hym to the eldryn hill,
 Vndernethe the grene wode lee,
Wher hit was derk as any hell,
 And euer water tille^k the knee.

Ther the space of dayes thre
 He herd but the noyse of the flode,
At the last he seid, " Wo is me !
 Almost I dye for fowte of fode."^l

^a damsel.	^b bower.	^c mars.	^d place.
^e place.	^f blue.	^g lead.	^h faded.
ⁱ woe.	^j give, deliver up.	^k To, up to	^l fault (or want) of food.

She led hym into a fayr herbere,[a]
    Ther frute growende [b] was gret plente,
Peyres and appuls bothe ripe thei were,
    The darte,[c] and also the damsyn tre:

The fygge, and also the white bery;
    The nyghtyngale biggynge [d] her nest,
The papyniay [e] fast about gan flye,
    The throstull song wolde haue no rest.

He presed to pul the fruy[t with] his honde
    As man for fode wexe ny honde [f] feynte.
She seid, " Thomas, let that ther stonde,
    Or ellis the feend [will] the ateynte. [g]

If thu pulle, the sothe to sey,
    Thi soule goeth to the fyre of hell;
Hit comes neuer out til domes day,
    But ther euer in payne to dwelle."

She seid, " Thomas, I the hight,[h]
    Come lay thi hed on my kne,
And thu shalle se the feyrest sight
    That euer saw mon of thi cuntre."

He leyd down his hed, as she hym badde,
    His hed vpon hir kne he leide ;
Hir to plecse he was full gladde,
    And then that lady to hym she seide:—

" Sees thu ȝonder vp fayr way
    That lyes oner ȝonder mounteyne;
ȝonder is the way to heven for ay,
    Whan synful soulis haue duryd ther peyne.

Seest thu now, Thomas, ȝonder way
    That lyse low under ȝon rise;
Wide is the way, the sothe to say,
    Into the joyes of paradyse.

Sees thu ȝonder thrid[i] way
    That lyes oner ȝonder playne;
ȝonder is the way, the sothe to sey,
    Ther[j] sinfull soules shalle drye [k] ther payne.

[a] arbour.   [b] growing.   [c] " date " in Sir W. Scott's copy.
[d] building.   [e] parrot.   [f] nigh hand, *ie.* almost.
[g] seize upon as a forfeit.   [h] call.   [i] third.
[j] where.   [k] suffer.

Sees thu now ȝonder fourt way
  That lyes ouer ȝonder felle;
ȝonder is the way, the sothe to say,
  Vnto the brennand fyre of hell.

See thu now ȝonder fayre castell
  That stondis vpon ȝonder fayre hill ;
Off towne and towre it berith the bell,
  In mydul erth is ther non like ther till.

In faith, Thomas, ȝonder is myne owne,
  And the kyngus of this cuntre:
But me were better be hongud and drawyn,
  Then he wist that thu lay be me.

My lorde is scrued at ilke·a messe
  With xxx^{ti} knyȝts fayre and fre,
And I shalle say, sittyng at the deese,[a]
  I toke thi speche be ȝonde the lee.

Whan thu comes to yonder castell gay,
  I pray the curtes [b] man to be,
And, what so euer any man to the say,
  Loke thu answer non but me."

Thomas stondyng in the stede,
  And he helde that lady gay,
She was feyre, and as rede,
  And as riche, on hir palfray.

Hir greyhoundis fillid with the dere blode,
  Hir rachis coupuld [c] be [d] my fay;
She blew hir horne, on hir palfray gode,
  And to the castell she toke the way.

Into a hall sothly [e] she went,
  Thomas folud [f] at hir hande:
Ladis come bothe faire and gent,
  Fful curtesly to hir kneland.

Harpe and fidul both thei fande,
  The gstorn, and also the sautry,
The lute and the ribybe both gangand,
  And alle maner of mynstralcy.

[a] dais, the high table in the hall.   [b] courteous.   [c] coupled.
[d] by.   [e] truly.   [f] followed.

Kny3ts dawnsyng be thre and thre,
　　Ther was reuel, both game and play;
Ther ware ladys fayre and fre
　　Dawnsyng with riche aray.

The gretist ferly ther Thomas tho3t,
　　When xxx^{ti} harts lay vpon flore,
And as meny dere in were broght,
　　That was largely long and store.

Rachis lay lappand on the dere blode,
　　The cokys ^a thei stode with dressyng knyves.
Brytnand ^b the dere as thei were wode;
　　Reuell was among [thaim] rife.

Ther was reuell, games, and play,
　　More than I yow say, parde ;
Tille hit fel vpon a day,
　　My lufly lady seid to me,

" Buske the, Thomas, for thu most gon,
　　Ffor here no lenger mayst thu be:
Hye the fast, with mode,^c and mone:
　　I shalle the bryng to eldyn tre."

Thomas answerid, with heuy chere,
　　" Lufly lady, thu let me be:
Ffor certenly I haue be here
　　But the space of dayes thre."

" Ffor sothe, Thomas, I the telle,
　　Thu hast bene here seuen 3ere ^d and more:
Ffor ^e here no longer may thu dwell,
　　I shal tel the the skyl ^f wherfore.

To morou on of hel, a fowle fende,
　　Among these folke shal chese his fee.
Thu art a fayre man and a hende,
　　Fful wel I wot he wil chese the.

Ffor alle the golde that euer myght be
　　Ffro heuen vnto the wordis ^g ende,
Thu beys ^h neuer trayed ⁱ for me:
　　Ffor with me I rede ^j the wende."

---

^a cooks.　　^b carving, cutting up.　^c mind.　　　^d years.
^e wherefore.　^f cause.　^g world's.　^h art.　ⁱ betrayed.　^j advise, counsel. .

She broght hym agayn to eldyntre,
    Vndernethe the grene wode spray,
In Hnntley banks, ther for to be,
    Ther foulys syng bothe ny3t and day.

" Ffor out ouer 3on mounten gray,
    Thomas, a fowken * makes his nest:
A fowkyn is an yrons b pray,
    Ffor thei in place will haue no rest.

Ffare wel, Thomas, I wende my way.
    Ffor me most ouer 3on bents brown."
This is a fytte: twayn ar to sey,
    Off Thomas of Erseltown.

THE MILLER AT THE PROFESSOR'S EXAMINATION.

There once came to England a famous foreign professor, and before he came he gave notice that he would examine the students of all the colleges in England. After a time he had visited all but Cambridge, and he was on his road thither to examine publicly the whole university. Great was the bustle in Cambridge to prepare for the reception of the professor, and great also were the fears of the students, who dreaded the time when they must prove their acquirements before one so famous for his learning. As the period of his arrival approached their fears increased, and at last they determined to try some expedient which might avert the impending trial, and for this purpose several of the students were disguised in the habits of common labourers, and distributed in groups of two or three at convenient distances from each other along the road by which the professor was expected.

He had in his carriage arrived at the distance of a few miles from Cambridge when he met the first of these groups of labourers, and the coachman drew up his horses to inquire of them the distance. The professor was astonished to hear them answer in Latin. He proceeded on his way, and, after driving about half a mile, met with

      a falcon.   b eagles.

another group of labourers at work on the road, to whom a similar question was put by the coachman. The professor was still more astonished to hear them give answer in Greek. "Ah!" thought he, "they must be good scholars at Cambridge, when even the common labourers on the roads talk Latin and Greek. It won't do to examine them in the same way as other people." So all the rest of the way he was musing on the mode of examination he should adopt, and, just as he reached the outskirts of the town, he came to the determination that he would examine them *by signs*. As soon, therefore, as he had alighted from his carriage, he lost no time in making known this novel method of examination.

Now the students had never calculated on such a result as this from their stratagem, and they were, as might well be expected, sadly disappointed. There was one student in particular who had been studying very hard, and who was expected by everybody to gain the prize at the examination, and, as the idlest student in the university had the same chance of guessing the signs of the professor as himself, he was in very low spirits about it. When the day of examination arrived, instead of attending it, he was walking sadly and mournfully by the banks of the river, near the mill, and it happened that the miller, who was a merry fellow and used to talk with this student as he passed the mill in his walks, saw him, and asked him what was the matter with him. Then the student told him all about it, and how the great professor was going to examine by signs, and how he was afraid that he should not get through the examination. "Oh! if that's all," said the miller, "don't be low about the matter. Did you never hear that a clown may sometimes teach a scholar wisdom? Only let me put on your clothes, with your cap and gown, and I'll go to the examination instead of you; and if I succeed you shall have the credit of it, and if I fail I will tell them who I am." "But," said the student, "everybody knows that I have but one eye." "Never mind that," said the miller; "I can easily put a black patch over one of mine." So they changed clothes, and the miller went to the professor's examination in the student's cap and gown, with a patch on his eye.

Well, just as the miller entered the lecture-room, the professor had tried all the other students, and nobody could guess the meaning of his signs or answer his questions. So the miller stood up, and the professor, putting his hand in his coat pocket, drew out an apple, and held it up towards him. The miller likewise put his hand in his pocket, and drew out a crust of bread, which he in like manner held out towards the professor. Then the professor put the apple in his pocket, and pointed at the miller with one finger: the miller in return pointed at him with two: the professor pointed with three: and the miller held out his clenched fist. "Right!" said the professor; and he adjudged the prize to the miller.

The miller made all haste to communicate these good tidings to his friend the student, who was waiting at the mill; and the student, having resumed his own clothes, hastened back to hear the prize given out to him. When he arrived at the lecture-room, the professor was on his legs explaining to the assembled students the meaning of the signs which himself and the student who had gained the prize made use of. "First," said he, "I held out an apple, signifying thereby the fall of mankind through Adam's sin, and he very properly held up a piece of bread, which signified that by Christ, the *bread* of life, mankind was regenerated. Then I held out one finger, which meant that there is one God in the Trinity; he held out two fingers, signifying that there are two; I held out three fingers, meaning that there are three; and he held out his clenched fist, which was as much as to say that the three are one."

Well, the student who got the prize was sadly puzzled to think how the miller knew all this, and as soon as the ceremony of publishing the name of the successful candidate was over he hastened to the mill, and told him all the professor had said. "Ah!" said the miller, "I'll tell you how it was. When I went in the professor looked mighty fierce, and he put his hand in his pocket, and fumbled about for some time, and at last he pulled out an apple, and he held it out as though he would throw it at me. Then I put my hand in my pocket, and could find nothing but an old crust of bread, and so I held it out in the same way, meaning that if he threw the apple at me I would throw the crust at him. Then he looked still more fiercely, and held out his one finger, as much as to say he would poke my one eye out, and I held out two fingers, meaning that if he poked out my one eye I would poke out his two, and then he held out three of his fingers, as though he would scratch my face, and I clenched my fist and shook it at him, meaning that if he did I would knock him down. And then he said I deserved the prize."

THE LAYING OF THE GHOST.

There lived in the town of ———, in that part of England which lies towards the borders of Wales, a very curious simple kind of a man; though, simple as he seemed, people all said there was more cunning in him than there appeared to be, and that he knew a good deal that other people did not know. Now there was in the same town a certain large and very old house, and one of the rooms was haunted by a ghost, which not only hindered people from making any use of that room, but was also very troublesome to them in other ways. The man whom I have just mentioned was reported to be very clever at dealing with ghosts, and the proprietor of the haunted house, by the advice of some of his friends, sent for him and asked him if he would undertake to make the ghost quit the house. Tommy, for that was the name the man generally went by, agreed to do this, on condition that he should have with him in the room which the ghost frequented three things, an empty bottle, a bottle of brandy with a tumbler, and a pitcher of water. So Tommy had a fine fire in the room, for it was a cold winter evening, and he locked the door safely in the inside and sat down to pass the night drinking brandy and water. Well, just as the clock struck twelve, he was roused by a slight noise, and looking up, lo! there was the ghost standing before him. Says the ghost, "Well, Tommy, how are ye?" "Pretty well, thank ye," says he, "but pray how did ye know my name?" "Oh, very well indeed," said the ghost. "And how did ye get in?" "Oh, very easily." "Not through the door, I'm sure." "No, not at all, but through the key-hole." "D'ye say so? none of your tricks upon me; I won't believe you came through the key-hole." "Won't ye? but I did." "I'm sure you can't get through the key-hole." "I'm sure I can." "Well, then," says Tommy, pointing to the empty bottle, which he pretended to have emptied, "if you can come through the key-hole you can get into this bottle, but I won't believe you can do either." Now the ghost began to be very angry that Tommy should doubt his powers of getting into the bottle, so he asserted most confidently that the thing was easy to be done. "No," said Tommy, "I won't believe it till I see you get in." "Here goes, then," said the ghost, and sure enough into the bottle he went, and Tommy corked him up quite tight, so that he could not get out, and he took the bottle to the bridge where the river was wide and deep, and he threw the bottle exactly over the key-stone of the middle arch into the river, and the ghost was never heard of after.

LEGEND OF THE ROLLRIGHT STONES.

Not far from the borders of Gloucestershire and Oxfordshire, and within the latter county, is the pretty village of Rollright, and near the village, up a hill, stands a circle of small stones, and one larger stone, such as our Celtic antiquaries say were raised by the Druids. As soon as the Druids left them, the fairies, who never failed to take possession of their deserted shrines, seemed to have had an especial care over these stones, and any one who ventures to meddle with them is sure to meet with some very great misfortune. The old people of the village, however, who generally know most about these matters, say the stones were once a king and his knights, who were going to make war on the King of England; and they assert that, according to old prophecies, had they ever reached Long Compton the King of England must inevitably have been dethroned,[a] and this king would have reigned in his place, but when they came to the village of Rollright they were suddenly turned into stones in the place where they now stand.

[a] The old rhyme runs,—
> If Long Compton thou can'st see,
> Then King of England thou shalt be.

See Hutchinson's *History of Cumberland*, i. 230.]

Be this as it may, there was once a farmer in the village who wanted a large stone to put in a particular position in an out-house he was building in his farm-yard, and he thought that one of the old knights would be just the thing for him. In spite of all the warnings of his neighbours he determined to have the stone he wanted, and he put four horses to his best waggon and proceeded up the hill. With much labour he succeeded in getting the stone into his waggon, and, though the road lay down hill, it was so heavy that his waggon was broken and his horses were killed by the labour of drawing it home. Nothing daunted by all these mishaps, the farmer raised the stone to the place it was to occupy in his new building. From this moment everything went wrong with him, his crops failed year after year, his cattle died one after another, he was obliged to mortgage his land and to sell his waggons and horses, till at last he had left only one poor broken-down horse which nobody would buy, and one old crazy cart. Suddenly the thought came into his head that all his misfortunes might be owing to the identical stone which he had brought from the circle at the top of the hill. He thought he would try to get it back again, and his only horse was put to the cart. To his surprise he got the stone down and lifted it into the cart with very little trouble, and, as soon as it was in, the horse, which before could scarcely bear along its own limbs, now drew it up the hill of its own accord with as little trouble as another horse would draw an empty cart on level ground, until it came to the very spot where the stone had formerly stood beside its companions. The stone was soon in its place, and the horse and cart returned home, and from that moment the farmer's affairs began to improve, till in a short time he was a richer and more substantial man than he had ever been before.

[Traditions that the large circles of stones to be seen in various parts of the country were once human beings, are to be met with elsewhere than at Rollright. The tradition is not limited to England. For instance, in India, about fifteen miles east of Murdan, in the district of Eusoofzye, is a remarkable circle of tall and upright stones.

The only tradition or legend the people have regarding the fabric is that the attendants of a marriage, while passing over the plain, were changed into these stones by some powerful magician or malignant demon. (*Journal of Asiatic Society of Bengal*, vol. xxxix. p. 59.)

Sometimes again the human element is left out. The only recorded tradition with regard to the stone circle at Stanton Drew represents Keyna, a holy virgin in the fifth century, the daughter apparently of a Welsh prince, obtaining a grant of the land on which the village of Keynsham now stands. She was warned, however, of the insecurity of the gift, in consequence of the serpents of a deadly nature that infested the place. She accepted the gift notwithstanding, and by her prayers converted the serpents into the stones we now see there. (Ferguson's *Rude Stone Monuments*, p. 151, quoting *Archæologia*, xxv. p. 189.)

The early traditions relating to great stones are an important subject connected with the primitive life of Britain, political as well as mythological, and it should be dealt with exhaustively for the Folk-Lore Society. Mr. Stuart has collected many important passages on stone-worship from the early chronicles and laws, in the second volume of his *Sculptured Stones of Scotland*, and Mr. Akerman contributed a valuable paper to the Numismatic Society " On the Stone Worship of the Ancients, illustrated by their Coins."]

THE STORY OF CONN-EDA;*

OR, THE GOLDEN APPLES OF LOUGH ERNE.

[Translated from the original Irish, by NICHOLAS O'KEARNEY, ESQ., and re-edited from *The Cambrian Journal* published under the auspices of the Cambrian Institute, vol. ii. pp. 101-115. London, 1855.]

HE following romantic tale, or *Fionn-sgeal*, is as wild as any told by the Arabian princess, and both curious and interesting, because it solely relates to Ireland. The story is a literal translation of an Irish one frequently told, or rather recited, by a professed story-teller, or *Ursgealaidhe*, named Abraham Mac Coy, during his professional engagements. The story-teller, possibly the last member of his profession known to have flourished in Ireland, was a living encyclopædia, replete with stories of the same nature, some of which have been rescued from oblivion, and may tend to throw light on the manners, customs, and forms of

* Some years ago two rude statues were found in Neale Park, county Mayo, the seat of Lord Kilmaine. One represented a unicorn, probably the goat, from whence the cornucopia was taken for Jupiter; the other a lion, or some such animal. The inscription found on those monuments of antiquity, as is stated, says that these were the "*Dié na feile*," gods of plenty, and were the gods adored by Conn and Eda. Hence the place has been called *Neale*, from the Irish words "*an fheile*" (pronounced a neile); and, because the Irish articles an, the, have been attached to the substantive, *the* Neale is the name by which the place has been known. The traditions of the people exactly correspond with this account. The statues, it is said, are still preserved in the park of Lord Kilmaine; but never having been in that part of the island, I have not seen them.

religious belief entertained by the pagan Irish, or, perhaps, help to elucidate some obscurities found dimming many pages of our ancient history.

It was long before the time the western districts of *Innis Fodhla** had any settled name, but were indiscriminately called after the person who took possession of them, and whose name they retained only as long as his sway lasted, that a powerful king reigned over this part of the sacred island. He was a puissant warrior, and no individual was found able to compete with him either on land or sea, or question his right to his conquest. The great king of the west held uncontrolled sway from the island of Rathlin to the mouth of the Shannon by sea, and far as the glittering Shannon wound its sinuous length by land. The ancient king of the west, whose name was Conn, was good as well as great, and passionately loved by his people. His queen was a *Breaton* (British) princess, and was equally beloved and esteemed, because she was the very counterpart of the king in every respect; for whatever good qualification was found wanting in one, the other was certain to indemnify the omission. It was plainly manifest that heaven approved of the career in life of the virtuous couple; for during their reign the earth produced exuberant crops, the trees fruit ninefold commensurate with their usual bearing, the rivers, lakes, and surrounding sea teemed with abundance of choice fish, while herds and flocks were unusually prolific, and kine and sheep yielded such abundance of rich milk, that they shed it in torrents upon the pastures; and furrows and cavities were always filled with the pure lacteal produce of the dairy. All these were blessings heaped by heaven upon the western districts of *Innis Fodhla*, over which the benignant and just Conn swayed his sceptre, in approbation of the course of government he had marked out for his own guidance. It is needless to state that the people who owned the authority of this great and good sovereign were the happiest on the face of the wide expanse of earth. It was during his reign, and that of his son and successor, that Ireland acquired the title of the "happy isle of the west" among

---

* *Innis Fodhla*, Island of Fate, as some think, an old name of Ireland.

foreign nations. Conn Mór and his good Queen Eda reigned in great glory during many years: they were blessed with an only son, whom they named Conn-eda, after both his parents, because the Druids foretold, at his birth, that he would inherit the good qualities of both. According as the young prince grew in years, his amiable and benignant qualities of mind, as well as his great strength of body and manly bearing, became more manifest. He was the idol of his parents, and the proud boast of his people; he was beloved and respected to that degree that neither prince, lord, nor plebeian swore an oath either by the sun, moon, stars, or elements, except by the head of Conn-eda. This career of glory however was doomed to meet a powerful but temporary impediment, for the good Queen Eda took a sudden and severe illness, of which she died in a few days, thus plunging her spouse, her son, and all her people, into a depth of grief and sorrow from which it was found difficult to relieve them.

The good king and his subjects mourned the loss of Queen Eda for a year and a day; and, at the expiration of that time, Conn Mór reluctantly yielded to the advice of his Druids and counsellors, and took to wife the daughter of his Archdruid. The new queen appeared to walk in the footsteps of the good Eda for several years, and gave great satisfaction to her subjects. But in course of time, having had several children, and perceiving that Conn-eda was the favourite son of the king and the darling of the people, she clearly foresaw that he would become successor to the throne after the demise of his father, and that her son would certainly be excluded. This excited the hatred and inflamed the jealousy of the Druid's daughter against her stepson to such an extent, that she resolved in her own mind to leave nothing in her power undone to procure his death, or even exile from the kingdom. She began by circulating evil reports of the prince; but, as he was above suspicion, the king only laughed at the weakness of the queen; and the great princes and chieftains, supported by the people in general, gave an unqualified contradiction; while the prince himself bore all his trials with the utmost patience, and always repaid her bad and malicious acts towards him with good and benevolent ones. The enmity of the queen towards Conn-eda knew no bounds

when she saw that the false reports she circulated could not injure
him. As a last resource, to carry out her wicked projects, she determined to consult her *Cailleach-chearc* (hen-wife), who was a reputed
enchantress.

Pursuant to her resolution, by the early dawn of morning she hied
to the cabin of the *Cailleach-chearc*, and divulged to her the cause of
her trouble. "I cannot render you any help," said the *Cailleach*,
"until you name the *duais*" (reward). "What *duais* do you require?"
asked the queen impatiently. "My *duais*," replied the enchantress,
"is to fill the cavity of my arm with wool, and the hole I shall bore
with my distaff with red wheat." "Your *duais* is granted, and shall
be immediately given you," said the queen. The enchantress thereupon stood in the door of her hut, and bending her arm into a circle
with her side, directed the royal attendants to thrust the wool into her
house through her arm, and she never permitted them to cease until
all the available space within was filled with wool. She then got on
the roof of her brother's house, and, having made a hole through it
with her distaff, caused red wheat to be spilled through it, until that
house was filled up to the roof, so that there was no room for another
grain within. "Now," said the queen, "since you have received your
duais, tell me how I can accomplish my purpose." "Take this chess-
board and chess, and invite the prince to play with you; you shall
win the first game. The condition you shall make is, that whoever
wins a game shall be at liberty to impose whatever *geasa* (conditions)
the winner pleases upon the loser. When you win, you must bind the
prince under the penalty either to go into *ionarbadh* (exile), or procure for you, within the space of a year and a day, the three golden
apples that grow in the garden, the *each dubh* (black steed), and
coilean con na mbuadh (hound of supernatural powers), called Samer,
which are in the possession of the king of the Firbolg race, who
resides in Lough Erne.* Those two things are so precious, and so well
guarded, that he can never attain them by his own power; and, if he
would rashly attempt to seek them, he should lose his life."

---

* The Firbolgs believed their elysium to be under water; and the Irish still
fancy that many of our lakes are peopled.

The queen was greatly rejoiced at the advice, and lost no time in inviting Conn-eda to play a game at chess, under the conditions she had been instructed to arrange by the enchantress. The queen won the game, as the enchantress had foretold ; but so great was her anxiety to have the prince completely in her power, that she was tempted to challenge him to play a second game, which Conn-eda, to her astonishment, and no less mortification, easily won. " Now," said the prince, " since you have won the first game, it is your duty to impose your *geis* first." " My *geis*," said the queen, "which I impose upon you, is to procure me the *each dubh* (black steed), and *cuilean con na mbuadh* (hound of supernatural powers), which are in the keeping of the king of the Firbolgs, in Lough Erne, within the space of a year and a day ; or, in case you fail, to go into *ionarbadh* (exile), and never return, except you surrender yourself to lose your head and *comhead beatha*" (preservation of life). " Well, then," said the prince, " the *geis* which I bind you by is, to sit upon the pinnacle of yonder tower until my return, and to take neither food nor nourishment of any description, except what red wheat you can pick up with the point of your bodkin; but, if I do not return, you are at perfect liberty to come down at the expiration of the year and a day."

In consequence of the severe *geis* imposed unexpectedly upon him, Conn-eda was very much troubled in mind; and, well knowing he had a long journey to make before he would reach his destination, immediately prepared to set out on his way, not however before he had the satisfaction of witnessing the ascent of the queen to the place where she was obliged to remain exposed to the scorching sun of summer, and the blasting storms of winter, for the space of one year and a day, at least. Conn-eda being ignorant of what steps he should take to procure the *each dubh* and *cuilean con na mbuadh*, though he was well aware that human energy would prove unavailing, thought proper to consult the Great Druid, Fionn Badhna, of Sliabh Badhna, who was a friend of his, before he ventured to proceed to Lough Erne. When he arrived at the *bruighean* of the Druid he was received with cordial friendship, and the *failte*, * as usual, was poured out before him; and, when he was seated, warm water was fetched, and his feet bathed, so that the fatigue he felt after his journey was greatly relieved.   The Druid, after he had partaken of refreshments, consisting of the newest of food and the oldest of liquors, asked him the reason for paying the visit, and more particularly the cause of his sorrow; for the prince appeared exceedingly depressed in spirit.   Conn-eda told his friend the whole history of the transaction with his step-mother, from the beginning to the end.   " Can you not assist me ? " asked the prince, with downcast countenance. " I cannot, indeed, assist you at present," replied the Druid, " but I will retire to my *grianan* at sun-rising on the morrow, and learn by virtue of my druidism what can be done to assist you." The Druid, accordingly, as the sun rose on the following morning, retired to his *grianan*, and consulted the god he adored, through the power of his *druidheacht*.   When he returned, he called Conn-eda aside on the plain, and addressed him thus :—" My dear son, I find you have been bound under a severe—an almost impossible—*geis*, intended for your destruction ; no person on earth could have advised the queen to impose it except the Cailleach of Lough Corrib, who is the greatest Druidess now in Ireland, and sister to the Firbolg King of Lough Erne.   It is not in my power, nor in that of the deity I adore, to interfere in your behalf ; but go directly to Sliabh Mis, and consult *Eánchinn-duine* (the bird with the human head), and, if there be any possibility of relieving you, that bird can do it; for there is not a bird in the western world so celebrated as that bird, because it knows all things that are past, all things that are present and exist, and all things that shall hereafter exist.   It is difficult to find access to his place of concealment, and more difficult still to obtain an answer from him; but I will endeavour to regulate that matter for you; and that is all I can do for you at present."

---

* *Failte* means welcome, but it means much more in original MSS. ; even the Irish contraction of the word means *fail*, a circle, and r, or re, the individual surrounded by friends.

The Archdruid then instructed him thus : — "Take," said he, " yonder little shaggy steed, and mount him immediately; for in those days the bird will make himself visible, and the little shaggy steed will conduct you to his place of abode. But, lest the bird should refuse to reply to your queries, take this precious stone (*leag longmhar*), and present it to him; and then little danger and doubt exist but he will give you a ready answer." The prince returned heartfelt thanks to the Druid; and, having saddled and mounted the little shaggy horse without making much delay, received the precious stone from the Druid, and, after having taken his leave of him, set out on his journey. He suffered the reins to fall loose upon the neck of the horse, according as he had been instructed, so that the animal took whatever road he chose.

It would be tedious to relate the numerous adventures he had with the little shaggy horse, which had the extraordinary gift of speech, and was a *draoidheacht* horse, during his journey.

The prince having reached the hiding-place of the strange bird at the appointed time, and having presented him with the *leag longmhar*, according to Fionn Badhna's instructions, and proposed his questions relative to the manner he could best arrange for the fulfilment of his *geis*, the bird took up in his mouth the jewel from the stone on which it was placed, and flew to an inaccessible rock at some distance, and, when there perched, he thus addressed the prince :—"Conn-eda, son of the King of Cruachan," said he, in a loud croaking human voice, " remove the stone just under your right foot, and take the ball of iron and the *corna* (cup) you shall find under it; then mount your horse, cast the ball before you, and having so done, your horse will tell you all the other things necessary to be done." The bird, having said this, immediately flew out of sight.

Conn-eda took great care to do everything according to the instructions of the bird. He found the iron ball and *corna* in the place which had been pointed out He took them up, mounted his horse, and cast the ball before him. The ball rolled on at a regular gait, while the little shaggy horse followed on the way it led, until they reached the margin of Lough Erne. Here the ball rolled into the water and became invisible. "Alight now," said the *draoidheacht*

pony, "and put your hand into mine ear; take from thence the small
bottle of *ice* (allheal) and the little wicker basket which you will find
there, and remount with speed, for just now your great dangers and
difficulties commence." Conn-eda, ever faithful to the kind advice of
his *draoidheacht* pony, did what he had been advised. Having taken
the basket and bottle of *ice* from the animal's ear, he remounted and
proceeded on his journey, while the water of the lake appeared only like
an atmosphere above his head. When he entered the lake the ball
again appeared, and rolled along until it came to the margin, across
which was a causeway, guarded by three frightful serpents; the
hissings of the monsters were heard at a great distance, while, on a
nearer approach, their yawning mouths and formidable fangs were
quite sufficient to terrify the stoutest heart. "Now," said the horse,
"open the basket, and cast a piece of the meat you find in it into the
mouth of each serpent; when you have done this, secure yourself in
your seat in the best manner you can, so that we may make all due
arrangements to pass those *draoidheacht peists*. If you cast the
pieces of meat into the mouth of each *peist* unerringly, we shall
pass them safely, otherwise we are lost. Conn-eda flung the pieces
of meat into the jaws of the serpents with unerring aim. "Bear
a benison and victory," said the *draoidheacht* steed, "for you are
a youth that will win and prosper." And, on saying these words, he
sprang aloft, and cleared in his leap the river and ford, guarded by
the serpents, seven measures beyond the margin. "Are you still
mounted, Prince Conn-eda?" asked the steed. "It has taken only half
my exertion to remain so," replied Conn-eda. "I find," said the pony,
"that you are a young prince that deserves to succeed,—one danger is
now over, but two others still remain." They proceeded onwards after
the ball until they came in view of a great mountain flaming with fire.
"Hold yourself in readiness for another dangerous leap," said the
horse. The trembling prince had no answer to make, but seated himself as securely as the magnitude of the danger before him would permit.
The horse in the next instant sprang from the earth, and flew like an
arrow over the burning mountain. "Are you still alive, Conn-eda,
son of Conn-mór?" inquired the faithful horse. "I am just alive

and no more, for I am greatly scorched," answered the prince. "Since you are yet alive, I feel assured that you are a young man destined to meet supernatural success and benisons," said the druidic steed. "Our greatest dangers are over," added he, "and there is hope that we shall be able to overcome the next, and last danger." After they proceeded a short distance, his faithful steed, addressing Conn-eda, said, "alight now, and apply a portion of the contents of the little bottle of *ice* to your wounds." The prince immediately followed the advice of his monitor ; and, as soon as he rubbed the *ice* (allheal) to his wounds, he became as whole and fresh as ever he had been before. After having done this, Conn-eda remounted, and, following the track of the ball, soon came in sight of a great city surrounded by high walls. The only gate which was visible was not defended by armed men, but by two great towers, which emitted flames that could be seen at a great distance. "Alight on this plain," said the steed, "and take a small knife from my other ear; with this knife you shall kill and flay me. When you have done this, envelop yourself in my hide, and you can pass the gate unscathed and unmolested. When you get inside you can come out at pleasure ; because, when once you enter, there is no danger, and you can pass and repass whenever you wish; and let me tell you that all I have to ask of you in return is that you, when once inside of the gates, will immediately return, and drive away any birds of prey that may be fluttering around to feed on my carcase; and more, that you will pour any little drop of that powerful *ice*, if such still remain in the bottle, upon my flesh, to preserve it from corruption. When you do this in memory of me, if it be not too troublesome, dig a pit and cast my remains into it."

"Well," said Conn-eda, "my noblest steed, because you have been so faithful to me hitherto, and because you still would have rendered me further service, I consider such a proposal insulting to my feelings as a man, and totally at variance with the spirit which can feel the value of gratitude, not to speak of my feelings as a prince. But as a prince I am able to say, ' Come what may—come death itself in its most hideous forms and terrors—I never will sacrifice private friendship to personal interest.' Hence I am, I swear by my arms

of valour, prepared to meet the worst,—even death itself,—sooner
than violate the principles of humanity, honour, and friendship!
What a sacrifice do you propose!" "Pshaw, man! heed not that:
do what I advise you, and prosper." "Never! Never!" exclaimed
the prince. "Well, then, son of the great western monarch," said the
horse, with a tone of sorrow, "if you do not follow my advice on this
occasion, I can tell you that both you and I shall perish, and shall
never meet again; but, if you act as I have instructed you, matters
shall assume a happier and more pleasing aspect than you may
imagine. I have not misled you heretofore, and, if I have not, what
need have you to doubt the most important portion of my counsel?
Do exactly as I have directed you, else you will cause a worse fate
than death to befall me. And, moreover, I can tell you, that, if you
persist in your resolution, I have done with you for ever."

When the prince found that his noble steed could not be dissuaded
from his purpose, he took the knife out of his ear with reluctance, and
with a faltering mind and trembling hand essayed experimentally to
point the weapon at his throat. Conn-eda's eyes were bathed in tears;
but no sooner had he pointed the druidic *scian* to the throat of his
good steed than the dagger, as if impelled by some druidic power,
stuck in his neck, and in an instant the work of death was done, and
the noble animal fell dead at his feet! When the prince saw his
noble steed fall dead by his hand, he cast himself on the ground, and
cried aloud until his consciousness was gone. When he recovered
he perceived that the steed was quite dead; and, as he thought there
was no hope of resuscitating him, he considered it the most prudent
course he could adopt to act according to the advice he had given
him. After many misgivings of mind, and abundant showers of
tears, he essayed the task of flaying him, which was only that of a
few minutes. When he found he had the hide separated from the
body, he, in the derangement of the moment, enveloped himself with
it, and proceeding towards the magnificent city in rather a demented
state of mind, entered it without any molestation or opposition. It
was a surprisingly populous city, and an extremely wealthy place;
but its beauty, magnificence, and wealth had no charms for Conn-eda,

because the thoughts of the loss he sustained in his dear steed were paramount to those of all other earthly considerations.

He had scarcely proceeded more than fifty paces from the gate, when the last request of his beloved *draoidheacht* steed forced itself upon his mind, and compelled him to return to perform the last solemn injunctions imposed upon him. When he came to the spot upon which the remains of his beloved *draoidheacht* steed lay, an appalling sight presented itself; ravens and other carnivorous birds of prey were tearing and devouring the flesh of his dear steed. It was but short work to put them to flight; and having uncorked his little jar of *ice*, he deemed it a labour of love to embalm the now mangled remains with the precious ointment. The potent *ice* had scarcely touched the inanimate flesh, when, to the surprise of Conn-eda, it commenced to undergo some strange change, and in a few minutes, to his unspeakable astonishment and inexpressible joy, it assumed the form of one of the handsomest and noblest young men imaginable, and in the twinkling of an eye the prince was locked in his embrace, smothering him with kisses, and drowning him with tears of joy. When one recovered from his ecstacy of joy, and the other from his surprise, the strange youth thus addressed the prince :—" Most noble and puissant prince, you are the best sight I ever saw with my eyes, and I the most fortunate being in existence for having met you ! Behold in my person, changed to the natural shape, your little shaggy *draoidheacht* steed ! I am brother of the king of this city; and it was the wicked Druid, Fionn Badhna, who kept me so long in bondage; but he was forced to give me up when you came to *consult* him, as my *geis* was then broken ; yet I could not recover my pristine shape and appearance unless you had acted as you have kindly done. It was my own sister that urged the queen, your step-mother, to send you in quest of the steed and powerful puppy hound, which my brother has long had in keeping. My sister, rest assured, had no thought of doing you the least injury, but much good, as you will find hereafter ; because, if she were maliciously inclined towards you, she could have accomplished her end without any trouble. In short she only wanted to free you from all future danger and disaster, and recover me from my relentless enemies through

your instrumentality. Come with me, my friend and deliverer, and
the steed and the puppy hound of extraordinary powers, and the
golden apples, shall be yours, and a cordial welcome shall greet you in
my brother's abode; for you deserve all this and much more."

The exciting joy felt on the occasion was mutual, and they lost no
time in idle congratulations, but proceeded on to the royal residence of
the King of Lough Erne. Here they were both received with demon-
strations of joy by the king and his chieftains; and, when the purport
of Conn-eda's visit became known to the king, he gave a free consent
to bestow on Conn-eda the black steed, the *coilean con-na-mbuadh*,
called Samer, and the three golden apples of health that were growing
in his garden, under the special condition, however, that he would
consent to remain as his guest until he would set out on his journey
in proper time, to fulfil his *geis*. Conn-eda, at the earnest solicita-
tion of his friends, consented, and remained in the royal residence of
the Firbolg King of Lough Erne, in the enjoyment of the most delicious and fascinating pleasures during that period.

When the time of his departure came, the three golden apples were
plucked from the crystal tree in the midst of the pleasure garden, and
deposited in his bosom; the puppy hound, Samer, was leashed, and
the leash put into his hand; and the black steed, richly harnessed, was
got in readiness for him to mount. The king himself helped him on
horseback, and both he and his brother assured him that he might not
fear burning mountains or hissing serpents, because none would impede
him, as his steed was always a passport to and from his subaqueous
kingdom. And both he and his brother extorted a promise from
Conn-eda, that he would visit them once every year at least.

Conn-eda took his leave of his dear friend, and the king his brother;
the parting was a tender one, soured by regret on both sides. He proceeded on his way without meeting any thing to obstruct him, and in
due time came in sight of the *dún* of his father, where the queen had
been placed on the pinnacle of the tower, in the full hope that, as it
was the last day of her imprisonment there, the prince would fail to
make his appearance, and thereby forfeit all pretensions and right to
the crown of his father for ever. But her hopes were doomed to meet

a disappointment; for when it had been announced to her by her couriers, who had been posted to watch the arrival of the prince, that he approached, she was incredulous ; but when she saw him mounted upon a foaming black steed, richly harnessed, and leading a strange kind of animal of the dog kind by a silver chain, she at once knew he was returning in triumph, and that her schemes laid for his destruction were frustrated.   In the excess of grief at her disappointment, she cast herself from the top of the tower, and was instantly dashed to pieces. Conn-eda met a welcome reception from his father, who mourned him as lost to him for ever, during his absence; and, when the base conduct of the queen became known, the king and his chieftains ordered her remains to be consumed to ashes for her perfidy and wickedness.

Conn-eda planted the three golden apples in his garden, and instantly a great tree, bearing similar fruit, sprang up. This tree caused all the district to produce an exuberance of crops and fruits, so that it became as fertile and plentiful as the dominions of the Firbolgs, in consequence of the extraordinary powers possessed by the golden fruit. The hound Samer and the steed were of the utmost utility to him ; and his reign was long and prosperous, and celebrated among the old people for the great abundance of corn, fruit, milk, fowl, and fish that prevailed during this happy reign.   It was after the name of Conn-eda the province of Connaught, or *Conneda*, or *Connacht*, was so called.

[The above story is communicated by Mr. Henry Charles Coote, F.S.A.   Having had occasion to refer to it while writing a paper for the Society, Mr. Coote suggested that it should be transplanted from its present position in the *Cambrian Journal*, where it is overlaid and lost, to these pages. Besides containing, says Mr. Coote, elements peculiar to Irish traditional story-telling, it has a good many of the general features of European Folk-Lore, such as " The Bird of Knowledge" (see Mad. D'Aulnoy's *La Belle Étoile et le Prince Cheri*); the slaying of the pony and his revival as a young prince; the appeasing of the serpents, each with a piece of meat; the taking objects necessary for the *dénouement* out of the pony's ears, &c. &c. A variant of the first part of this story is to be found in one of the numerous Irish chapbooks published by James Duffey, of Dublin. This chapbook is called *Hibernian Tales*, and the story "The Black Thief and Knight of the Glen." Here there are three princes instead of one. The Knight of the Glen answers to the King of Lough Erne, and the Black Thief is the means of the success of the princes, instead of the pony. The pony does not appear at all, and the Black Thief saves the lives of the princes from the vengeance of the Knight of the Glen by telling stories. The two stories are very nearly identical in the opening portion, containing the jealousy of the step-mother, the means taken to accomplish her designs, the game of chess and the double result; but the latter portion differs considerably.]

NOTES, QUERIES, NOTICES, AND NEWS.

NOTES.

[Communications for these columns should be addressed to the Hon. Secretary.]

i. *Extracts from old Chapbooks, &c.* — Professor Dr. George Stephens, F.S.A., of Copenhagen, sends the following extracts from out-of-the-way sources. They serve well to illustrate the value of the cheap popular literature of former times, a comprehensive study of which is so much desired.

Elves, Gasts, Ghosts, &c.—" The ghosts, like old horses, go all night for fear they are seen, and be made to carry scate or fish or be carted ; and witches are the worst kind of devils, and make use of cats to ride upon, or kill-kebbers, and besoms, and sail over the seas in cockle-shells, and witch lads and lasses, and disable bridegrooms.   As for Willy-and-the-Wisp, he is a fiery devil, and leads people off their road in order to drown them, for he sparks sometimes at your feet, and then turns before us with his candle, as if he were two or three miles before us. Many a good boat has Spunkie drown'd ; the boats coming to land in the night-time, they observe a light off the land, and set in upon it and drown."—*History of Buck-haven in Fifeshire.* Chapbook. Glasgow. 8vo. p. 22, 23.

" Fairies are terrible troublesome, they gang dancing round fouks lums, and rin through the houses they haunt, and play odd tricks, and lift new-born bairns from their mothers, and none of them is safe to lie with their mothers, a night or two after they are born, unless the mother gets a pair of men's breeches under her head for the first three nights; when the fairies are frighted, they will leave an old stock with the woman, and whip away the child. One tried to burn an old stock that the fairies left in the cradle; but, when the fire was put on, the old stock jumped on upon a cat and up the lum."—*Id.* p. 23.

" And here I make a vow, either to get the conquest, or else never to come in your sight, and to say as I was wont:

> What, Himp and Hamp?
> Here will I neuer more grinde nor stamp.
>   Yours in choller, *Robin Good-fellow*."

From *Robin Goodfellowves Epistle*, prefixt to *The Cobler of Canter-burie*, London, 1608, sm. 4to. See Halliwell, *Tarlton's Jests*, p. 110. (Above verses printed as prose). " Hob Thrust, Robin Goodfellow, and such like spirites."—Halliwell, *Tarlton's Jests*, 8vo. Lond. 1844, p. 55 (Shakespear Soc.)

" The kelpy is a sly devil, he roars before a loss at sea, and frightens both young and old upon the shore."—*History of Buck-haven*. Chapbook (as above), p. 23.

" Which [figure] he took no doubt for the ' Whooffey Brow bogle,' or ' Old Serat ' himself."—*Cumberland Pacquet*. Quoted in *Morning Chronicle*, Nov. 5, 1858, p. 8, col. 6.

Brownie, his sitting on an ale-cask, and his game at ball.—*Thrummy-Cap*. Chapbook.

Boc.—"Boc bulbagger, as some use to feare children withal."—*Jack of Dover*. (Chapbook, reprint, p. 27.)

Bell, Bellman.—Bell at Dalkeith used by the Popish clergy, which would " rive" (rend) at touch of a guilty person.—*Jokes of G. Buchanan*. (Chapbook, pt. i. p. 20.)

" The Night before he was to suffer Death, the Bellman coming as usual at Night to put him in mind of his approaching End, by repeating some Mementos of Mortality: quoth he, ' The Deel blaw my Bladder full of Pebble Stones if this Mon may not as well sing Psalms to a dead Horse as prate thus to me.'   Next Day, riding along in the Cart, which stopped under the Wall of St. Sepulchre's Churchyard, whilst a Man performed the Ceremony of ringing a Bell, and giving other Admoni-tions tending to the exhorting him to consider of a future State: quoth he, ' This is the strangest Country Ise e'er was in, that a Man can't go to the Gallows in Peace.   Ise swear, if Ise am damn'd, it is because I'm hanged after this Superstitious wan.'   But what seemed more irreligious in him was his having, instead of a Prayer Book, the

Ballad of ' Chevy Chase' in his hand."—Smith, *Lives of Highwaymen*, vol. ii. London, 1719; pp. 193-4 (in *Life of Sawney Douglas*). The custom is explained in the same work (vol. iii. Lond. 1720, pp. 45, 48). It was establisht by Eliz. Elliot, temp. James I. she leaving £250 to pay a man for ringing a bell under Newgate, between 11 and 12 of the night before any one was to be hanged, repeating a solemn exhortation; and again next day, under St. Sepulchre's churchyard, the bell in the steeple tolling for them, and the cart stopping for that purpose, while the bellman repeats another pious address.

Chastity.—" Bevis answered: by the Lions not hurting thee, I know thou art a pure Virgin."—*Sir Bevis of Southampton*. (Chapbook, Newcastle, p. 16.)

May-Day.—" In summer season howe doe the moste part of our yong men and maydes in early rising and getting themselues into the fieldes at dauncing ? What foolishe toyes shall not a man see among them! What vnchast countenances shall not be vsed then among them! Or what coales shall there be wanting that maye kindle cupid's desire ! Truly none. Through this dauncing many maydens haue been vnmaydened, whereby I may saye it is the store-house and nurserie of bastardie. What adoe make our yong men at the time of May ! Do they not vse night-watchings to rob and steale yong trees out of other men's grounde, and bring them home into their parishe with minstrels playing before? And when they haue set it up they will decke it with floures and garlandes, and daunce round (men and women together, most vnseemely and intoler-able, as I haue proued before,) about the tree."— Collier's *Northbrooke's Treatise*, 1577, p. 176.

St. David's Day.—" With other Materials, as Shoes, Hat, Stockings, and Periwig, which he made up much like such a Figure, which was wont to be hung up for a Show on St. Taffy's Day."—Smith's *Lives of Highwaymen*, vol. i. Lond. 1719, p. 122.

Corpse Arrest.— " Nay, hast thou not seen the very corpse of thy departed brother arrested, and uncharitably stayed ; who, though he had paid his debt to nature, yet must receive no *burial* till his poor corpse has discharged his debt unto his creditor ? And hast thou sought to satisfy his hard-hearted creditor that those due funeral rites might be performed to thy brother?"—R. Braithwaite. *The Penitent Pilgrim*, 1641, reprint. Pickering, Lond. 1853, p. 109.

"At the bottom of Cloth Fair the corpse was arrested at the suit of an old herb-woman for elevenpence halfpenny, which had been due a long time to the hag for cabbages and cucumbers which the deceased had in his life-time."—*Fun upon Fun, or the Comical Merry Tricks of Leper the Taylor.* Chapbook, Glasgow, 1817, p. 23.

Three Drops of Blood.—

> *Dowglas*—Last Night, no sooner was I laid to Rest,
> But just three Drops of Blood fell from my Nose,
> And stain'd my Pillow, which I found this Morning,
> And wonder'd at.
>
> *Queen Mary.*—That rather does betoken
> Some Mischief to thy self.
>
> *Dowglas.*—Perhaps to Cowards,
> Who prize their own base Lives; but to the Brave,
> 'Tis always fatal to the Friend they Love.

Banks, *The Albion Queens.* London, 1735, p. 39. (First printed 1684).*

Old Maids.—1. Lead apes in hell. 2. In London and its vicinity they say, that in the next world they mend the old bachelors' breeches; others say that they shall sew their buttons on, but the more they sew the faster they fall off again. If the old maids are very diligent in the above labour, they may return to this life again and have another chance. 3. In Longfellow's *Evangeline*, ii. 1, we have quite a different tradition. Is it American only, or also English? Or is it originally French?—"Come, give him thy hand and be happy! Thou art too fair to be left to braid St. Catherine's tresses."

Hares.—"The fishers look on all maukens (hares) to be devils and witches, and, if they but see a sight of a dead mauken, it sets them a

[* Horace Walpole records a variant of this. "Three drops of blood fell from the nose of Alfonso's statue. Manfred turned pale, and the princess sank upon her knees. Behold! said the friar, mark this miraculous indication that the blood of Alfonso will never mix with that of Manfred."—See *Castle of Otranto*, cap. iv.]

trembling."—*History of Buck-haven in Fifeshire.* Chapbook, 8vo. Glasgow, p. 22.

"The bucky lads and lasses, when they go to gather bait, tell strange stories about ghosts, witches, Willy-with-the-wisp, and the kelpy, fairies, maukens, and bogles of all sorts."—*Id.* p. 22.

Burials.—"Within the coffin, along with herself, she got a pair of new brogues, a penny candle, a good hard-headed old hammer, with an Irish sixpenny-piece to pay her passage at the gate, and what more could she look for?"—*The Comical Sayings of Paddy from Cork.* Chapbook, Stirling, p. 13.

Dancing.—"Insomuche that in some places they shame not in the tyme of divine service to come and dance about the churche, and without [? withal] to have naked men dauncing in nettes, which is most filthie; for the heathen, that had never further knowledge than the light of nature, have counted it shamefull for a player to come on the stage without a slop."—Stockwood's *Sermon,* 1578. Quoted in Collier's *Northbrooke's Treatise,* p. xiv.

ii. *Excerpts made from two Lists of Obsolescent Words of East Cornwall,* contained in *The Journal of the Royal Institution of Cornwall,* Nos. i. and xi. (subsequently reprinted at Truro), and from MS. additions made thereto by the compiler Thomas Quiller Couch, F.S.A. of Bodmin:—

Airy-Mouse, the Bat.—The village boys at Polperro address the bat, as it flits above them, in the following rhymes:—

> "Airy mouse, airy mouse! fly over my head,
> And you shall have a crust of bread;
> And when I brew and when I bake,
> You shall have a piece of my wedding cake."

"Friday in Lide" Festival.—This Anglo-Saxon name of the month of March still lingers in the Blackmoor tin district. "Friday in Lide" (the first Friday in March) is observed by the tinners as a festival now chiefly marked by a serio-comic custom of sending a young lad to the highest "bound" or hillock of the work, and allowing him to sleep there as long as he can; the length of his nap being the measure of the mid-day nap of the tinners throughout the ensuing twelve months. The weather usually characterising " Friday in Lide " is, it need hardly be said, not very favourable to prolonged sleep. In Saxon times labourers generally were allowed their mid-day sleep, and it is still permitted to husbandmen in some parts of East Cornwall during a stated period of the year. Tusser speaks of the custom:

> " From May to mid-August an hour or two
> Let Patch sleep a snatch howsoever ye do ;·
> Though sleeping one hour refresheth his song,
> Yet trust not Hob Greathead for sleeping too long."

There is a saying in Luxulgan that " ducks will not lay till they have drunk Lide water."—Appendix to List of Obsolescent Words in No. XI. of *The Journal of the Royal Institution of Cornwall.*

Neck.—A miniature sheaf of wheat with four plaited arms, intertwined with " everlasting " and the more durable of flowers.

The stalks of wheat brought down by the last sweep of the scythe are brought home in thankful triumph, and woven as described, and in the evening taken into the mowhay [stackyard], where are assembled all the harvest party. A stout-lunged reaper proclaims loudly and slowly :

> " I hav'en! I hav'en! I hav'en!"

Another loud voice questions :

> " What hav'ee ? What hav'ee ? What hav'ee ?"
> " A neck! A neck! A neck!"

is the reply; and the crowd take up in their lustiest tones the chorus of " wurrah." General merriment follows, and the songs are loud, and the draughts of ale or cyder deep.

The neck may be seen hanging to the beam in many of our farmhouses between harvest and Christmas eve, on which night it is given to the master-bullock in the stall. " Hollaing the neck " is in some parts of Cornwall still heard, and is one of the cheerfulest of rural sounds.

Wad.—A bundle ; a *wad* of straw. "Joan the Wad" is the name of a *Pisky.*

> " Jack the lantern, Joan the wad,
> That tickled the maid and made her mad,
> Light me home, the weather's bad."
>
> (*Polperro.*)

Church-hay.—Churchyard.   This word is going out of use, but is often heard in the adage—

> " A hot May
> Makes a fat church-hay."

The terminal *hay* is the Anglo-Saxon *hœs* or *heze*, a hedge or inclosure.

Corrat.—Pert, impudent, sharp in rejoinder, saucy.

> " As corrat as Crocker's mare."
>
> *Proverb.*

Heal.—To hide or conceal—

> " The healer is as bad as the stealer."
>
> *Cornish Proverb.*

Louster.—To work hard—

> " He that can't schemey (or skill) must louster."
>
> *Local Proverb.*

Lawrence.—The rural god of idleness—

> " He's as lazy as La'rence."
> " One would think La'rence had got hold o'n."

Roper's News.—Something heard before—

> " That's roper's news."
>
> *Bodmin Phrase.*

Rish or Rush, i. e. A list.   Our people, instead of " turning over a new leaf," " begin a new rish."   I have thought that this may have been derived from a primitive way of keeping a tally, by stringing some sort of counters on a *rush*.   THOMAS SATCHELL.

iii. *Players' Superstitions.*—The superstitions of players are many and various, and are astonishing by reasons of their simplicity.   Recently, in a pleasant after-dinner conversation, Mr. Boucicault made a series of curious revelations.   He remarked especially upon the superstitions of ballet dancers.   Every grade of the ballet in England and on the Continent is a slave to superstition.   For instance, in his *Babil and Bijou* a première danseuse and twenty coryphées rebelled at the full-dress rehearsal, because the scene in which they had to dance was entirely in blue, without any adornments of silver. Blue is an unlucky colour among players, all the world over, silver being its only saving relief. In the English theatres, to trip on entering on the scene on the first night of a play is a sure sign of success. To receive a bouquet at the stage-door before the play begins is an omen of failure. In America, too, some strange superstitions prevail. When the *Black Crook* was ready for production at Niblo's Garden, under the management of Mr. Wheatley, Mr. Jarrett, and Mr. Palmer, the first-named was very nervous about it. Every thing depended on its success. Failure meant ruin, and he could not view the situation as calmly as his partners did. The theatre was all lighted up, the carpenters had "set" the first two scenes, and Flanagan, the janitor, had his hand on the bolts ready to throw open the stained-glass doors that kept out the clamorous crowd that had gathered in the hallway. Mr. Wheatley, standing beside the gate with his partners, gave the signal for opening the doors, and the rush began. The first person who reached the ticket-taker was a lady, accompanied by a little boy. Mr. Wheatley leaned over the rail, and thrust her outside, at the same time pushing a man, the next in turn, inside the railing. Then, raising his hat politely to the lady, he apologized and escorted her to the usher himself. "It would never do," he afterwards said to a friend, "to allow a woman to be the first to enter the theatre on a first night. It's unlucky; let a man in first, and you are all right." *The Crook* was very successful, and no argument could convince Mr. Wheatley that he had not saved it by thrusting a man in first.

A few more words on this subject. In America, as in England, the player has a superstitious objection to rehearsals on the Sabbath. During the rehearsals of *Leo and Labis* at Niblo's Garden there were two Sunday-night rehearsals, and at each it was found necessary to lock the doors at 11 P.M. to keep the dancing girls from running away. Even then some got out of the green-room windows into Crosby Street, climbed over the iron railings, and escaped. It is believed that salaries will not be paid regularly during the run of a piece rehearsed on Sundays, or that the piece itself will be a failure, or that a death will occur in the company. This was predicted at the Sunday rehearsals of *The Crook*, and the croakings of the ballet girls were verified by the sudden death of a soubrette. At the Grand Opera House, during Mr. Fisk's term of management, Sunday rehearsals were enforced in spite of the protests of the Company. When the great spectacle *Lalla Rookh* was preparing there were three Sunday representations, and the birds of ill-omen were loud in their predictions of disaster. Mr. Fisk was shot and killed before the fourth Sunday-night revel, and the piece, although magnificently presented to the public, did not prove remunerative.—See *The Theatre*, Sept. 1879, p. 106.

WILLIAM GEORGE BLACK.

iv. *Superstitions of Weardale, Durham.*—Friday.—The same ideas are held as in West Sussex. See *Folk-Lore Record*, vol. i. Nos. 49, 50, 51.

May Cat.—It is believed that a cat born in the month of May will suck the breath of a baby in the cradle if the opportunity offers.

Worms.—To cure this complaint, a trout is to be obtained and placed alive upon the bowels of the patient, and bound with a bandage, and kept there all night. The writer remembers this being done to a boy about seven years old about the year 1830.

Witches.—In passing a witch, doubling the thumbs under the forefingers was considered a preventive to being bewitched.

Pigs.—When pigs are seen to carry straw in their mouths it is considered to be a sure sign of wind.

Witch Wood.—A piece of wood cut from the mountain-ash was considered a preventive of bewitching, if carried about the person.

Repeating the Lord's Prayer backwards, it was said, would cause the devil to raise his head through the floor ; the only way of appeasing him was to present him with a black hen.

Lay two straws, in the form of a cross, and say—

> " Rain, rain, go away,
> Din'nt come back till Christmas Day,"

was considered to prevent a wet day.

J. G. FENWICK.

v. *Witchcraft in Cornwall,* 1844.—Not long since the resting-place of
the dead at Phillack, near Hayle, was made the scene of transactions
which would have blackened the darkest ignorance of bygone ages. It
appears that several persons afflicted with disease, and who, for want
of moral courage, would not submit to the directions of their medical
advisers, very readily caught hold of and applied every nostrum that
gossips made known. Experience proving that the boasted remedies
were of no avail, their imaginations were put to the utmost stretch, in
order that they might avoid the only method by which they could be
cured. Fortunately a blazing light shot across their darkened way,
and their gloomy reflections were dissipated by its brilliancy. It was
a revelation ; and they denounced their ignorance, because they did
not sooner find out the cause of their malady. To believe that they
were ill-wished was only the work of a moment, but to discover a
person who could break the spell was not so easily accomplished.
Every thought and action were centered in attaining their darling
object. Finally, their wish was consummated, and a scatterer of
witch-spells stalked forth from Helston, to whom they disclosed every
incident of their lives, fraught with uncertainty, as tending to good or
evil. The day was chosen, the dreaded hour of midnight fixed, and
the abode of the silent clod of all that once was living was named as
the place of assignation. The hour drew near, but their purpose
became known from the impulse of their ecstacies, and their stealthy
actions were closely watched. The asked-for fee was immediately
given, and, after silence was enjoined, the churchyard wall was scaled.
Then the spell-breaker commenced the mysteries of his art, by making
mysterious sounds and performing mysterious actions, as he walked
over the dead, hotly pressed by his frightened dupes. Having walked
many times round the church, the doors and windows opened and shut
at his bidding. Then he commanded them to remain open, and, as
they were passed in succession, he brought the persons who had ill-
wished them to their face. Thus the spell was broken and dissolved,
and a faith given that their cure would be speedily effected. Some
days have since elapsed, and either their faith has failed, or the witch-
spell is not broken, for their disease still maintains its ground, the

effect of a visible cause.— *West Briton,* quoted in the *Times,* 9th Sept. 1844.

vi. *Consulting a Witch.—Gross Superstition in Devonshire.*—At the village of Charles, in the extreme north of Devon, considerable gossip and excitement have been caused by the visit of a personage known as "The White Witch." A small farmer in the parish, with a deal of credulity scarcely credible in these days, believed that he had been bewitched by a relative, and accordingly went off to visit "The White Witch," who ostensibly carries on the business of herbalist at Exeter, and vends a charm which will cure all diseases of humanity. This was, however, too serious a matter to be dealt with by mere potions, and the "Witch Doctor" persuaded his victim that it would be necessary to accompany him in order to find out the whereabouts of and exorcise the evil spirit. On arriving at the house proceedings were commenced by the "White Witch." A mixture of incense was placed on a plate and lit, and a sort of incantation gone through, those present being strictly enjoined to silence on pain that the whole proceeding would be violated. Somehow or other the spell failed to work, and the "witch" intimated that he would have to return to the farmer's house, and stay a week in order to effect a perfect cure, being fed meanwhile on beef, which would alone strengthen him sufficiently to enable him to perform his task satisfactorily. It seems that the farmer's wife was somewhat less credulous than her liege lord, and declined to be imposed upon in this way, and the result was an inquiry into and exposure of the whole trick. It is said that in remote parts of Devonshire such instances of credulity are far from uncommon, and in most instances the impostors succeed in bleeding their victims to a considerable extent.— *Yorkshire Post,* August 20, 1879.

vii. *Burning a Witch.*—St. Petersburg, Oct. 27.—Seventeen peasants have been tried for burning a supposed witch to death near Nijni-Novgorod. All the prisoners were acquitted with the exception of three, who were sentenced to Church penance.— *Daily Telegraph,* Oct. 28, 1879.

viii. *Witchcraft in Norfolk,* 1879.—A local paper reports the fol-

lowing case of alleged witchcraft, which was recently heard at the
East Dereham petty sessions:—William Bulwer, of Etling-green, was
charged with assaulting Christiana Martins, a young girl, who resides
near the Etling-green toll-bar. Complainant deposed that she was
sixteen years of age, and on Wednesday, the 2nd inst., the defendant
came to her and abused her. The complainant, who looked scarce
more than a child, repeated, despite the efforts of the magistrate's
clerk to stop her, and without being in the least abashed, some of
the worst language it was possible to conceive—conversation of
the most gross description, alleged to have taken place between
herself and the defendant. They appeared to have got from words
to blows, and, while trying to fasten the gate, the defendant hit
her across the hand with a stick. She alleged that there was no
cause for the abuse and the assault, so far as she knew, and, in
reply to rigid cross-examination as to the origin of the quarrel,
adhered to this statement. Mrs. Susannah Gathercole also corrobo-
rated the statement as to the assault, adding that the defendant said
the complainant's mother was a witch. Defendant then blazed forth
in righteous indignation, and, when the witness said she knew no
more about the origin of the quarrel, he said: Mrs. Martins is an
old witch, gentlemen, that is what she is, and she charmed me, and I
got no sleep for her for three nights, and one night, at half-past eleven
o'clock, I got up because I could not sleep, and went out and found a
'walking toad' under a clod that had been dug up with a three-
pronged fork. That is why I could not rest; she is a bad old woman;
she put this toad under there to charm me, and her daughter is just
as bad, gentlemen. She would bewitch any one; she charmed me,
and I got no rest day nor night for her, till I found this 'walking
toad' under the turf. She dug a hole and put it there to charm me,
gentlemen, that is the truth; she is a bad old witch. I got the toad
out, and put it in a cloth, and took it upstairs and showed it to my
mother and 'throwed' it into the pit in the garden. I can bring it
and show it to you, gentlemen. Mr. Hyde: What do you say, she
bewitched you? Defendant: Yes, Sir. She went round this here
'walking toad' after she had buried it; and I could not rest by day

or sleep by night till I found it. She is a bad old witch, and is not going to come it over me though. Her daughter is as bad as she is and encourages her in it. The Bench: Do you go to church? Defendant: Sometimes I goes to church and sometimes to chapel, and sometimes I don't go nowhere. Her mother is bad enough to do anything; and to go and put the "walking toad" in the hole like that, for a man which never did nothing to her, she is not fit to live, gentlemen; to go and do such a thing, is not as if I had done anything to her. She looks at lots of people, and I know she will do some one harm. The Chairman: Do you know this man, Superintendent Symonds? Is he sane? Superintendant Symonds: Yes, Sir, perfectly. Defendant: It is quite true, gentlemen, I showed the toad to my mother, and I can bring it for you to see. The Chairman said he was very sorry the defendant was so foolish as to believe such rubbish, and he would be fined 1*s*. and 12*s*. 6*d*. costs.—*The Rock*, 25 April, 1879.

ix. *Curious Superstition.*—On some parts of the Tweed there is still a belief amongst some illiterate persons in the power of fairies, who are supposed to affect the produce of the fisheries, and it is the custom of these, not only to impregnate the nets with salt, but also to throw some of that commodity into the water for the purpose of blinding the mischievous elves, who are said to prevent the fish from falling victims to the snares laid for them. This practice was observed near Coldstream the other day, and, strange to say, the net when drawn to land, instead of being empty, as usual, contained two fine salmon.—*Newcastle Daily Journal* (March, 1879).

JOHN GEORGE FENWICK.

x. *Milton Well-dressing.*—The ninth anniversary of this popular festival took place on Monday and Tuesday, June 23rd and 24th, 1879, in a large field near the church, admirably suited for the purpose of giving full scope to the numerous and varied amusements provided by the Committee. The wells were artistically dressed with choice flowers, representing scenes and devices, mottoes, &c. &c. The procession started from the principal well at one o'clock each day, headed by the Burslem Volunteer Band (which was engaged to play for dancing), followed by the May Queen, Maids of Honour, May-pole dancers, &c. &c. May-pole dance each day at four and seven p.m.

xi. *The Magic Mirror of Japan.*—Professor Ayrton lectured last week at the Royal Institution, his subject being "The Magic Mirror of Japan." In Japan there is, he said, an absence of house walls, interior and exterior, the houses consisting of a roof supported on only a few posts inclosing very little but empty space, and sliding screens alone divide off compartments. Why, in this comparative absence of all that we should call furniture, does one article pertaining to the ladies' toilette—the bronze mirror with its stand—hold so prominent a position? This mirror is usually circular, from 3 in. to 12 in. in diameter, made of bronze, and with a bronze handle covered with bamboo. The reflecting face is generally more or less convex, polished with a mercury amalgam, and the back is beautifully ornamented with a gracefully executed raised design. Some for the rustic population have also polished letters. The explanation of the fact that the mirror is almost *par excellence* the entire furniture is found partly in the elaborate head-dresses of the Japanese ladies and the painting of their faces, and partly from the belief, that, as the sword was "the soul of the Samouri," so is the mirror the " soul of woman." It therefore constituted the most valuable of all her possessions, and two mirrors form part of the trousseau of every bride. The characteristic qualities of the mirror must, it is believed, be in accordance with the constitution of the possessor, and "second sight" is resorted to in the selection of a mirror. But why is the mirror so important in the Imperial palace, where the Court ladies, still preserving the fashion of old days, comb back their hair in the simplest style? Why does the fortune-teller, instead of looking at a girl's palm, regard the reflection in a mirror? Why, instead of referring to the book of the recording angel, does the Japanese Plato bring before the boatman his evil deeds reflected in a mirror? And why does the mirror hold so important a place in Japanese temples? The mirror ranks far higher in Japanese history than has been supposed; it, in fact, takes the place of the cross in

Christian countries. Professor Ayrton read the myth of the origin of the worship of the mirror. The main points in it are that when gods alone inhabited the earth the sun-goddess one day hurt her hand with her shuttle, having been suddenly frightened by a practical joke of her brother the god of the sea. She indignantly retired to a cave. Darkness followed, and the goddess had to be appeased. The wisest of the gods suggested making an image of her more beautiful than herself. The Japanese Vulcan fashioned a mirror in the shape of the sun, and all the gods laughed and shouted, " Here is a deity who surpasses even your glory." Woman's curiosity could not stand this. The goddess peeped out, and while admiring herself in the mirror was caught and dragged out b⁓ a rice rope. The national traditions have it that this sun-goddess (Amaterasu ô mi Kami), sending her adopted grandson, who was also the great-grandfather of the first Emperor of Japan, to subdue the world, made him three presents : the *maga-tama* (the precious stone, emblematical of the spirit of woman), the sword (emblematical of the spirit of man), and the mirror (emblem of her own soul). " Look," she said, " on this mirror as my spirit, keep it in the same house and on the same floor with yourself, and worship it as if you were worshipping my actual presence."—*Times*, 4 February, 1879.

xii. *A Burmese Ceremony.*—Mr. R. Hope Pilcher, junior secretary to the Chief Commissioner in British Burmah, writing from Rangoon, April 18, sends us, by direction of the Chief Commissioner, the following description of a ceremony which was held on February 7 last, near the eastern frontier of the Akyab district, on the occasion of the reconciliation of two clans or villages of the Chin (or Khyeng) tribe named Bainbah and Mantin, between which a blood feud had previously existed. " The description," Mr. Pilcher adds, " may perhaps be valuable for ethnological purposes:— . . . . These preliminaries being completed, the ceremony of taking the oath of friendship was carried out—a ceremony of a unique and peculiar character, of which the following is a description:—At the foot of a Nyoung Bin, supposed to be the residence of a ' Nat,' a pot of khoung was placed half

buried in the earth. In the orifice of the pot some fresh leaves of
the tree were placed, and through them, into the liquor, were thrust
two pipes to suck with, a gun, a spear, a dah, alligators' teeth, tigers'
tusks, and some bamboo sticks with notches, cuts, and splits of a
mystic character. This being ready, one of the oldest of the Toung-
min (hill chief) present killed a small pig, extracted its heart, and,
filling the pot with water, commenced a harangue invoking the
'Nat' to pour down his wrath on the two Mantin and Bainbah men
sitting by the pot, and cause their destruction by any of the ways
indicated by the different articles thrust into the pot, if they bore
each other ill-will and did not remain friends thenceforth and for ever.
This invocation being over, Mantin took up the pig's heart, and,
pressing a drop of blood from it into the liquor, the two men ex-
changed words and commenced sucking up the liquor, adding more
water. After them two other representatives of the two villages had
a suck, and then the different implements, &c. were removed, and all
the other Chins present began drinking (by suction) out of the same
pot and another one supplied for general use, and they all seemed to
enjoy the liquor immensely, and the effects soon became apparent on
several of them. Some war-dances were performed, and we went
back to our camp the other side of the stream, and the Chins then
cooked the pig, ate, drank, and were merry. The khoung pots were
filled with fermented rice, to which water was added as required, and
the smell showed the mixture had no small intoxicating properties.
The oath thus administered is said to be most binding on Chins, and,
once taken, seldom, if ever, violated. . . . . Note.—'Bin' is the
Burmese for tree. 'Nyoung' includes a large number of the ficus
tribe. 'Nat' is the Burmese word used to translate the Indian 'Deva.'
Originally it denotes a local divinity, often a Hamadryad. 'Khoung'
is a kind of rice-beer made and used by the hill-tribes all over Burmah."
—*Times*, 23 May, 1879.   HENRY ASTON WALKER.

xiii. *Sporting Ceremony (France).*—The *Monde* describes a ceremony
once general among sportsmen, but now surviving only at Chantilly,
the Mass and Blessing of the Dog on St. Hubert's day, the 3rd of

November. The degenerate race of sportsmen, the *Monde* complains, imitate St. Hubert's cynegetic passion rather than his prodigies of penitence, and consider the slaughter of an innocent rabbit equal to the death of the mystical dragon overcome by the hero of the Ardennes. The Duc d'Aumale, however, keeps up the tradition, and at four in the morning he and his guests assembled in the parish church, where his chief huntsman, Hourvari, held in a leash Rabagas, the oldest member of the pack. Gravely seated on the steps of the altar, Rabagas seemed to receive with some surprise the holy water and the Orleans cockade which was attached to his neck, but he committed no indecorum like his predecessor Corbeau, who last year devoured a wax candle. At the elevation of the host, the six huntsmen sounded on the trumpet the blast of St. Hubert, and on leaving the church they gave the " Reveil du Veneur," the " Condé," and the " D'Orleans." At eleven o'clock the Orleans Princes and 300 guests hunted a stag, which, after a fine chase, was despatched in the Comelle Ponds.—*Times*, 5 Nov. 1879.

JOHN FENTON.

xiv. *An old Shrove Tuesday Custom.*—My mother, who is an old Nottinghamshire woman, between 70 and 80 years of age, tells me that when she was a little girl it was a custom in the Ollerton district of Nottinghamshire to always give the first piece of the first pancake to the cock. If the country folk who were dining were not in possession of fowls of their own, a piece of the first pancake was always cut off as soon as cooked and carried by a child or some other person to a cock belonging to some near neighbour. Dinner was never commenced till the cock had consumed the piece of pancake.

W. G. SMITH.

xv. *Chapbook Bibliography*, ante, vol. i. p. 244.—Allow me to correct an oversight on this subject, where it is said that Nisard's *Histoire des Livres populaires ou de la litterature du Colportage* (2 vols. 8vo. Paris 1854) is the only complete history of foreign Chapbooks. Nisard, of which a second edition, " *considerablement augmentée*," was published in·1866, is a history of French Chapbooks only. Goerres published at Heidelberg, as long ago as 1807, a history of German Chapbooks, *Die Teutschen Volksbücher*, which contains notices of forty-eight of them, many of which, of course, illustrate our English Chapbooks on the same subjects.   M. N. S.

xvi. *Funeral Custom in Scotland.*—It consists in placing the coffin on a table, tables, or chairs at the door of the house before the procession moves. After the coffin is taken off for interment the chairs or tables are placed upside down, and allowed to remain so for a considerable time. This formula was observed by the Rev. John Stevenson, of Glamis, at the funeral of one of the Earls of Aberdeen, and it is remarkable that such a custom should be observed in a family which might be supposed to be above such superstition.   W. G. SMITH.

xvii. *Bibliography of the Romance of Sir Tristem.*—In vol. ix. of *The Journal of the Bombay Branch of the Royal Asiatic Society* Dr. Edward Tyrrel Leith describes at length the migration of the story of Sir Tristem, and, as bibliographies of this nature are specially valuable, I have compiled the following from Dr. Leith :—

> Fragment of Welsh poem said to be at least as old as the tenth century [Tristan mentioned in].· See translation in Appendix to Scott's edition of Sir Tristrem.
>
> A Latin version by Rusticien de Puise (1110-1120).
>
> Manuscript in the Royal Library at Paris, published by Von der Hagen (temp. Richard I. John, or Henry III.) [From Michel's work.]
>
> Lai du Chevercfoil of Marie de France, dating from commencement of the thirteenth century. [From Michel's work.]
>
> Sir Walter Scott, Poetical Works of. .Edinburgh, Constable, 1825. vol. iv. From the Auchinlech MS. attributed to the Scottish bard, Thomas of Erceldoune, in the thirteenth century.
>
> Gottfried von Strassburg. Epic of Tristan and Isolde. (Commencement of the thirteenth century.)
>
> Ulrich von Thurheim, continued Gottfried about 1250.
>
> Heinrich von Friberg, continued Gottfried about 1300.
>
> Segehart von Bunbemberg. A metrical version. (Latter half of the fourteenth century.)

Eilhart von Oberge, a poet in the train of Henry the Lion. A fragment
only of the romance by this author now exists.

Morte d'Arthur. Books viii. ix. x. xii. Compiled from the old French
writers by Sir Thomas Malory, and first printed by Caxton in 1485.

Hans Sachs. The Tragedy of the strong love of Sir Tristrant for the fair
Queen Isalde. 1553.

Buesching und Von der Hagen. Buch der Liebe. Berlin, 1809. (A collection of old romances from the sixteenth century.)

Von Groote. Tristan, von Meister Gotfrit von Strassburg, mit der Fort-
setzung des Meisters Ulrich von Thurheim. Berlin, 1821.

Mone. Einleitung in C. von Groote's Ausgabe von Tristan und Isolde.
Also Ueber die Sage von Tristan, &c. Heidelberg, 1822.

Francisque Michel. Tristan, recueil de ce qui reste des poemes relatifs à
ses aventures, &c. Londres, 1835.

Immerman. Tristan und Isolde, &c. Duesseldorf, 1841.

Kurtz. Tristan und Isolde. Gedicht von Gottfried von Strassburg. Stutt-
gart, 1847.

Simrock. Tristan und Isolde, von Gottfried von Strassburg. Leipsig, 1855,

Ludwig Schneegans. Tristan, Trauerspiel, &c. Leipsig, 1865.

Welsh Triads (down to the seventh century) [Tristan mentioned in]. See
The Myvyrian Archæology of Wales.

Manuscript in the Library of Bern. [From Michel's work.]

Two fragments of Douce (mentioned by Sir Walter Scott in his edition of
Sir Tristrem). [From Michel's work.]

Extract from Le Donnez des Amans, in a MS. of Sir Thomas Phillipps.
[From Michel's work.]

This list is very imperfect of course, not being obtained from
original sources. But printing it as it stands may bring some cor-
rective notes and some additional information. What is wanted in each
case is an exact bibliographical title for each volume quoted. At all
events, it is a step, even if a faint one, in the direction of gathering
together such important facts as are here indicated.

G. L. Gomme.

xviii. *The Crow and the Fox* (ante, vol. i. p. 238).—These lines
are simply a metrical paraphrase of one of Æsop's Fables, the only
difference being that in Æsop the crow takes a piece of cheese from a
cottage window instead of the crust from a pedlar's pack.

Geo. L. Apperson.

QUERIES.

i. *The arcana of Night.*—The *Pall Mall Gazette* of 10th July, 1879, contains a critique on " Travels with a Donkey in the Cevennes," by Robert Louis Stevenson, and the following extract from the work is quoted, " What seems a kind of temporal death to people choked between walls and curtains is only a light and living slumber to the man who sleeps afield. All night long he can hear nature breathing deeply and freely ; even as she takes her rest she turns and smiles, and there is one stirring hour unknown to those who dwell in houses when a wakeful influence goes abroad and all the outdoor world are on their feet. It is then that the cock first crows, not this time to announce the dawn, but, like a cheerful watchman, speeding the course of night. Cattle awake in the meadows ; sheep break their fast on dewy hill-sides and change to a new lair among the ferns ; and houseless men, who have lain down with the fowls, open their dim eyes and behold the beauty of the night . . . . . . Even shepherds and old country folk, who are the deepest read in these arcana, have not a guess as to the means or purpose of this nightly resurrection. Towards two in the morning they declare the thing takes place, and neither know nor inquire further." This description is extremely interesting. I have often witnessed the phenomenon, but have never seen it described. About two hours before the break of day a restless spirit seems to pervade the whole animal race, and with humanity it is the time when physical and moral courage are at their lowest ebb. A strange feeling of depression comes over us, and the vital powers are painfully languid. Now it is that those who watch beside the beds of dying men observe the first symptoms of impending dissolution, though death does not usually take place before dawn. The accuracy of these observations has been lately confirmed to me by a distinguished medical man, who has long been aware of the facts above-mentioned, but cannot account for them. Perhaps some of the readers of the *Folk-Lore Record* can supply some information on this subject.

F. G.

ii. *Legend of Parsloe, Essex.*—I have been on the look-out for many years for a remarkable legend connected with Parsloe, near Romford, the old seat of the Fanshaws, concerning an ancestor of the family who for some reason is condemned at certain times to drive about, headless himself, in a carriage drawn by headless horses. Can any Essex member of the Folk-Lore Society supply further particulars?

M. N. S.

iii. *Royal Superstition.*—Can any of the members refer me to the origin of the following? "In the twelfth year of King Stephen he wore his crown during Christmas at Lincoln, which no king, from some superstitious feeling, had before ventured to do."—*Henry of Huntingdon*, bk. viii. See *Notes and Queries*, 5th scr. xii. p. 490.

G. L. GOMME.

iv. *The House that Jack built.*—Can any member tell me the origin or history of "The House that Jack built?" I have asked several gentlemen versed in literature, and who were likely to be interested in folk-lore, but can obtain no information from them. In a little book entitled *Service for the First Nights in Passover*, a poem is introduced so like the one in question that I think they must be connected in some way. The latter begins with "One *only* kid which my father bought for two zuzine," and then goes on with the feats of the cat, dog, staff, fire, water, ox, which last is slain by the angel of death; "then came the Most Holy, blessed be He, who slew the angel of death;" when the series goes back regularly to the "One *only* kid which my father bought for two zuzine." The author (Rev. A. P. Mendes) says, "this poem is generally regarded as a parable, descriptive of incidents in the history of the Jewish nation, with some reference to prophecies yet unfulfilled."—*Service of the First Nights of Passover according to the Custom of the German and Polish Jews.* (By the Rev. A. P. Mendes.)

ELIZA BELL.

NOTICES AND NEWS.

BOOKS ON FOLK-LORE LATELY PUBLISHED.

It is advisable that members of the Society should have their attention drawn to works on folk-lore which have been issued during the year; and it is well to put on record, in our yearly volume, any notes that refer to the doings of the students of folk-lore beyond the range of the Society. One of the objects of the Society is to encourage the study and the collection of folk-lore, and certainly it is not an unimportant indication of the encouragement thus afforded to bring into notice the books published during the year. Let it be observed, however, that these notices are simply intended to give a general idea as to the subject and worth of each book, not a detailed and critical review.

(1) BY MEMBERS OF THE SOCIETY.

i. *Demonology and Devil-Lore.* By Moncure Daniel Conway, M.A. With numerous illustrations. (Chatto and Windus, 1879.) [Vol. i. pp. xvi. 428; vol. ii. pp. xii. 472.]

This book, considered in the light of a great collection from all parts of the world of faiths, beliefs, and superstitions connected with demons, devils, and the like, must be very welcome to the student of folk-lore. Mr. Conway had prepared himself for the task by gradual approaches to his subject, only towards the last fully realizing how much there was to collect and how much there was to say about his collection. He placed himself outside all such faiths and beliefs before he began to comment upon them and study them, and this position, in one sense greatly enhances the value of his work.

The book is divided into four parts. The first part, entitled "Demonolatry," treats of the genesis of demons, and points out the difference between demon and devil. We then have a chapter on the degradation of deities which is indicated in their names and in still-existing legends of their fall ; and here is quoted the familiar tradition of Wayland the Smith, who in Scott's romance is a mere impostor, though the character to which he makes pretence belongs to the genuine Teutonic legend. Deities became degraded also and demonized by conquest—the conquering people adopting the deities of the conquered as demons.

In the next part, devoted to "the Demon," we have a classification of demons, which Mr. Conway arranges according to the evils which mankind has had to contend against in all ages. Thus then are demons of heat, cold, and the elements ; animal demons, indicating the animal power to harm mankind; man-demons from hostile tribes or countries ; demons of hunger and famine, darkness, disease, and death ; and demons arising from natural obstacles, such as mountains, rocks, &c., and from illusions, such as Will-o'-the-Wisp.

The third part treats of the decline of the demons and the rise of "the Dragon." This deals with dragon superstitions and traditions from all parts of the world, and the portions especially mentioning the dragons of Great Britain might be usefully compared with the chapter devoted to dragons in Mr. Henderson's *Folk-Lore of the Northern Counties*.

The fourth part, dealing with "the Devil," occupies the whole of the second volume. We have the devil distinguished from the dragon of the preceding part, and then the questions of new gods diabolized, Ahriman, the divine devil, Viswàmitra, the theocratic devil, paradise and the serpent, Adam and Eve, and the whole Hebrew traditions of the devil treated of at some length. Finally witchcraft and the legends of the Wild Huntsmen are brought to bear upon the question of devil-lore.

The book is illustrated throughout with many useful wood-cuts from sources not easily accessible, and there is a fairly good index. Although many of the theories and much of the comment with which Mr. Conway has surrounded his facts may not be acceptable to students, the book is a great storehouse of new facts and extensive researches, and altogether makes a valuable contribution to folk-lore material.

ii. *British Goblins: Welsh Folk-Lore, Fairy Mythology, Legends, and Traditions.* By Wirt Sikes. With Illustrations by T. H. Thomas. (London: Sampson Low and Co., 1880.) [1 vol. pp. xvi. 412.]

This work seeks to bring Welsh folk-lore within the reach of the student of comparative folk-lore. Now and again, indeed, the author himself turns aside to show some of the paths which lead from Welsh to comparative folk-lore; but, strictly speaking, his work deals with Welsh folk-lore only, and the collection now placed before the student is both useful and extensive. Mr. Sikes, the United States Consul, it appears, loves Wales and the Welsh sufficiently well to have devoted some of his time to wandering among "the people" and collecting their superstitions and their legends. He divides his work into four books: Book I. The Realm of Facrie. II. The Spirit World. III. Quaint Old Customs. IV. Bells, Wells, Stones, and Dragons.

As the arrangement of materials for folk-lore books has now become so clearly a matter of concern to the student, it is well to notice how Mr. Wirt Sikes deals with his material. "The fairies of Wales," he says, "may be divided into five classes, if analogy be not too sharply insisted on. Thus we have: 1. The Ellyllon, or elves; 2. The Coblynau, or mine fairies; 3. The Bwbachod, or household fairies; 4. The Gwragedd Annwn, or fairies of the lakes and streams; and 5. The Gwyllion, or mountain fairies." Mr. Sikes proceeds to tell all he knows and has learnt about these fairies. In particular, he notes Shakespeare's peculiar knowledge of Welsh folk-lore in several instances.

The Welsh spirit-world is treated equally exhaustively as the realm of faerie. The phantoms are always picturesque, they are often ghostly; sometimes they are amusing to the point of risibility, but besides they are instructive to him whose purpose in studying is to know (p. 138). In treating of customs, says Mr. Sikes, no other classification is useful than their arrangement in orderly sequence in two divisions; first those which pertain to certain days and seasons; second, those relating to the most conspicuous events in common human life, courtship, marriage, and death (p. 252). Accordingly under this classification Welsh quaint old customs are arranged. The plan cannot, perhaps, be objected to as it follows that adopted by most authors dealing with customs and superstitions ; and therefore becomes more ready for comparison with the customs of other places. But the time has certainly come when the whole subject of arrangement and classification must be discussed and settled upon a properly ascertained basis.

Among the most curious of Welsh wedding customs is that of horse-weddings, a relic of the bride-lifting of primitive man. But in attempting to explain the origin of this Mr. Sikes altogether misses its importance when he refers the Welsh survival to a Roman origin suggested by the well-known Rape of the Sabines. The Welsh horse-wedding and the Roman Rape of the Sabines are more nearly connected than by the unwelcome origin of conqueror imposing upon conquered—the two customs belong to that primitive Aryan world from which Roman and Welsh alike came. The division devoted to bells, wells, stones, and dragons is valuable, as it brings together much useful information not otherwise procurable. If Mr. Sikes, however, had dived a little deeper into primitive life, he would have found other theories for the origin of many of these customs than those advanced. The stone chair, mentioned in page 362, for instance, should have been compared with that engraved by Mr. Stuart in *Proceedings of the Society of Antiquaries of Scotland,* and referred to a very primitive political custom—all the more valuable now because the Scotch instance has found a parallel from Wales.

iii. *Folk-Lore : or Superstitious Beliefs in the West of Scotland within this Century.* By James Napier, F.R.S.E. F.C.S. &c. (Paisley : Alex. Gardner, 1879) [1 vol. pp. vii. 190.]

Mr. Napier gives an interesting account of " some of those superstitions now either dead or in their decadence, but which, within the memory of persons now living, had a vigorous existence in the west of Scotland." His book is the more valuable that it is not a compilation merely, but the result of personal observation and intercourse for the past sixty years with friends and neighbours. These beliefs and observances he has compared, in many instances, with those of other parts

of Scotland and other countries generally, and he has endeavoured to
trace their origin and development from Pagan to Protestant times·
The work comprises chapters on Birth and Childhood, Marriage,
Death, Witchcraft, Second Sight and the Black Art, Charms, Divi-
ning, Superstitions relating to animals and plants.   There is also an
Appendix on the different festivals, showing the probable relation of
the modern feast-day to ancient sun and fire worship as exemplified by
the Yule and Beltane festivities.   The chapter on marriage gives some
interesting particulars of that ceremony, and that on charms and
counter-charms is equally valuable.   The book is clearly written,
and there is also the advantage of a good index.

(2) BY NON-MEMBERS OF THE SOCIETY.

i. *Folk-Lore Journal.* Edited by the Working Committee of the South
   African Folk-Lore Society. Vol. I.; parts i. ii. iii. iv. January
   to July, 1879; pp. iv. 97. (Cape Town: Darter Brothers and
   Walton. London: David Nutt.)

In the first volume of the *Folk-Lore Record* it was announced that
Miss Lloyd would probably start a periodical devoted to Bushman,
Hottentot, and Kaffir Folk-Lore.   This plan has now happily been
carried out under the auspices of a newly formed " South African
Folk-Lore Society."   Four parts of the first volume of the *Folk-Lore
Journal*, as the periodical.has been christened, have been printed, and
these parts contain some very valuable materials.   There are ten
folk-tales, namely, " The Story of Long Snake," giving some important details of the Kaffir manners of courtship ; " The Lion and
the Ostrich," a piece of native literature in Setshuâna ; A " Nursery
Tale" of the Batlaku tribe, a version of a frequently repeated tale
in which a bird comes to the assistance of children whose lives are
endangered by the attack of one or more cannibals; " Ulusanana,"
a boy deliverer, about whom no other stories are known ; "Story of
Little Red Stomach," who is swallowed by an animal (which usually
lives in water) and who survives and lives for an indefinite time afterwards; " Story of Five Heads," when the hero, a snake, is married to a
young girl, thereby giving some marriage customs; "The story of a

Dam " from the Hottentots; " The Romance of Unyengebule;" " News from Zululand," a legend believed to refer to the event which took place on 22 Jan. 1879, a few miles from Rorke's Drift; and " The Story of Ngaugezwe and Mnyamana," one of the many stories to be met with all over the world, relating the jealousy of a stepbrother and step-mother of a king's eldest son and the ultimate triumph of the hero.

Besides these there are some contributions to the customs and superstitions of South Africa. It was always reported that the Basuto had no gods, but from a remarkable passage in the diary of a Berlin missionary this is shown to be an error. The " customs and superstitions among the Betshuâna " are detailed, and an account is given of the curious ceremony of Dipheku, a kind of yearly sacrifice which is intended to protect the tribe from all the ills which might befall it during the year. One part is specially devoted to some of the customs of the Ovahereró, and we have a valuable collection relating to customs at birth, circumcision, filing of the teeth, shaving of the head, fasten-ing of the false hair, betrothal, marriage, death, burial, sacrifice of the deceased, customs performed at graves, and resurrection.

Considering the many difficulties which attend the production of these journals—difficulties which begin with the first great essential, namely, the want of means for printing, the South African Folk-Lore Society is to be congratulated upon its success and thanked for its endeavours. Communications from the lips of the aborigines, written down in their own language and words, and accompanied by a trans-lation in English, must be of enormous value to the students of comparative folk-lore, for the benefit of whose branch of science, says the preface to the first part, the journal is chiefly intended.*

ii. *Old Celtic Romances.* Translated from the Gaelic. By P. W. Joyce, LL.D., T.C.D., M.R.I.A. (London : C. Kegan Paul and Co. 1879.) [1 vol. pp. xx. 420.]

In the preface to this most interesting collection of folk-tales, Dr. Joyce has done what all collectors should do if they want their works

* Members of the Society desirous of subscribing for the *South African Folk-Lore Journal* should communicate with Mr. Nutt, 270, Strand.

to find a place in the student's library as well as in the nursery—he has explained at length the sources from which his materials have been obtained. Thus the eleven tales here given to the public, practically for the first time, are selected and translated from the manuscripts of Trinity College and of the Royal Irish Academy. These old manuscripts represent the link, and a most important one too, be it observed, between the original professional storyteller and the literary reproduction of modern times. They are older than the printing era and not so old as the traditional story-telling era; and a careful comparison and collation of different MSS. is a work to be welcomed most highly by folk-lore students. It settles at once any question of literary adaptation from one country to another. Is Dr. Joyce quite right, however, in saying that this book is "the first collection of the old Gaelic prose romances that has ever been published in fair English translation?" For there exists a little volume, not too extensively known, it is true, but still fully recognised by students of folk-tales, namely, Patrick Kennedy's *Fire-Side Stories of Ireland*.

Dr. Joyce gives the following stories:—"The Fate of the Children of Lir, or the Four White Swans;" "The Fate of the Children of Turenn, or the Quest for the Eric-Fine;" "The overflowing of Lough Neagh, and the Story of Liban the Mermaid;" "Connla of the Golden Hair and the Fairy Maiden;" "The Voyage of Maildun;" "The Fairy Palace of the Quicken Trees;" "The Pursuit of the Gilla Dacker and his Horse;" "The Pursuit of Dermat and Grania;" "The Chase of Slieve Cullinn;" "The Chase of Slieve Fuad;" and "Oisin in Tirnanoge, or the Last of the Feni." These stories do not, perhaps, lead so thoroughly into the realms of comparative folk-lore as the generality of the folk-tales, being chiefly derived from quasi-historical personages of ancient Ireland. But the work of comparison must be accomplished before absolutely saying that the form of these stories is not older than ancient Erin. They most undoubtedly contain an old stratum of the primitive folk-tale—the talking pony, the transformation of children into swans, the magic clue of thread, and other characteristics being specially noticeable. As they stand, also, they afford many glimpses into archaic life and manners. There is that fairy-land so common to all branches of popular mythology; there are descriptions of some very primitive political institutions—some old meeting-places and popular assemblies for example; there is the prevalence of the most favourite amusement of the ancient Irish chiefs, the game of chess (already noticed in the story of Conn-eda, *ante*, page 184), and many other glimpses into primitive life which cannot now be mentioned. Dr. Joyce has also added a list of proper names, with their original Gaelic forms and their meanings, to make the whole work a most acceptable addition to folk-lore libraries.

iii. *Popular Romances of the Middle Ages.* By Sir George W. Cox, M.A., Bart., and Eustace Hinton Jones. Second edition. (C. Kegan Paul and Co. 1880.) [1 vol. pp. viii. 514.]

The re-appearance of this old favourite is sure to be welcomed. What has been said, however, in the previous notice relative to the necessity of collating all the old manuscripts of popular romances, is all the more applicable in the present case. One of the most fitting tasks for members of the Society to work upon would be to take Sir George Cox's book in hand and thoroughly examine the literary sources of his collection, both English and foreign. The result of such an examination would give a bibliographical study of great value. There are no hints upon this subject in the preface to this volume, such as were so gladly welcomed in Dr. Joyce's *Old Celtic Romances.* We are only told that "the tales are partly found in books not easily accessible;" but what should be made known to the student of folk-lore is—what are the books here mentioned; where are they to be found; and from what sources were they printed.

For mediæval romances have their special folk-lore value, as well as the early tales. They frequently contain many important survivals of olden-time institutions and customs, and often themselves can be traced to an olden-time original. The story of Sir Tristrem, for example, has been thus traced by Dr. Edward Tyrrel Leith in the *Journal of the Bombay Branch of the Royal Asiatic Society* (see vol. ix. pp. 101-133), perhaps not altogether satisfactorily, but still with sufficient skill and learning to make one thankful for the attempt and its result. And again the mediæval romance has the same sort of career as the primitive folk-tale. It lives not by the influence of literature, but by the influence of popular appreciation. It grows up, may be, by accretion, each version gaining something more of the popular life, and now and again something of an old story that has thus lived to find a home under a mediæval hero instead of a mythological.

Sir George Cox's volume however contains, as is well known, other stories than those properly belonging to mediæval heroes. The stories of Beowulf, of the Volsungs, the Nibelung, and Burnt Njal are known to all students of early Teutonic and Scandinavian history. They were popular in the middle ages, as they are popular now, because they represented what was passed and gone.

iv. *Teutonic Mythology.* By Jacob Grimm. Translated from the fourth edition, with Notes and Appendix, by James Steven Stallybrass, vol. i. pp. viii. 437. (W. Swan, Sonnenschein, and Allen, 1880).

Remembering most vividly the delight with which, more than forty years ago, we cut the leaves and worked our way, as well as we could, through the first edition of Grimm's *Deutsche Mythologie*, those who will make their first acquaintance with this treasure-house of folk-lore, through the English version of it by Mr. Stallybrass, of which the first volume is now issued, are almost to be envied their pleasure. It will be in three volumes, like the fourth edition of the original, of which the last volume has not been issued many months. Upon the death of Jacob Grimm, the superintendence of this fourth edition was entrusted by his family to Professor E. H. Meyer, of Berlin, who has included in it such additional matter as the author had collected in his Note Books for future use. We are glad to see, too, that the Appendix, consisting of a short treatise on the *Anglo-Saxon Genealogies* and the collection of *Superstitions* of the Teutonic nations, which formed so marked a feature in the first edition, will be included in this; for the satisfaction with which we received the second edition and found the text enlarged from 680 to just upon 1,200 pages was diminished when we missed the Appendix, which Mr.

Stallybrass is in error in supposing did appear in such second edition. The translator in his short and intelligent preface announces two or three modifications in the arrangement of the book, which will we have no doubt meet the approval of English readers—two will certainly do so, namely, the addition of a full classified Bibliography, and an accurate and detailed index to the whole work. Though the 42 columns of index to the 1835 edition have in the fourth edition been extended to 64, it has no claim to be considered a "detailed" index.

The work is fittingly dedicated to Professor Max Müller, who, when the Society first thought of undertaking the translation, took so much interest in the good work as to promise a translation of some of the chapters himself, even though his labours in other fields were so great.*

v. *Basque Legends:* Collected, chiefly in the Labourd, by Rev. Wentworth Webster, M.A. With an Essay on *The Basque Language*, by M. Julian Vinson. Together with Appendix: *Basque Poetry*. Second edition. (London: Griffith and Farran, 1879.) [1 vol. pp. xvi. 276.]

This second edition was much wanted, and besides the original material in the first edition an appendix has been added upon Basque Poetry. Everything in connection with the Basques is most valuable to the student of primitive man. Almost alone among European people, they represent in language and customs a period of European history which is far behind the literary era. These legends have been collected from those who knew the Basque language only, and the author has compared some of them to stories in Miss Frere's *Old Deccan Days*, Campbell's *Popular Tales of the West Highlands*, and other well-known works. But the work of comparison could be very easily extended and indeed ought to be done thoroughly with all these collections of primitive world lore. Turning to Patrick Kennedy's

---

* It should be remembered that the publishers, Mr. Sonnenschein being a member of the Society, kindly consented to allow members of the Society to purchase this book at ten shillings instead of twelve, the ordinary publishing price.

Fireside Stories of Ireland, for instance, there is "The Lazy Beauty"
on all fours with "The Pretty but idle Girl" of the Basque, and a
tale in the Chapbook *Hibernian Tales*, "The Farmer and his Ser-
vant," quadrates with "The Three Brothers, the Cruel Master and
Matron." The story of Peau d'Âne, too, is here. But, besides the
materials for comparison, there are the materials for tracing out survivals of archaic life and institutions in these Basque legends. The
book is, however, already too well known to need any further comment.

We have been favoured by Dr. Liebrecht with some observations
upon our Society and its first publication, which are to the following
effect :—

"We see from the list of members that the Folk-Lore Society includes a goodly show of English *literati* of note. We have a right,
therefore, to assume that, if the participation of the members be something more than the payment of their subscriptions, the Society will
eventually take up an important position in this department of
literature.

"The first volume opens with 'Some West Sussex Superstitions.'
Amongst the superstitious notions there mentioned very many are
known elsewhere, as well as in other provinces of England. It is of
importance, however, to note the differences which appear in their
separate versions. As Mrs. Latham does not enter into any comparisons with the superstitions existing in other countries, we will
adduce some of these resemblances :—In regard to the magpie (18),
there is still a magpie cultus in Porton, where it is usual to tie a
bunch of heather or laurel upon the top of a high tree 'to honour the
magpie,' because the bird by its cry warns the inhabitants of the
approach of the wolf. To kill a magpie brings great misfortune.
This must have reference to its sanctity; in other words, its divinity.
Other magpie beliefs from Norway are given in my recent book, *Zur
volkskunde*. The egg superstition (23) is found in Germany, Holland, and Portugal. To rock an empty cradle (35) is in many
places forbidden, even in China, but different reasons are assigned.

(69.) Of a peasant who had murdered his wife, it is said in a Swedish tale that he was turned into a cuckoo by our Lord as he was once walking about with S. Peter, and to the present day he retains his murderous nature. (83.) Lucretius gives another reason (4, 986). (85) is also a Swedish and Irish superstition. (103.) Compare Wuttke, *Der deutsche volksaberglaube.* (115.) Thorburn (*Bannu, or our Afghan Frontier*) heard the mother of a child who had quinsy say, ' I'll go out on the road to-morrow, and ask the first horseman I see riding a grey horse what remedy to apply, and whatever he says I'll do.' (127.) A prayer against toothache. A similar prayer is found in Wuttke from Westphalia and in Liège. (128.) This refers to a symbolical new birth. (See my observations on ' Gervase of Tilbury,' and in *Zur volkskunde.*) (140, 141.) These are founded on the great homœopathic idea that what hurts also cures (see *Zur volkskunde*). (193.) This is also a Norwegian superstition (see *Zur volkskunde*), according to which even the hens have a so-called ' unrest feather' on their body. (194.) The idea lying at the bottom of these superstitions I have discussed in the *Zur volkskunde.* (195.) This belief is found elsewhere (see Grimm's *Deutsche Myth.* &c. &c.) Notes on Folk Tales—This essay is in the highest degree worth reading. The tale of ' Susa No and the Oroche ' (Some Japan Folk Tales) is found in Campbell's *Circular Notes.* A folk-tale of the Hidatsa Indians—see my *Zur volkskunde* (Three Souls.) Mr. Thoms's paper—the third point (Saint Peter's Sextus) remains unexplained. Plant-Lore Notes, No. 64; the warning against nutting is in other countries more explicitly given, as it is meant against levity of conduct, for which the nutting season gave occasion. Divination by the Blade-bone—to the authorities add Tylor's *Primitive Culture*, Grimm's *Deutsche Mythologie*, Giraldus Cambrensis, *Itin. Cambriæ*, Capt. Raverty's *Selections of the Poetry of the Afghans*, Jaubert's *Idrisi.* Some Italian Folk-Lore—in Campbell's *Tales of the Highlands*, the slipper is of glass. The Merry Dun of Dover—the author's query is answered by reference to Müllenhof's '*Sagen, &c. aus Schleswig-holstein und Lauenberg*,' No. 323; the very same incident occurs in a story there given."

Mr. James Britten, F.L.S. is carrying out his intention of indexing the Folk-Lore contributions to *Notes and Queries*, and the Rev. Charles Swainson has kindly promised to assist in the work.

Mr. C. Pfoundes, a member of the Society, is preparing a volume on *The Folk-Lore of Old Japan: a Budget of Notes about Nipon*, which Messrs. Griffith and Farran will publish at an early date. Mr. Pfoundes has resided for over twelve years with the Japanese people, and has lived the native life amongst the intelligent better class in that country. Adopting that which is best in the classifications of the leading folk-lore authorities, Mr. Pfoundes does not profess to make an exhaustive collection, but simply to give under each heading the most characteristic illustrations derived from the native literature.

Mr. Robert Charles Hope, a member of the Society, is going to publish by private subscription a reprint of *The Popish Kingdome: or, Reigne of Antichrist, written in Latin verse by Thomas Naogeorgus, and englyshed by Barnabe Googe*. 1570. Of this exceedingly rare and curious work only one perfect copy is known to exist, viz. that in the Cambridge University Library, from which this reprint is taken. To the student of philology and folk-lore this work is invaluable. Both Brand and Hone quote largely from it, and the account which it contains of popular and other superstitions, particularly those relating to saints' days, is unusually interesting. Intending subscribers should address Mr. Hope, at Albion Crescent Villa, Scarborough.

Mr. Furnivall has reprinted book iv. of *The Popish Kingdome* as an appendix to one of his publications for the New Shakspere Society.

The Devonshire Association for the Advancement of Science, &c. has appointed a committee, consisting of Mr. P. F. S. Amery, Mr. G. Doe, Mr. R. Dymond, Rev. W. Harpley, Mr. P. O. Karkeek, and Mr. J. Brooking Rowe, for the purpose of collecting notes on Devonshire Folk-Lore. Four Reports have already been issued.

Messrs. W. Satchell, Peyton, and Co. are publishing a volume of Tuscan Tales collected from the peasantry.

Mr. Whitley Stokes has recently printed at Calcutta, for private circulation, a volume of *Indian Fairy Tales*, containing thirty stories, the greater part of which were told in Hindústání by native servants to his daughter, Miss M. S. H. Stokes, and afterwards written down in English by that very young lady, and excellently annotated by the late Mrs. Stokes. The book, which is full of instruction as well as interest, will probably be published here before long, edited, with a prefatory essay on the connection of Indian with European folk-tales, by Mr. W. R. S. Ralston. It is to be hoped also that Mr. Murray will soon publish a new edition of Miss Frere's *Old Deccan Days*, that delightful work being now out of print.—*Athenæum*.

The Council have decided to issue *The Folk-Lore Record* in future in two half-yearly parts instead of a yearly volume. They think that as this publication is the chief means of intercommunication between members, and will contain some of the papers read at the Evening Meetings, current news on folk-lore, notes, queries, and general announcements, the new plan will be found more acceptable to the members than the present method. The parts will be issued in paper covers.

By the wish of many members, the Council have arranged for four meetings of the Society for the reading and discussion of papers, to be held at the rooms of the Royal Asiatic Society, 22, Albemarle Street, at eight o'clock, on Tuesday, 9th December, 1879 ; Tuesday, 10th February, 1880; Tuesday, 9th March, 1880; and Tuesday, 13th April, 1880. The paper read on Tuesday, the 9th December, was " Catskin, the English and Irish Peau d'Âne," by Henry Charles Coote, Esq. F.S.A.; and papers for the other meetings will be duly announced. Members may introduce, personally or by card, non-members of the Society to the above meetings.

The publication for the year 1878 was—

THE FOLK-LORE RECORD, Part I.

CONTAINING

Some West Sussex Superstitions lingering in 1868. By Mrs. Latham.
Miscellaneous:—

Notes on Folk-Tales. By W. R. S. Ralston, M.A.
The Folk-Lore of France. By A. Lang, M.A.
Some Japan Folk-Tales. By C. Pfoundes.
A Folk-Tale and various superstitions of the Hidatsa Indians. Communicated by Dr. E. B. Tylor.
Chaucer's Night-Spell. By William J. Thoms, F.S.A.
Plant-Lore Notes to Mrs. Latham's West Sussex Superstitions. By James Britten, F.L.S.

Yorkshire Local Rhymes and Sayings.

Divination by the Blade-bone. By William J. Thoms, F.S.A.

Index to the Folk-Lore in the First Series of Hardwicke's "Science-Gossip." By James Britten, F.L.S.

Some Italian Folk-Lore. By Henry Charles Coote, F.S.A.

Wart and Wen Cures. By James Hardy.

Fairies at Ilkley Wells. By Charles C. Smith.

Notes, Queries, Notices and News.

The issues for 1879 are—

Notes on the Folk-Lore of the Northern Counties of England and the Borders. By William Henderson. A new edition with considerable additions by the Author. (Published for the Society at 12s. by Messrs. W. Satchell, Peyton, and Co. Tavistock Street, Covent Garden.)

Aubrey's Remains of Gentilisme and Judaisme, with the additions by Dr. White Kennet. Edited by James Britten, F.L.S.

The Folk-Lore Record, vol. ii. (with the Annual Report for 1878).

The issues for 1880 will be selected from the following (all of which are advanced):—

The Denham Tracts. To be edited by James Hardy.

Folk-Lore and Provincial Names of British Birds. By the Reverend Charles Swainson.

Notes on the Folk-Lore of the North-East of Scotland. By the Reverend Walter Gregor.

Together with—

The Folk-Lore Record, vol. iii. (in two half-yearly parts).

Other works are in active preparation. They include the following:—

The Bibliography of Folk-Lore. Compiled and edited by Thomas Satchell.

Excerpts from two Early-English Folk-Lorists.

Notes for a History of English Chapbooks and Penny Histories.

East Sussex Superstitions. By the Reverend W. D. Parish.

Folk-Medicine. By William George Black.

The Merry Tales of the Wise Men of Gotham. To be edited, with illustrative Notes and an Introductory Essay on English Noodledom, by William J. Thoms, F.S.A.

The Folk-Lore of Lincolnshire. By Edward Peacock, F.S.A.

The Folk-Lore contained in the Gentleman's Magazine. By G. Laurence Gomme, F.S.A.

Index to the Folk-Lore in "Notes and Queries." By James Britten, F.L.S.

On Madagascar Folk-Lore. By the Reverend J. Sibree.

British Fairies.

The Folk-Lore contained in the Statistical Accounts of Scotland.

INDEX TO VOLS. I. AND II.

The Folk-Lore Society.

FIRST ANNUAL REPORT OF THE COUNCIL,
29 MAY, 1879.

IN presenting the First Annual Report to the Members of the Society, the Council think they have great reason for congratulation upon the very general welcome that has been afforded to the undertaking, both by the general public and the press. The formation of the Society, first proposed in *Notes and Queries*, was supported by other literary journals, and from the commencement a steady increase in the number of Members has been made. The preliminary list contained 129 names; in December, 1878, the number was 180, and at the present moment the roll shows over 220 Members.

The Council, convinced by the experience of the past year that the establishment of a Folk-Lore Society had become thoroughly necessary to the student-world, think it is not an inopportune moment to state shortly what special branches of knowledge seem to them to be embraced under the term " Folk-Lore."

The origin of the term " Folk-Lore " is no doubt pretty generally known, but the Council think that the First Report of the Society should contain a full reference to the source from which the term is derived. In *The Athenæum* of the 22nd August, 1846, the following letter was printed :—

August 12.

Your pages have so often given evidence of the interest which you take in what we in England designate as Popular Antiquities, or Popular Literature (though by-the-bye it is more a Lore than a Literature, and would be most aptly described by a good Saxon compound Folk-Lore—*the Lore of the People*)—that I am not without hopes of enlisting your aid in garnering the few ears which are remaining scattered over that field from which our forefathers might have gathered a goodly crop.

No one who has made the manners, customs, observances, superstitions, ballads, proverbs, &c. of the olden time his study, but must have arrived at two conclusions:—the first, how much that is curious and interesting in these matters is now entirely lost—the second, how much may yet be rescued by timely exertion. What Hone endeavoured to do in his "Every-day Book," &c. the *Athenæum*, by its wider circulation, may accomplish ten times more effectually—gather together the infinite number of minute facts, illustrative of the subject I have mentioned, which are scattered over the memories of its thousands of readers, and preserve them in its pages, until some James Grimm shall arise who shall do for the Mythology of the British Islands the good service which that profound antiquary and philologist has accomplished for the Mythology of Germany. The present century has scarcely produced a more remarkable book, imperfect as its learned author confesses it to be, than the second edition of the "*Deutsche Mythologie;*" and what is it?—a mass of minute facts, many of which, when separately considered, appear trifling and insignificant—but, when taken in connexion with the system into which his master-mind has woven them, assume a value that he who first recorded them never dreamed of attributing to them.

How many such facts would one word from you evoke, from the north and from the south—from John O'Groat's to the Land's End! How many readers would be glad to show their gratitude for the novelties which you, from week to week, communicate to them, by forwarding to you some record of old Time—some recollection of a now neglected custom—some fading legend, local tradition, or fragmentary ballad!

Nor would such communications be of service to the English antiquary alone. The connexion between the FOLK-LORE of England (remember, I claim the honour of introducing the epithet Folk-Lore, as Disraeli does of introducing Father-Land, into the Literature of this country) and that of Germany is so intimate that such communication will probably serve to enrich some future edition of Grimm's Mythology.

Let me give you an instance of this connexion.—In one of the chapters of Grimm, he treats very fully of the parts which the Cuckoo plays in Popular Mythology—of the prophetic character with which it has been invested by the voice of the people; and gives many instances of the practice of deriving predictions from the number of times which its song is heard. He also records a popular notion "that the Cuckoo never sings till he has thrice eaten his fill of cherries." Now I have lately been informed of a custom which formerly obtained among children in Yorkshire, that illustrates the fact of a connexion between the Cuckoo and the Cherry,—and that, too, in their prophetic attributes. A friend has communicated to me that children in Yorkshire were formerly (and may be still) accustomed to sing round a cherry-tree the following invocation:—

> Cuckoo, cherry-tree,
> Come down and tell me
> How many years I have to live.

Each child then shook the tree,—and the number of cherries which fell betokened the years of its future life.

The Nursery Rhyme which I have quoted is, I am aware, well known. But the manner in which it was applied is not recorded by Hone, Brande, or Ellis;—and is one of those facts which, trifling in themselves, become of importance when they form links in a great chain—one of those facts which a word from the *Athenæum* would gather in abundance for the use of future inquirers into that interesting branch of literary antiquities—our Folk Lore.

AMBROSE MERTON.

P.S.—It is only honest that I should tell you I have long been contemplating a work upon our *Folk-Lore* (under *that title*, mind Messrs. A. B. and C., so do not try to forestall me);—and I am personally interested in the success of the experiment which I have in this letter, albeit imperfectly, urged you to undertake.

The suggestion thus made met with the kindly and cordial support of the Editor of the *Athenæum*, Mr. Dilke. It was followed up a fortnight later by a second letter from "Ambrose Merton," suggesting special subjects of inquiry, such as elves, fairies, pixies, headless steeds, howdening, the barguest, local feasts, &c., and led to a large number of very interesting letters, which are to be found in the subsequent numbers of the *Athenæum*. A generation has almost passed away since "Ambrose Merton" wrote this letter—it is now one of the records of past literary history—yet perhaps there are but few members of the Folk-Lore Society who do not know that under that name its valued Director, Mr. Thoms, first publicly proposed the collection of Folk-Lore, which after thirty-two years he has seen practically carried out by the establishment of the Society.

Since the time when it was first introduced the term Folk-Lore has found favour both with the antiquary and the scientist. It is now duly incorporated in English dictionaries, and has also extended beyond English-speaking countries, having been adopted in Germany.

It is more difficult to explain what branches of knowledge are properly understood to be included under this generic title. The study of Folk-Lore has been extended far beyond the original conception. Stated broadly, it may be said to stand towards the history of a people in a position exactly corresponding to that in which the famous " unwritten law" stands towards statute law—and may be defined as unwritten history. Moreover it is the unwritten history of primitive times. During the development of civilised life many of the old manners, customs, observances, and ceremonies of olden times are, as it were, thrown off by the leading sections of society, and they gradually become the superstition and traditions of the lower classes. Again, many of the deeds of warlike men or of local heroes and heroines are told and retold to those whose kith and kin or whose local habitation give more than a passing interest to the subject, and thus is formed the legendary ballad or tale and the proverb. Lastly, when the household god and the tribal or national mythology gave way to the influences of Christianity, the old religion was not entirely eradicated from the memory or the associations of the people; it survived in the nursery tale and in the surperstitious reverence for certain rites and ceremonies.

Thus, Folk-Lore may be said to include all the " culture " of the people which has not been worked into the official religion and history, but which is and has always been of self growth. It represents itself in civilised history by strange and uncouth customs; superstitious associations with animals, birds, flowers, trees, and topographical objects, and with the events of human life; the belief in witchcraft, fairies, and spirits; the traditional ballads and proverbial sayings incident to particular localities; the retention of popular names for hills, streams, caverns, springs, tumuli, fountains, fields, trees, &c., and all such out-of-the-way lore. In savage life all these things are extant, not as survivals but as actual portions of the prevalent state of society. The Folk-Lore survivals of civilization and the Folk-Lore status of savage tribes both, therefore, belong to the primitive history of mankind; and in collecting and printing these relics of one epoch, from two such widely different sources, the Folk-Lore Society will produce that necessary comparison and illustration which is of so much service to the anthropologist.

It should be pointed out, however, that the main work of the Society belongs essentially to the department of *collecting materials*. The equally important work of illustrating these collections, of placing them rightly in the scientific divisions of human history, can only be a subsequent work.

In the first prospectus issued by the Council the following divisions were made in the scope of the Society's labours :—

1. The reprinting of scarce books or articles on English Folk-Lore, and the collection and printing of scattered materials now existing in English olden-time literature.
2. The publication of original communications on Folk-Lore.
3. The printing of accounts of Folk-Lore of the Colonies and of foreign countries.
4. The collection and printing of the Folk-Lore of savage tribes.

The Council, keeping these objects steadily in view, have established the "Folk-Lore Record," for the purpose of publishing all papers and contributions not suitable for various reasons (such as length, &c.) for separate publication; and they think this volume, together with the list of proposed subjects already in preparation for publication, will be found to cover some portion of the ground over which their labours extend.

The publication for the year 1878 was—

THE FOLK-LORE RECORD, Part I.

CONTAINING

Some West Sussex Superstitions lingering in 1868. By Mrs. Latham.
Miscellaneous:—
 Notes on Folk-Tales. By W. R. S. Ralston, M.A.
 The Folk-Lore of France. By A. Lang, M.A.
 Some Japan Folk-Tales. By C. Pfoundes.
 A Folk-Tale and various superstitions of the Hidatsa Indians. Communicated by Dr. E. B. Tylor.
 Chaucer's Night-Spell. By William J. Thoms, F.S.A.
 Plant-Lore Notes to Mrs. Latham's West Sussex Superstitions. By James Britten, F.L.S.
 Yorkshire Local Rhymes and Sayings.
 Divination by the Blade-bone. By William J. Thoms, F.S.A.
 Index to the Folk-Lore in the First Series of Hardwicke's "Science-Gossip." By James Britten, F.L.S.
 Some Italian Folk-Lore. By Henry Charles Coote, F.S.A.
 Wart and Wen Cures. By James Hardy.
 Fairies at Ilkley Wells. By Charles C. Smith.
  Notes.   Queries.   Notices and News.

The difficulties in obtaining anything like a complete collection of Folk-Lore during the first year were necessarily very great, and the Society is much indebted to the Rev. W. D. Parish for so valuable a contribution as the West Sussex superstitions of Mrs. Latham, whose work had been the collection of many years.

The Council feel grateful for the very ready acknowledgment of approval which this volume has received from almost all quarters. They might have met the wishes of some Members who had expected a larger volume if they had adopted a plan, which in their opinion is not an advisable one, namely, to mortgage the future income of the Society. But they feel sure that when the Members see from the Auditors' statement that not only has the Society been able to meet all the preliminary expenses, but all the expenses of the first publication, out of the income of the first year, they will feel perfectly satisfied with the judgment of the Council in this matter.

The Folk-Lore Record will as far as possible be issued annually and be considered essentially the *Members' volume.* Although the Council have decided not to restrict in all cases the issue of their publications to the Members of the Society only, they think that it will be on all hands advisable to keep the " Record " as the Member's volume, and not to offer it to the public.

The issues for 1879 will be—

Notes on the Folk-Lore of the Northern Counties of England and the Borders. By William Henderson. A new edition with considerable additions by the Author.

Aubrey's Remains of Gentilisme and Judaisme, with the additions by Dr. White Kennet. To be edited by James Britten, F.L.S.

The Folk-Lore Record, Part II.

The Council received a most generous proposal from Mr. Henderson with reference to the re-issue of his valuable work. It is not necessary to state here the detail of these proposals, but the practical effect is that the Council are enabled to issue this volume to every Member of the Society, and in all probability will reap a substantial pecuniary benefit besides.

The new edition will contain many important additions, collected by the author since the first edition was published, and a very carefully compiled index has been prepared by Mr. Thomas Satchell. The Council have decided to offer this work for sale to the public at a price exceeding the proportion subscribed by Members, and they have appointed Messrs. W. Satchell, Peyton, and Co. publishers to the Society for this purpose.

Members should forward to the Honorary Secretary, as early as possible, papers intended for the *Folk-Lore Record, Part II.* Every paper is submitted to a reading committee of the Council.

The following papers have been accepted :—

The Néo-Latin Fay. By Henry Charles Coote, F.S.A.
Malagasy Folk-Lore and Popular Superstitions. By the Reverend J. Sibree, Jun.
The Folk-Lore of Modern Greece. By A. Lang, M.A.
The Folk-Lore of Chaucer. By the Reverend F. G. Fleay.

Other works are in active preparation. They include the following :—

Excerpts from two Early-English Folk-Lorists.
Notes for a History of English Chapbooks and Penny Histories.
East Sussex Superstitions. By the Reverend W. D. Parish.
Folk-Medicine. By William George Black.
Folk-Lore and Provincial Names of British Birds. By the Reverend Charles Swainson.
The Merry Tales of the Wise Men of Gotham. To be edited, with illustrative Notes and an Introductory Essay on English Noodledom, by William J. Thoms, F.S.A.
The Folk-Lore of Lincolnshire. By Edward Peacock, F.S.A.
The Folk-Lore contained in the Gentleman's Magazine. By G. Laurence Gomme, F.S.A.
The Denham Tracts. To be edited by James Hardy.
Notes on the Folk-Lore of the North-East of Scotland. By the Reverend Walter Gregor.
Index to the Folk-Lore in "Notes and Queries." By James Britten, F.L.S.
On Madagascar Folk-Lore. By the Reverend J. Sibree.

In April of last year it will be remembered that the Council prepared and issued forms for the compilation of a Bibliography of English Folk-Lore. But almost immediately a Member came forward and offered the use of his valuable collection, made for a bibliography of superstitions and religious belief, which was the result of many years' work, involving among other labours the complete perusal of the British Museum catalogues. Although this collection was only in part available for the Society's purposes, and did not cover all the ground which the Bibliography of Folk-Lore will occupy, the Council very thankfully accepted this offer, and they are able to announce as approaching completion

The Bibliography of Folk-Lore. Compiled and edited by Thomas Satchell.

The Council hope that the Members will always make a point of communicating to the Honorary Secretary any scraps, even the smallest, relating to Folk-Lore. Such scraps may not be used immediately on all occasions, but they will be classified and arranged for use when opportunity shall arise. As a parallel to this, Members who are engaged in making collections of any particular branch of Folk-Lore are invited to communicate with the Honorary Secretary, so that at the first opportunity their objects may be made known to the other Members, thereby creating co-operation in the work of the Society.

The following subjects may now be mentioned as coming under the latter requirements :—

1. Notes on Folk-Lore of Plants should be sent to Mr. James Britten, British Museum.

2. Notes on the Folk-Lore of Birds to the Rev. Charles Swainson, Rectory, Old Charlton, S.E.

3. Collections of Field Names and Legends connected therewith to the Hon. Secretary.

4. Popular names and legends applied to natural and artificial topographical objects such as Hills, Streams, Wells, Fountains, Tumuli, Trees, &c., to the Hon. Secretary.

5. Local Rhymes and Sayings to the Hon. Secretary.

6. Notes on Folk Medicine to Mr. W. G. Black, 1, Alfred Terrace, Hillhead, Glasgow.

7. Legends and superstitions connected with Wells and Fountains to Mr. Robert Charles Hope, Albion Crescent Villa, Scarborough.

It has been suggested that a Library of Folk-Lore books should be formed for the use of Members of the Society. The

Council would most gladly urge the adoption of this suggestion, but do not see their way clear, at present, to recommend the expenditure of any portion of the income of the Society for this object.

The Council early last year promulgated the following code of Rules which they recommend to the Members for confirmation:—

I. "The Folk-Lore Society" has for its object the preservation and publication of Popular Traditions, Legendary Ballads, Local Proverbial Sayings, Superstitions and Old Customs (British and Foreign), and all subjects relating to them.

II. The Society shall consist of Members being subscribers to its funds of One Guinea annually, payable in advance on the 1st of January in each year.

III. A Member of the Society may at any time compound for future annual subscriptions by payment of Ten Guineas over and above the subscription for the current year.

IV. An Annual General Meeting of the Society shall be held in London at such time and place as the Council from time to time appoint. No Member whose subscription is in arrear shall be entitled to vote or take part in the proceedings of the Meeting.

V. The affairs of the Society, including the admission of Members, shall be conducted by a President and a Council of twelve Members, who shall from among themselves elect a Director, Treasurer, and Secretary. The Council shall have power to fill up occasional vacancies in their number.

VI. At each Annual General Meeting all the Members of the Council shall retire from office, but shall be eligible for re-election.

VII. The accounts of the receipts and expenditure of the Society shall be audited annually by two Auditors, to be elected at the General Meeting.

VIII. Any Member who shall be one year in arrear of his subscription shall cease to be a Member of the Society.

IX. Every Member (whose subscription shall not be in arrear) shall be entitled to a copy of each of the ordinary works published by the Society.

X. No alteration shall be made in these rules except at a Special General Meeting of the Society, and upon the requisition of at least five Members, nor then unless at least one month's previous notice of the change to be proposed shall have been given in writing to the Secretary. The alteration proposed shall be approved by at least three-fourths of the Members present at such Meeting.

Signed by order of the Council,

VERULAM, *President.*

G. Laurence Gomme, *Hon. Secretary.*

THE FOLK-LORE SOCIETY.

TREASURER'S ACCOUNT OF RECEIPTS AND EXPENDITURE *for the year ending 31st December*, 1878.

RECEIPTS.

1878.		£	s.	d.
Jan. 1st to Dec. 31st	On account of Subscriptions due 1st January, 1878	121	7	9
	On account of Subscriptions due 1st January, 1879	5	5	0
	On account of Subscriptions due 1st January, 1880	1	1	0
		£127	13	9
1879.				
Jan. 1st	Balance at Bankers	95	18	9

EXPENDITURE.

1878.			£	s.	d.
Feb. 11.	Cheque-book		0	4	2
April 27.	Messrs. Nichols and Sons, General Printing		9	17	6
Oct. 18.	Mr. J. Cooper, engraving title-page block		1	10	0
Oct. 30.	Copying MS. at the British Museum ...		10	0	0
	Honorary Secretary for Postages, Stationery, Carriage, &c. as under:—				
	24 April	6 7 6			
	25 July	2 6 0			
	18 Oct.	1 9 10			
			10	3	4
Dec. 31.	Balance at Bankers		95	18	9
			£127	13	9

Examined and found correct, 15 May, 1879.

EDWARD HAILSTONE, } Auditors.
JOHN TOLHURST,

W. R. DRAKE, *Treasurer.*

STATEMENT OF THE AUDITORS.

WE, the Auditors appointed to examine the Accounts of the Folk-Lore Society, hereby certify that the Treasurer has produced to us the Bankers' pass-book and the accounts and vouchers for the year ending 31st December, 1878, and we also certify that the above statement of Receipts and Expenditure is correct. We have received a statement from the Honorary Secretary to the effect that a further sum of £73 10s. 0d. has been received during the present year on account of the subscriptions for 1878, and that the amount of the outstanding liabilities on 31st December, 1878, was £122 7s. 0d.

EDWARD HAILSTONE.
JOHN TOLHURST.

15 *May*, 1879.

ANNUAL MEETING.

The First Annual Meeting of the Folk-Lore Society was held on Thursday, 29th May, 1879, at the Rooms of the Royal Asiatic Society, 22, Albemarle Street, at 4 o'clock p.m.

The Earl of VERULAM, President, in the Chair.

The PRESIDENT opened the Meeting with a short address and moved the adoption of the Report of the Council.

The Secretary having read the Report,

Mr. W. J. THOMS seconded the motion of adoption, and pointed out that though the Report stated that the origin of the word Folk-lore was due to him, the origin of the Society was really due to the suggestion of a lady correspondent of *Notes and Queries*, whom he could not name beyond saying that she wrote under the signature of St. Swithin.

The Secretary then read the Treasurer's Account and the Statement of the Auditors.

It was proposed by General ALLAN, and seconded by Mr. A. NUTT, "That the account and statement be approved and adopted, and that the thanks of the Meeting be given to the Auditors and Treasurer."

The Secretary having read the names of the Members of the Council, it was moved by Mr. TOLHURST, and seconded, "That the Council for the past year be re-elected."

It was moved by Mr. HILL, and seconded, "That Mr. Edward Hailstone and Mr. John Tolhurst be the Auditors of the Society for the ensuing year."

It was proposed by Mr. SOLLY, and seconded by Mr. CHURCHILL, "That the thanks of the Meeting be given to Mr. William J. Thoms, F.S.A., for his services as Director."

It was proposed by Mr. CHURCHILL, and seconded by Mr. BRITTEN, "That the thanks of the Meeting be presented to Mr. Vaux, and the Royal Asiatic Society, for the privilege of meeting in their rooms."

The foregoing Resolutions were all carried unanimously.

It was proposed by Mr. W. R. S. RALSTON, seconded, and carried unanimously, "That this Meeting desires to express its best thanks to the Earl of Verulam for presiding at this—the first General Meeting of the Society."

Officers and Members of the Society.

PRESIDENT.
THE RIGHT HON. THE EARL OF VERULAM, F.R.G.S.

COUNCIL.

JAMES BRITTEN, F.L.S.	PROFESSOR MAX MÜLLER, M.A.
HENRY C. COOTE, F.S.A.	F. OUVRY, F.S.A.
SIR W. R. DRAKE, F.S.A.	W. R. S. RALSTON, M.A.
G. L. GOMME, F.S.A.	EDWARD SOLLY, F.R.S. F.S.A.
HENRY HILL, F.S.A.	WILLIAM J. THOMS, F.S.A.
A. LANG, M.A.	EDWARD B. TYLOR, LL.D.

DIRECTOR.—WILLIAM J. THOMS, F.S.A.

TREASURER.—SIR WILLIAM R. DRAKE, F.S.A.

HONORARY SECRETARY.—G. L. GOMME, F.S.A., Castelnau, Barnes, S.W.

AUDITORS.—E. HAILSTONE, ESQ. F.S.A.
JOHN TOLHURST, ESQ.

BANKERS.—UNION BANK OF LONDON, CHARING CROSS BRANCH,
to whom all Subscriptions should be paid.

MEMBERS.

George H. Adshead, Esq., 9, Strawberry Terrace, Pendleton.

Major-General Stuart Allan, F.S.A.Scot. Shene Lodge, Richmond.

George L. Apperson, Esq., The Common, Wimbledon.

The Society of Antiquaries, Burlington House, W.

Mrs. Arnott, 6, Freesland Road, Bromley, Kent.

Edward I. Aydon, Esq., St. John's Chambers, Grainger Street West, Newcastle-on-Tyne.

William E. A. Axon, Esq., Bank Cottage, Barton-on-Irwell.

James Backhouse, Esq., West Bank, York.

Jonathan E. Backhouse, Esq., Bank, Darlington.

J. E. Bailey, Esq., F.S.A., Egerton Villa, Stretford, Manchester.

James Bain, Esq., 1, Haymarket, S.W.

Alexander Baird, Esq., 251, Great Western Road, Glasgow.

J. Davies Barnett, Esq., 28, Victoria Street, Montreal, Canada.

J. Bawden, Esq., Kingston, Canada.

Charles H. Bayley, Esq., West Bromwich.

William Rutter Bayley, Esq., Cotford House, near Sidmouth, Devon.

The Earl Beauchamp, 13, Belgrave Square, S.W.

Miss Bell, Borovere, Alton, Hants.

Rev. H. J. Bigge, F.S.A., Stoke Albany House Market Harborough.

Isaac Binns, Esq., Batley, Yorkshire.

William George Black, Esq., 1, Alfred Terrace, Hillhead, Glasgow.

J. F. Boaler, Esq., Woodrhydding, Ilkey-in-Wharfdale, Yorkshire.

The Boston Athenæum, Boston, U.S.

H. Courthope Bowen, Esq., 49, Gloucester Place, Portman Square, W.

Rev. Henry U. Bradshaw, Morley Rectory, Derby.

Mrs. Woodhouse Braine, 56, Maddox Street, W.

James Britten, Esq., F.L.S., British Museum, W.C.

Percy W. Britton, Esq., 13, Park Square, Leeds.

William E. Brough, Esq., Leek, Staffordshire.

The Lord Brougham and Vaux.

Henry Thomas Brown, Esq., Chester.

M. Loys Bruèyre, 11, Rue de la Ville l'Evèque, Paris.

The Right Rev. Bishop Callaway, Caffraria, South Africa.

J. M. Campbell, Esq., Kelvin Grove, Glasgow.

Henry Campkin, Esq., F.S.A., Reform Club.

Rev. J. L. Carrick, Spring Hill, Southampton.

Rev. J. W. Cartmell, Christ's College, Cambridge.

William Chappell, Esq , F.S.A., Strafford Lodge, Oatlands Park, Weybridge.

H. B. Churchill, Esq., Weiland House, Reigate.

Rev. George Christian, Redgate, Uppingham.

Hyde Clarke, Esq., D.C.L., 32, St. George's Square, S.W.

Edward Clodd, Esq., Rosemount, Tufnell Park, N.

D. F. Cogan, Esq., Hibernian Bank, Swinford, Mayo.

John Collett, Esq., 12, Fopstone Road, Kensington, W.

J. Payne Collier, Esq., F.S.A., Riverside, Maidenhead.

The Library of Congress, Washington, U.S.

Moncure D. Conway, Esq., Hamlet House, Hammersmith.

Henry C. Coote, Esq., F.S.A., Walwyn House, Richmond Road, West Brompton

F. W. Cosens, Esq., F.S.A., 27, Queen's Gate, Kensington.

James Curtis, Esq., 12, Old Jewry Chambers, E.C.

Daniel Daulby, Esq., Biggleswade.

Hugh Welch Diamond, Esq., M.D., F.S.A., Twickenham House, Twickenham.

Thomas Dixon, Esq., 15, Sunderland Street, Sunderland.

James H. Dormer, Esq., 48, Devonshire Street, Queen's Square, W.C.

Sir William R. Drake, F.S.A., Oatlands Lodge, Weybridge (Treasurer).

J. Dalrymple Duncan, Esq., 225, West George Street, Glasgow.

John M. Dunn, Esq., F.R.G.S., 30, Claverton Street, St. George's Square, S.W.

E. D. Durrant, Esq., 90, High Street, Chelmsford.

Rev. T. F. Thiselton Dyer.

Charles W. Empson, Esq., 1, Southwood Terrace, Highgate, N.

John Evans, Esq., LL.D. F.R.S. V.P.S.A. Nash Mills, Hemel Hempstead, Herts.

J. T. Godfrey Fawssett, Esq., Lichfield.

John Fenton, Esq., Elm Tree House, Hampstead.

John George Fenwick, Esq., Moorlands, Newcastle-on-Tyne.

David Fitzgerald, Esq., 3, Porten Road, Hammersmith, W.

Rev. F. G. Fleay, 33, Avondale Square, S.E.

Augustus W. Franks, Esq., M.A., F.R.S., Dir.S.A.

Edwin Freshfield, Esq., F.S.A., 5, Bank Buildings, E.C.

William Garnett, Esq., Quernmore Park, Lancaster.

The Right Hon. W. E. Gladstone, M.P., Harley Street, W.

F. W. Goddard, Esq., Seymour Lodge, St. James's Road, Brixton.

Frederick J. Gomme, Esq.

G. L. Gomme, Esq., F.S.A., Castelnau, Barnes, S.W. (Hon. Secretary).

The University Library, Gottingen.

Thomas B. Green, Esq., Summerstown, Oxford.

Rev. Walter Gregor, Pitsligo, Fraserburgh, Aberdeenshire.

B. P. Grimsey, Esq., Stoke Lodge, Ipswich, Suffolk.

Rev. A. B. Grosart, LL.D. F.S.A., Park View, Blackburn, Lancashire.

Rev. T. R. Grundy, Elbury Lodge, Newton Abbot.

Arthur Gunn, Esq., Haverstock Hill, Hampstead.

Mrs. Gutch, Holgate Lodge, York.

Robert Guy, Esq., Ferncliff, Pollockshaws, near Glasgow.

Edward Hailstone, Esq., F.S.A., Walton Hall, Wakefield (Auditor).

John Hamer, Esq., Ladywell, Dartmouth Park Hill, N.

James Hardy, Esq., Oldcambus, Cockburnspath.

H. S. Harris, Esq., 26, Porchester Square, W.

Mrs. Harrison, Shirley House, The Avenue, Beckenham, Kent.

Fred. J. Harte, Esq., 3, Clifton Square, Lytham, Lancashire.

E. Sidney Hartland, Esq., 8, Brunswick Place, Swansea.

William Henderson, Esq., Ashford Court, Ludlow, Shropshire.

Henry Hill, Esq., F.S.A., 2, Curzon Street, Mayfair, W.

Robert Holland, Esq., Norton Hill, Runcorn, Cheshire.

Robert Charles Hope, Esq., Peterhouse, Cambridge.

J. Devenish Hoppus, Esq., Church Cottage, Woburn Sands, Bedfordshire.

David Howard, Esq., Rectory Manor, Walthamstow, E.

H. E. Hubbart, Esq., 6, Thurland Street, Nottingham.

Rev. Canon Hume, D.C.L., All Saints Vicarage, Liverpool.

A. Granger Hutt, Esq., 8, Oxford Road, Kilburn, N.W.

Rev. E. F. Drummond Hutton, D.D., St. Silas, Glasgow.

Count Takatsgu Irouyé, M.R.A.S., University College, Gower Street.

Francis W. Jackson, Esq., Botton Percy, Tadeaster.

Joseph J. Jenkins, Esq., 67, Hamilton Terrace, N.W.

Mrs. Jobling, 97, Rathgar Road, Dublin.

The John Hopkins University, Baltimore, U.S.

Joseph Jones, Esq., Abberley Hall, Stourport.

Rev. W. Rodwell Jones, Hanley, Oxfordshire.

G. H. Kinahan, Esq., Ovoca, Ireland.

Mrs. Henry Kingsley, Attrees, Cuckfield.

Alfred Kingston, Esq., Record Office, Fetter Lane.

John Kirsop, Esq., 6, Queen's Crescent, Glasgow.

C. J. Knight, Esq., F.S.A., York Terrace, Regent's Park.

Rev. W. S. Lach-Szyrma, M.A., St. Peter's Vicarage, Penzance.

Alexander Laing, Esq., LL.D., Newburgh-on-Tay, Scotland.

A. Lang, Esq., M.A., 1, Marloes Road, Kensington.

Henry C. Lea, Esq., 706, Sansom Street, Philadelphia.

F. de M. Leathes, Esq., 17, Tavistock Place, W.C.

Dr. Felix Liebrecht, Liège, Rue de Mouton Blanc 13.

Professor Lindsay, D.D., Free Church College, Glasgow.

John Lockett, Esq., Market Drayton.

The London Institution, Finsbury Circus.

The London Library, St. James' Square, S.W.

J. Long, Esq., 19, Adam Street, W.C.

Sir John Lubbock, High Elms, Beckenham, Kent.

J. W. MacCarthy, Esq., British Legation, Yedo, Japan.

Edgar MacCulloch, Esq., F.S.A., Guernsey.

John Machair, Esq., Moray Place, Edinburgh.

Alex. Mackay, Esq., Trowbridge, Wilts.

Rev. Clement W. Mackey, Alveley Vicarage, Bridgnorth.

William L. Mackie, Esq., 23, Yonge Park, Holloway, N.

Surgeon-General Mackinnon, 3, Camp Villas, Colchester.

William MacLennan, Esq., 317, Drummond Street, Montreal, Canada.

Sir Henry Sumner Maine, K.C.S.I., LL.D., F.R.S., 27, Cornwall Gardens.

Mrs. E. M. Mann, Manor House, Shropham, Thetford, Norfolk.

Ch. Elkin Matbews, Esq., 7, Hamilton Terrace, Highbury Park, N.

The Mercantile Library, Philadelphia, U.S.

H. E. Michelsen, Esq., 9, James Street, Westbourne Terrace.

J. Middleton, Esq., Westholme, Cheltenham.

The Mitchell Library, Glasgow.

John Moore, Esq., Oakwood, Beckenham, Kent.

James Earl Moreton, Esq., F.R.C.S., Tarvin, near Chester.
Rev. A. B. Morris, Keighley, Yorks.
Professor Max Müller, M.A., Norham Gardens, Oxford.
James Napier, Esq., Maryfield, Bothwell.
The Lady Caroline Nevill.
The Newcastle Literary and Philosophical Society, Newcastle-on-Tyne.
Robert Cradock Nichols, Esq., F.S.A., 5, Sussex Place, Hyde Park.
James Nicholson, Esq. Murton, Berwick-upon-Tweed.
" Notes and Queries," The Proprietor of.
Alfred Nutt, Esq., Rosendale Hall, Dulwich.
Frederic Ouvry, Esq., F.S.A., 12, Queen Anne Street, Cavendish Square.
William L. Sharp Page, Esq., 4, Upton Vale Terrace, Torquay.
Cornelius Paine, Esq., 9, Lewes Crescent, Kemp Town, Brighton.
Edward Palmer, Esq., 7, The Crescent, Tressilian Road, St. John's Street.
George L. I. Palmer, Esq., Trowbridge, Wilts.
M. Gaston Paris, Membre de l'Institut, 7, Rue de Regard, Paris.
Rev. W. D. Parish, The Vicarage, Selmeston, Lewes.
W. Payne, Esq., Hatchlands, Cuckfield, Sussex.
Edward Peacock, Esq., F.S.A., Bottesford Manor, Brigg, Lincolnshire.
C. Pfoundes, Esq., Custom House, London.
John South Phillips, M.A., Barton Lodge, Bury St. Edmund's.
Mrs. W. F. Phillpotts, 3, Gloucester Terrace, Campden Hill, W.
William Duncombe Pink, Esq., Leigh, Lancashire.
Mrs. Pollard, 5, Belsize Crescent, N.W.
Hon. Gerald Ponsonby, 54, Green Street, Grosvenor Square, W.
R. T. Porter, Esq., Raleigh, Beckenham, Kent.
D'Arcy Power, Esq., 37A, Great Cumberland Place, Hyde Park.
The Earl of Powis, 45, Berkeley Square, W.
Mrs. Priestley, 17, Hertford Street, Mayfair, W.
W. R. S. Ralston, Esq., M.A., 8, Alfred Place, Bedford Square.
Thomas Ratcliffe, Esq., Worksop.
Isaac J. Reeve, Esq., Newhaven, Sussex.
W. Napier Reeve, Esq., F.S.A., Leicester.
J. H. Rivett-Carnac, Esq., C.I.E., F.S.A., M.R.A.S., F.G.S., Ghazipùr, India.
Josiah Rose, Esq., Leigh, Lancashire.
Henry Ross, Esq., F.S.A., Chestham Park, Henfield, Sussex.
Rev. G. Stringer Rowe, Harrogate.
George Augustus Sala, Esq., Mecklenburg Square.
The Lady Salt, Maplewell, Loughborough.
Thomas Satchell, Esq., Downshire Hill House, Hampstead.
J. Ebenezer Saunders, Esq., F.S.A., F.L.S., 9, Finsbury Circus, E.C.
Rev. A. H. Sayce, Queen's College, Oxford
George Scharf, Esq., F.S.A., National Portrait Gallery, South Kensington.

L. A. Shaltuck, Esq., Boston, U.S.

Frederick Sherlock, Esq., 1, Lombard Street, Belfast.

Rev. J. Sibree, jr., 4, Welland Terrace, Upper Winchester Road, Blythe Hill.

Mrs. Singleton, Great Girendale, Pocklington.

A. Russell Smith, Esq., 36, Soho Square.

Charles C. Smith, Esq., Bradley, near Kildwick, Yorkshire.

George Smith, Esq., F.S.A., 62, Hamilton Terrace, St. John's Wood, N.W.

Edward Solly, Esq., F.R.S., F.S.A., Sutton, Surrey.

William Swan Sonnenschein, Esq., 15, Paternoster Square, E.C.

J. G. Sowerby, Esq., Gateshead-upon-Tyne.

Professor Dr. George Stephens, F.S.A., Copenhagen.

C. H. Stephenson, Esq., Lilian Road, Castelnau, Barnes, S.W.

Dr. A. P. Stewart, 75, Grosvenor Street, W.

Rev. Charles Swainson, The Rectory, Old Charlton.

Hon. Wirt Sykes, Cardiff.

Edward Taylor, Esq., Hockerville, Bishops Stortford.

William J. Thoms, Esq. F.S.A., 40, St. George's Square, S.W. (Director).

Samuel Timmins, Esq., F.S.A., Elvetham Lodge, Birmingham.

John Tolhurst, Esq., Glenbrook, Beckenham, Kent (Auditor).

The Torquay Natural History Society.

Miss Henrietta Townsend, South End House, Croydon.

George M. Traherne, Esq., St. Hilary, Cowbridge, Glamorganshire.

Dr. Edward B. Tylor, Linden, Wellington, Somersetshire.

J. S. Udal, Esq., 4, Harcourt Buildings, Temple, E.C.

Professor J. Veitch, LL.D., Glasgow University.

Rev. Precentor Venables, The Precentory, Lincoln.

The Right Hon. the Earl of Verulam, Gorhambury, St. Albans (President).

R. H. Wallace, Esq., Newton Hall, Kennoway, Fife, N.B.

John Walker, Esq., Eastfield House, Corbridge-on-Tyne.

Horace Walpole, Esq., India Office, Whitehall.

Chas. Walton, Esq., The Manor House, East Acton, W.

C. Staniland Wake, Esq., 74, Wright Street, Hull.

Mrs. Wartnaby, Market Harborough.

Alfred White, Esq., F.S.A., F.L.S., West Drayton.

George White, Esq., St. Briavels, Epsom.

William A. White, Esq., C.B., H.B.M.'s Consul-General, Belgrade.

Hamilton Whiteford, Esq., 17, Courtenay Street, Plymouth.

Rev. J. Whitmee, F.R.G.S., C.M.Z.S., 5, Dacre Park, Blackheath.

Adin Williams, Esq., Kempsford, Fairford, Gloucestershire.

Charles Williams, Esq., Moseley Lodge, near Birmingham.

J. Remington Wilson, Esq., Petworth, Sussex.

William Wilson, Esq., West Lodge, Pollockshields, Glasgow.

Miss E. A. Winfield, North Circus Street, Nottingham.

Miss G. M. Zornlin, 11, Clifton Terrace, Winchester.

ADDITIONAL LIST OF MEMBERS.

T. Adkins, Esq., Smethwick, near Birmingham.
J. B. Andrews, Esq., Villa Piganti, Mentone.
Edward W. Brabrook, Esq., F.S.A., 11, Limes Villas, Lewisham, S.E.
The Countess of Caledon.
Signor Comparetti, Florence.
Richard B. Cragg, Esq., Skipton.
Rev. Prebendary Davies, M.A., Moor Court, Kington, Herefordshire.
Ernest Foreman, Esq., 1, Gresham Villas, Stanstead Road, Forest Hill, S.E.
Colonel Francis Grant, 4, Fairholme Road, West Kensington, S.W.
J. Guerrin, Esq., Leelands, Trinity Road, Upper Tooting.
James E. A. Gwynne, F.S.A., 97, Harley Street, and Folkington Manor, Sussex.
Lord Hanmer, F.S.A., 59, Eaton Place, S.W., and Bettisfield Park, Whitchurch,
    Salop.
Harvard College Library.
Dr. Reinhold Köhler, Weimar.
Rev. W. E. Layton, Cranbourne, Windsor Forest.
Alexander Macmillan, Esq., Bedford Street, Covent Garden.
Manchester Free Library, King Street, Manchester.
E. Marston, Esq., Crown Buildings, Fleet Street.
Middlesbrough Free Library.
W. G. Palgrave, Esq.
Professor Z. Consiglieri Pedroso, Lisbon.
Plymouth Institution and Devon and Cornwall Nat. Hist. Society.
Arthur Porter, Esq., Brookhurst, South Norwood, Kent.
John Edward Price, Esq., F.S.A., M.R.S.L., 60, Albion Road, Stoke Newington, N.
C. Riestonigee, Esq., Ghazipùr, India.
Miss Sandars, Lower Soughton, Northop, Flintshire.
Surgeon-Major Sartoris, Ghazipùr, India.
Royal Library of Stockholm.
Lieutenant R. Carnac-Temple, India.
P. C. Wheeler, Esq., Bengal Civil Service, Ghazipùr, India.
Sparks Henderson Williams, Esq., F.S.A., 5, Essex Court, Temple.
Sydney Williams, Esq., Henrietta Street, Covent Garden.
R. H. Wood Esq., F.S.A., F.R.G.S., Penrhos House, Rugby.

9783744776790